First ACT Shakespeare

First ACT
Shakespeare

Illustrated by
**Clive
Francis**

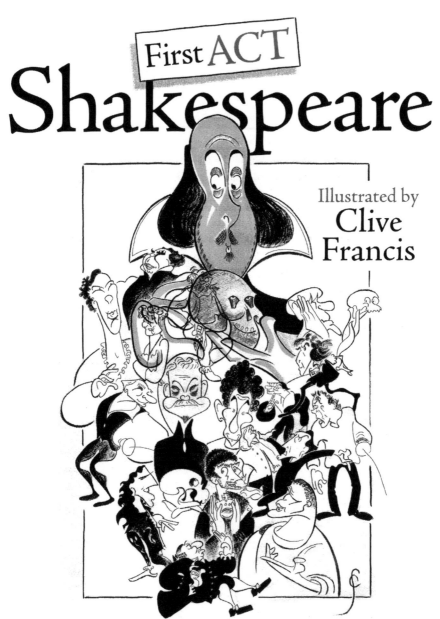

Robert Pennant Jones

First published in Great Britain in 2021 by The Seven Stars Project

Edited, designed and produced by Tandem Publishing
http://tandempublishing.yolasite.com

ISBN: 978-1-5272-8828-7

10 9 8 7 6 5 4 3 2 1

A CIP catalogue record for this book is available from the British Library.

Printed and bound in Great Britain by CPI Group (UK) Ltd, Croydon CR0 4YY.

For Lily and Alana

And to the memory of Penny Tuerk

Contents

The History Plays

The Natural World • The Individual • Worldly Realities •
Endgame • The Theatre • Tools of the Theatre: Words and
Music • The Imagination • Supremacy of the Poet

Foreword

Ian McKellen

In our late teens, Robert Pennant Jones and I were at the same Cambridge college, studying English Literature over three years and acting together in undergraduate productions of Bernard Shaw, Turgenev, Tennessee Williams, John Whiting and of Shakespeare, too.

After three years, I started out as a professional actor and Robert kept on as an amateur.

Neither of us thinks less of an actor just because he isn't paid to play the part. How could I, when in the middle of playing King Lear for the Royal Shakespeare Company, I saw Robert triumph in the same part for The Tower Theatre Company, the most active amateur troupe in inner London?

As I proceeded, doing Shakespeare on stage, on television and radio and on film, Robert's shared passion brought us together in defence of the remains of the Rose Theatre where Shakespeare's earliest plays were first performed, on the banks of the River Thames.

He showed me his archive of theatre designs by Bill Dudley,

whose first job was to design *Hamlet* for Nottingham Playhouse. And whenever we met, I was treated to Robert's strongly-held views on his latest theatre-going. His knowledge of Shakespeare's 37 plays is more substantial than my own and if he ever approves of my work, I am grateful – and relieved.

Student, actor, director and above all audience member, all-in-all, he has earned the right to add another book to the many thousands already written about Shakespeare.

His book is, as I would expect, unlike all the others. It is a guide not from a pedagogue but from an actor/director who thinks that the best way to appreciate Shakespeare is to act in his plays. That is an extreme position, acting not being for everybody, even though all we men and women are merely players.

Here is a guide to any of us planning to embark on a Shakespeare voyage, at school or college, or for one of the hundred groups in the Little Theatre Guild, where Robert is an experienced stalwart. He gives us not a rule book but plenty of sensible advice and strong views, some of which, some will question. Teaching, quite rightly, stimulates discussion and disagreement and argument.

As it was for Robert, my teachers at primary and secondary schools were crucial to discovering the power and delights of live theatre: so, for us both, was actually going to see plays performed, many of them by Shakespeare. It wasn't reading the plays round the class-room which enchanted me but rather seeing them on stage – and hearing them too, which is what *audiences* primarily do.

Trying to get to grips with Shakespeare through reading is not easy. Best to see the play first and only then read it and study it, preparing you for the next production.

So I wish you well with the Pennant Jones approach, practical and illuminating in every chapter. As you read them all, you will want to discover those plays you don't yet know.

If you are further encouraged to be involved in bringing one of them to life on-stage, Robert's scholarship and imagination will have been rewarded.

Happy reading, happy acting and happy theatre-going.

— Ian McKellen,
London, 2021

Preface

I was taught a love of Shakespeare by two of my school masters, Leslie Wilson and David Raeburn. I acted Shakespeare at university, under some distinguished directors such as John Barton and Toby Robertson. I subsequently acted and directed Shakespeare non-professionally during my business career and, on retirement, professionally too. In recent years I have taught Shakespeare at schools. I want to pass on my experience to those who may not have, or have had, teachers of such enthusiasm and practical encouragement as I had.

I was lucky in my masters who encouraged me to act in the school plays. At that point of my student career I was sufficiently encouraged by the nice things said of these performances to think I might become a professional actor. At university, where theatre was a serious business for many of my contemporaries, I quickly realised that whereas I was good enough to be cast in whatever undergraduate production I wanted to be in, it was usually as an attendant lord and was once as a mute soldier. I did play a few nice roles, but the really good parts went to actors who subsequently distinguished themselves in the profession. While I admire those who set out on this course, and particularly those who did so for forty years, the satisfactions and the financial rewards will have been both variable and unpredictable. Several other actors whom I considered equal to the best decided that a career in the theatre was not for them because of this. And so did I.

During my business career I found time in the evenings and at weekends to act in and direct plays non-professionally. Such is the stigma attached to "am. dram." that I prefer to refer to this work as non-professional, which is to say that I try to work to professional standards, and choose not to be paid for it. I do it because I love it and am therefore an amateur in the true meaning of the word, which has also been debased in this context.

Now retired, I work professionally too, though I often waive my professional fees if that enables me to do work that would otherwise not be done on economic grounds. I am fortunate that my business earnings enable me to do this.

The economic point needs to be addressed by anyone wanting to act or direct Shakespeare. Shakespeare's plays need significant resources: acting talent supported by designers, musicians, sound and lighting creators and significant costs of sets, props and costumes. By and large the plays with the bigger casts cost more to put on than those with smaller casts. With the exception of the great subsidised acting companies, it is seldom possible to mount fully professional productions of Shakespeare without economic loss. Non-professional productions can cover their costs simply because the actors are not paid. This is the moment to suggest that anyone considering being involved in Shakespeare might consider this question for himself or herself. For students involved in school productions, it is too soon to decide whether or not to continue with Shakespeare professionally. Drama school students need to recognise that professional opportunities to play Shakespeare are likely to be limited. For the rest it is likely that any future involvement in Shakespeare will be non-professional.

My purpose in writing this book is to put as many of you as possible in a position to enjoy Shakespeare as much as I do, whether you choose the professional or non-professional route; whether you act, direct or support the actors backstage; whether or not English is your first language. I believe that every aspiring Shakespearean should:

ACT Shakespeare rather than SEE Shakespeare

SEE Shakespeare rather than READ Shakespeare

READ Shakespeare rather than IGNORE Shakespeare.

This was the first of the three points I tried to teach in my FIRST ACT SHAKESPEARE lessons for schools. The second point was:

learn to use your IMAGINATION

and the third:

learn as much Shakespeare as you can BY HEART while you are young.

I used to explain the last point by noting that whereas I still remember much of what I learned by the time I was twenty, I now have difficulty in recalling what I may have learned and performed recently.

The purpose, then, is to enable anyone who would like to act Shakespeare to do so. The factual information in the play pages will enable you to choose the most appropriate play for your purposes.

I must here mention the subject of Shakespeare as part of exam syllabuses. Most of us are introduced to Shakespeare in this way, and for many the experience is a turn-off, often for life. I was lucky that my teachers directed my interest beyond examinations. I would simply ask you to keep an open mind about Shakespeare until you have had the pleasure of Acting Shakespeare, and not allowing a set text to blight your enjoyment.

Why put ACTING at the top of the list? I believe that it is only by confronting the lines of your character, working out what they mean and performing them in a way that an audience will understand, that reveals the ultimate pleasure of Shakespeare. Part of this process is the solving of the syntactical problems that Shakespeare inevitably sets us today. Shakespeare's language is not easy to a modern ear, but it is not insoluble either. Once you have learned to understand and to speak it, assisted of course by his incomparable verse rhythms, Shakespeare's difficult syntax becomes a revelation and a pleasure. Many feel Shakespeare is "boring" when they really mean "I hardly understood any of it, and even if I did understand it was irrelevant to me". My contention is that the understanding of even the most obscure and archaic language is solved by acting it, and often becomes relevant to modern experience. To those parents and grandparents who feel "I only did Shakespeare for exams, and hated it" I would say please give your children, your grandchildren the chance to experience Shakespeare outside the examination room. SEEING Shakespeare in the theatre, on TV or on film, is the next best thing to ACTING Shakespeare, and I can thoroughly recommend the films of Olivier, Welles, Zeffirelli, Kurosawa, Luhrmann, Branagh and Brook.

For my generation, however, Shakespeare in the theatre has been the more important medium, in that the plays are constantly revived. In my country the great subsidised companies, Royal Shakespeare Company (RSC mainly Shakespeare) and the National Theatre (NT more occasional Shakespeare), and the newer (unsubsidised) Shakespeare's Globe (mainly Shakespeare) have resulted in as many as 10 or 12 different productions in any given year. A strong regional theatre has mounted many productions and Shakespeare has been widely available throughout the country. Add to this many non-professional productions at all levels and it can be demonstrated that Shakespeare is alive and well in the theatre in the UK.

In the USA, Canada, Australia too, Shakespeare is widely played and important work is also done in Japan, Germany, France and many other countries where English is not the main language. India has a long tradition of playing Shakespeare too. By all means see Shakespeare wherever he is played. But do so, if possible, with the experience of acting Shakespeare under your belt. Unlike films, past productions can seldom be revisited and never in the conditions of the original productions.

While theatre is still the obvious medium for acting Shakespeare for yourself, I should also note that today other media are available for such experience. Film cameras are now cheap, digital technology makes editing easy and computers can supply a host of abilities previously available from film professionals at high cost.

There is no reason why you should not 'film' performances, remembering, however, that the immediacy of theatrical performance may be more exciting. We all deserve that pleasure in Shakespeare that I have enjoyed as actor, director, script writer, broadcaster and playgoer. I suggest the best time for this is when minds are young, where imagination is second nature and where good opportunities of involving friends and colleagues exist. For those that aspire to become professional actors this book is perhaps only a stepping stone for there will be further acting opportunities at university and drama school. The would-be professional will get plenty of opportunity to build on these precepts. While Shakespeare is only part of a professional's career, I believe that most great actors will have been challenged by Shakespeare, and distinguished themselves in his plays. It may not be too much to say that great actors must have had success in Shakespeare at one stage or other of their careers. For those of us who will experience Shakespeare as amateurs or non-professionals, widespread fringe and non-professional theatres present opportunities to play Shakespeare.

To act Shakespeare at schools, in dramatic societies and at university and other tertiary education, we all need experienced and enthusiastic guidance. This may be less available today than it was to me, i.e. an enthusiastic and supportive teacher with a wide experience of performing the plays. Today you may have to do it without such help, what with the demands of the curriculum and other extra-mural activities on teachers. The play pages may help to provide such advice and inform your choices based on the needs of the plays and the resources available to you. If I can shorten the work or suggest suitable directions to take, that will be all to the good. But it is your imaginations that must take over from then. And a knowledge of some or all of the quotations I suggest as suitable to learn will encourage you to persevere even when it looks all too difficult to contemplate your own performances.

Of course if you cannot mount a full production you can do an abridgement or even perform an anthology of scenes. And opportunities to see Shakespeare should not be ignored. But for those unlucky enough not to be able to ACT Shakespeare or SEE Shakespeare, all that remains if you are not to IGNORE Shakespeare is to READ Shakespeare. But for all the reasons already mentioned, for a modern reader this is not easy. Live performance is a great assistance in sorting out confusions of plot, of identity and of syntax. I urge all would-be Shakespeareans to embrace this assistance by seeing Shakespeare if possible and acting Shakespeare yourselves.

The second part of this book is a Sampler of Shakespeare's thoughts included in the plays, but of less relevance to the character speaking the lines than his own life philosophies. Many can profitably be learned by heart but all, I suggest, are important insights into topics that are still relevant today.

And the wonderful illustrations by Clive Francis of eminent Shakespearean actors are provided as a tribute to many performances I have seen or would like to have seen.

The Purpose and Use of the Play Pages

In an earlier draft of this book I produced a set of cards to enable comparisons to be made quickly between plays in the practicalities of acting and staging them. In this book the cards are reproduced on the play pages. There is a wealth of information about Shakespeare that is universally available. Apart from the many fine editions of the plays themselves, there is a host of books on Shakespeare the man; the authorship; audition pieces; glossaries; concordances; reviews and scholarly criticism – a choice almost too rich to contemplate let alone digest, particularly by those who do not have mentors or tutors available with wide experience to suggest which play to perform. The play pages can assist with choosing the right play.

I sincerely hope that many of you will wish to ACT Shakespeare, by which I mean choosing a play, thinking of a particular audience and having in mind the personal and technical resources to act it successfully. Acting Shakespeare need not be limited to choosing a complete play. Plays can be cut or modified, individual scenes can be chosen, or an assortment of extracts be performed or filmed. For this a knowledge of the entire range of possibilities is not necessary, and practically any choice is bound to be a success. However, the pages may help in identifying which plays need cutting, on grounds of length, size of cast or technical difficulty, and a quick appraisal of your available resources may be of assistance in deciding which play to choose.

The Play Pages

Without considerable experience there is no easy way to compare plays quickly and accurately. This is the purpose of the play pages. These are designed to include all the relevant data that you will need to make an informed choice of which play to ACT, in a quick and convenient way.

Once a shortlist has been derived according to your own criteria, the information can be augmented by the chapters on the individual plays, where more data is listed and where three 'cruxes' are identified.

The cruxes are my views on the three most crucial points in each play that need to be considered in any production. I invite you to develop your own ideas on how these cruxes should be 'solved'. Of course you can decide to ignore my cruxes. Nevertheless I feel it may be helpful to think about the cruxes if only to discard them from your planning.

I have tried to include all the practical information about the 37 plays to enable comparisons between plays to be made. I shall give one example later to show you how simple it is to make such comparisons.

INFORMATION IN THE PLAY PAGES

1 Comedy/tragedy/history

This trilogy is the traditional (i.e. First Folio) categorisation of plays. I prefer the term tragicomedy to describe plays such as *The Winter's Tale, Measure for Measure* or *Cymbeline* but the traditional system will generally be understood and accepted.

2 Date

The dates when the plays were written are often not exactly known. The dates are usually given as a range where scholars are in doubt. An exact date will not be of much material assistance in choosing a play but the identification of the three categories may have its use:

Early plays (1589–1594)	*EARLY*
Middle period (1595–1602)	*MID*
Late plays (1603–1613)	*LATE*

3 Popularity

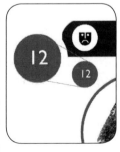

The plays are numbered according to my own research into the popularity of each play. The research (up to 1995) was based on 40 years of box office receipts at RSC Stratford and reflects the experience at that company at that time. *Twelfth Night* was the most popular play and *Titus Andronicus* the least. Of course there will have been changes since, and it may be (though I doubt it) that *Twelfth Night* is no longer Number 1 nor *Titus Andronicus* Number

37. Plays may have slipped down or moved up the charts but in terms of whether a play is popular (1–12), of average popularity (13–26), or not popular (27–37), I believe the ranking remains broadly accurate.

Popularity is important especially for box office unless you have a captive audience or are heavily subsidised. It may also indicate comparative merit, and when starting on a Shakespeare adventure I would expect most choices to be made from the top two categories rather than the third.

4 Playing time

This is calculated to the nearest 5 minutes estimating that 1,000 lines will take an hour to perform plus 15 minutes for an interval. The three categories are:

Category	est. playing time	announce
Short	120–170 minutes	under 3 hours
Medium	170–190 minutes	around 3 hours
Long	195–265 minutes	over 3 hours

A long play would probably be a mistake for an early foray into Shakespeare. In my experience, too, it is better to have an early curtain-up time rather than to overrun the last transport home with an overlong play. Always announce an estimated finishing time.

5 Number of lines

This is crucial information to enable you to judge two vital matters: how long an audience will have to sit in the theatre (see previous item) but also how much rehearsal time you will need to devote to the play. If you plan to spend the same amount of rehearsal time on *King Lear* as you would on *Comedy of Errors,* say, you will

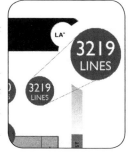

probably have a poorly prepared production of *King Lear*. You can of course cut a play and in most cases there are obscure speeches which will not be missed. Even removal of secondary and tertiary characters is possible, though it needs a sure touch. The number of lines will indicate what extent the cuts should be, or if no great cuts are made, how long you will need to prepare.

6 Recommended cast

Shakespeare's given cast lists range from 17 (*Comedy of Errors*) to 65 (*Henry VI, Part 2*). These are identified roles with lines to speak. In addition all plays would benefit from a number of attendants – non-speaking roles whose function is to assist with set changes, dress the stage with bodies, and other generally thankless tasks that are often described as spear-carrying. In suggesting a recommended cast size I am ignoring all non-speaking attendant roles on the understanding that if such help is available (e.g. in school productions) and if these roles can be combined with other interesting offstage work, productions will be considerably enhanced. I envisage that the speaking actor will also, whenever available, become an attendant lord, or soldier or attendant.

In these plays I suggest a range of casts from 11 (*Comedy of Errors*), to 27 (*King Henry VI, Parts 1 & 2*), I am primarily doing so on two grounds – satisfaction of the actors through doubling and even trebling parts, and the costs in terms of money and effort needed.

I suggest a particular assignment of roles in the appendix which aims to make practical sense – as far as possible avoiding more than one role per act, and avoiding unnecessary costume changes back and forth. In some cases I suggest that the sex of a minor character is ignored if an actor of the opposite sex is available. However, I have concentrated on suggesting a total cast number that can by such means do the whole play, often with difficult but pleasing challenges for the doubling and trebling actors. You can play around with the casting to suit your resources, but I doubt if the plays can be done with fewer actors than I have identified.

7 **Balance of star roles to ensemble roles**
The roles in each play are set out in order of importance as they might appear on a theatre billboard. In casting a play the order will assist in assigning the right actor to the right part. It seems pointless to contemplate acting *Hamlet* say, if you haven't an obvious Hamlet for the role. And the same goes for any play needing either a superstar (which I

define as having over 1,000 lines) or star (500+). Such roles are identified on the play pages (at the top of the bill, so to speak) in bold capitals (with superstars given a slightly larger size of letter).

The next range of parts is also of great importance and is also differentiated by size of role:

LEADING   250+ lines   CAPS
SUPPORTING   100+ lines   CAPS

Ensemble roles are defined as having less than 100 lines and are not generally named.

The *King Henry IV, Part 1* play page tells us the following. There are three stars (Falstaff, Prince Hal and Hotspur) that each has more than 500 lines. In total they have 57% of the lines of the play. There is one leading player (Henry IV) who has more than 250 lines, in this case 11% of the lines of the play.

Two actors have more than 100 lines (Worcester and a composite role of Northumberland, Glendower and one other) and these account for a further 10% of the lines of the play. There are a further 15 ensemble roles which together take the remaining 22% of the lines of the play.

8 Balance of age and sex

It may be useful to know the balance

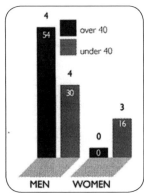

between ages and sexes in the plays, though I do not wish to overplay this as, in general, there are relatively few women's roles in Shakespeare; and actors should be able to play older, or even younger than they really are.

The plays have quite different balances, and the bar chart is designed to give a quick visual check on those roles of 100+ lines, plus a few important roles that have fewer lines, e.g. Lavinia, Lady Macduff, and a few others. Sometimes deciding whether a character is over or under 40 is more a matter of opinion than fact, but I am generally happy with the detail for each play. The example of *Henry IV, Part 1* tells us that:

> *51% of the lines are spoken by 4 men aged 40+*
> *47% of the lines are spoken by 3 men aged 40-*
> *2% of the lines are spoken by 1 woman aged 40-*
> *And thus there is a 51%/49% balance between the older and younger roles.*

9 Technical difficulty

There are three categories:

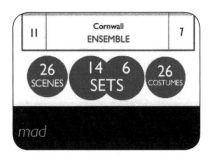

1. SCENES

Antony and Cleopatra has 42 scenes while *The Tempest*, *Love's Labour's Lost* and *A Midsummer Night's Dream* have only 9. There are two points to consider. First that a change of scene takes time, and sometimes special efforts must be made to reduce that time (in the case of *Antony and Cleopatra*) by overlapping entrances, etc. Even an average of 10 seconds per change will extend the running time by 6 or 7 minutes. The second point is that scene changes, if they also entail a set change, will inevitably incur a further time penalty.

Few scenes	9–16
Average scenes	17–23
Many scenes	24–42

2. Sets

Sets were not a feature of Shakespeare's theatre, and the days of elaborate sets, especially involving construction, are long gone. However, I have listed the settings as specified to remind directors and actors that identity of place, whether by set or some other means, should not be overlooked. There is a great variety in complexity and the number of sets specified may not be generally useful, though once the choice of play has been made it will serve as a checklist for the designer. Of more use in planning may be the number of simplified sets in which, for example, a room in a palace in Paris, say, is considered the same as a room in a palace in London, a single set being differentiated by banners, props and furniture. Plains, open places and battlefields can also be simplified into one set. The range is as follows:

	SPECIFIED SETS	SIMPLIFIED SETS
Few	1–8	1–5
Average	9–11	6
Many	12–21	7–10

3. Costumes

This figure is simply the number of characters in Shakespeare's cast list (with lines), assuming each character would have a distinctive costume even though (in the case of guards also appearing as messengers) a degree of rationalisation is possible. But it seems a good indication of the size of task for the wardrobe department.

Few costumes	18–24
Average costumes	25–40
Many costumes	41–65

10 Summary recommendation

The facts in these pages will enable anyone to have an informed opinion as to the ease or difficulty likely to be encountered in the light of which criteria are important to them. I provide a boxed summary on each card of my personal recommendation derived from my own experience of the relative attractiveness and challenges of each play.

11 Key quote

A phrase from the play chosen to remind the reader of the theme, or one of the themes, of the play.

USING THE PLAY PAGES

I mentioned I would provide an example of how to produce a shortlist or lists of plays to be considered.

I will assume that I have a relatively small and inexperienced company of actors available, with perhaps two who could become stars one day, and with relatively few ensemble players. As we are an inexperienced company I plan to rule out those plays that are considered difficult, reducing the plays from 37 to 25.

Next I put to one side those plays which indicate a large ensemble (12 or more), a total of eight in the example. I also take out one further play that requires a large overall cast (22 or more). I would also take out the two plays that have a high percentage of lines for the stars for which we have no obvious star players. Fourteen plays are now left.

At this point the example has perhaps demonstrated its usefulness in throwing up candidate plays for further consideration.

Depending on what other criteria are important to your group you can refine the list further, confident that your final choice will meet, as far as possible, your requirements.

The speed with which these shortlists can be made, or dismantled, is far greater than could be achieved by all but the most experienced practitioners.

The crucial idea is that to understand Shakespeare you have to ACT Shakespeare, and I hope I have persuaded a number of my readers to do just that. If so I cannot but conclude this chapter with the best advice that can be given to young actors, indeed to all actors, and even to us all as a precept for life. It comes from an unlikely character, the would-be actor of all the best parts, Bottom, at the end of the rehearsal scene in *A Midsummer Night's Dream*. Astoundingly, this is given in only five words:

> Take pains, be perfect; adieu!

Attaining perfection would indeed be a good precept for life, though Bottom is only asking that you learn your lines, of which I venture to translate:

> Try your best; learn your lines; trust in the Lord.

But use Shakespeare's words for all your acting. To update the stories and abandon Shakespeare's language seems to me to be villainous. By all means update the settings, but by no means abandon the language. Remember, if the actors know what they are doing, and understand what they are saying, through ACTING Shakespeare, the audience will easily understand the plays, and some of them will, as a result, want to ACT Shakespeare too. That's the point.

TWELFTH NIGHT

OLIVIA Mark Rylance   **MALVOLIO** Stephen Fry

TWELFTH NIGHT
Youth's a stuff

Viola and Sebastian, twin sister and brother, are shipwrecked off the coast of Illyria and are separated, each thinking the other drowned. With the help of a captain, Viola disguises herself as a boy, Cesario, and is accepted at Duke Orsino's court where she is soon employed by the Duke to woo Olivia, a Countess, on his behalf, not realising that Viola is about to fall in love with him. Olivia is indifferent to Orsino's suit, but falls for the charms of Cesario.

In Olivia's household is a sponging uncle, Sir Toby Belch, who is living off Sir Andrew Aguecheek, a foolish suitor for his niece's hand. Olivia's steward, Malvolio, is gulled by Sir Toby, Maria, Olivia's gentlewoman, and Feste, a clown, into thinking that his mistress loves him. Malvolio is encouraged to declare his love for Olivia, and is confined on grounds of suspected madness in a darkened room, where Sir Toby and Feste avenge themselves on him for personal and professional slights.

Sebastian was not drowned, and, assisted by Antonio, an old enemy of Orsino, is at large in Illyria. Cesario is challenged to a duel. Sebastian is mistaken by Olivia for Cesario and accepts Olivia's offer of marriage.

Orsino is enraged by Cesario's apparent perfidy but these confusions are cleared up as Antonio and the priest, who married Olivia and Sebastian, are found. Viola and Sebastian are reunited. This leaves Orsino free to marry Viola, and Sir Toby marries Maria. Malvolio, Sir Andrew and Feste are disappointed. Feste loses his job to Fabian, a younger member of Olivia's household.

*T*welfth Night* is, by my reckoning, the most popular of Shake-speare's plays. It has a small cast, so practically every part is of interest and importance and the costs of production are low. It lasts barely 2 ½ hours. It ends happily, with only Feste (out of a job) and Malvolio (planning revenge) in the slightest way disaffected. It has taught us much about professionalism, identity and sex. A perfect comedy in fact. I see no reason why it should ever lose its popularity.

Twelfth Night needs 14 actors of whom three only could be described as bit parts. There are seven settings which can be simpli-fied to five and, as is usual in Shakespeare, none of these actually needs elaborate set construction. Some thought must be given to how to stage the darkened room in which Malvolio is tormented by Feste – I had him below the stage with only Malvolio's hands visible – "Pare thy nails Dad" then becoming the final insult as Feste stamps on his fingers.

The first crux is to decide the degree of physical similarity between the twins Viola and Sebastian. With modern aids such as film and projection, or ancient ones like mirrors, it is possible for one actor to play both twins, with body doubles for the final moments where both twins are on together. However, I would recommend using two actors in this play even if it is hard to find two actors suffi-ciently alike.

The second crux is of sexual identity. With boy actors playing the original Viola, Olivia and Maria, the male/female identities were mixed indeed. A boy actor plays Viola, a girl who dresses to disguise herself as a boy, who falls in love with Duke Orsino, a young man who thinks he is in love with a countess (Olivia) played by another boy, who is enamoured of the Duke's messenger Cesario, apparently a boy but actually a girl played by a boy, and who precipitately woos and weds the twin brother of the androgynous messenger. Today with actresses in these female roles there still remains the sexual confusions of Orsino's regard for Cesario and Olivia's for Viola, not to mention the slight sexual ambiguity of Orsino's court. And what to make of Olivia's grief at the death of a brother that causes her to withdraw from all romantic contact for the period of her mourning?

My third crux is of professionalism. I was in the dressing room of the cast of *Twelfth Night* and in Feste's place I saw a pile of stage money that the character had been given during the course of the previous evening's performance. Feste is a professional and, unlike many of the nobility and gentry in the play, has to earn his living; which he does by a mixture of singing, cajoling and begging, getting paid for his wit and performance. It is his personal tragedy that he is turned away at the end of the play – he has lost his job and another would-be professional, Fabian, has got it. The moment when this is decided is when he tells Olivia of Malvolio's madness in histrionic detail. He does this as a matter of professional revenge since Malvolio had previously questioned his competence to Olivia. Fabian gets Feste's job since his treatment of Malvolio has been less a matter of personal revenge and thus more acceptable to Olivia. It should be noted, too, that Malvolio is a professional in that he is a gentleman without a personal income and is forced to earn a living as a steward. He mistakes Olivia's gentle treatment of his professional stewardship for the idea that he is beloved of her. His behaviour to Olivia is in marked contrast to Sir Toby's, whose fortunate birth and riotous appetites mean that he must sponge off his niece, and extract from Sir Andrew as much money as he can to live like a gentleman and feed his debaucheries; a professional of necessity. Maria, Olivia's waiting gentlewoman, is also a professional. Like Feste she lives on her personality and wit. It may be a major misjudgement for her to marry Sir Toby. One final point is that of age, particularly Feste's. I believe that Feste is in the twilight of his years, that the loss of employment is probably a financial catastrophe for an older man. The youth of the play is attractive, but it is offset by our feeling of autumn where Feste, Sir Toby and Malvolio are concerned. Sir Andrew might well be a considerably younger man than these, but for him, too, time is pressing and his simpleness is probably tinged with melancholy.

This is a multi-faceted play that, despite its familiarity, always needs to be rethought in the light of the resources available to mount it. Most choices can be justified by the text, so beautifully balanced (and ambiguous) are the relationships and the narrative. It may even be a play about which the last word cannot ever be written. No wonder it is so popular.

The modern tendency to assign characters a different gender than the text requires is both understandable and regrettable. *Twelfth Night* is a good test case. Giving Viola, Olivia and Maria to female actors, rather than to boys as in Shakespeare's time, is to be applauded. However, the decision to cast Malvolio and Feste with female actors, as the National Theatre has recently done, is to my mind regrettable. Take Malvolio, gulled into believing that Olivia, a woman in the text and now in fact, is in love with him. Is this Malvolia's lesbian infatuation? Or is this Malvolio, a gay steward, acting against the character of the written text?

And to play Feste as a young female is entirely against character as I have argued above. However talented the actors involved, such choices diminish the play.

The illustration shows Mark Rylance as Olivia in a highly acclaimed West End production. In his artistic directorship of Shakespeare's Globe, he played the same role in an all-male cast: a production reverting to Shakespeare-era casting. Though his later Cleopatra was a brilliant success, I nevertheless remain unconvinced that cross-gender casting is right for modern productions. Rylance remains a great Shakespearean (though not, I believe, a Stratfordian), for his outstanding achievements in establishing the Globe's opening seasons, which included these gender reversals of the cast.

However, I do applaud giving female actors parts written for men, where the basic story does not suffer. The role of Timon of Athen's steward, Flavius, also at the National Theatre, became Flavia, with no ambiguity to Timon's predicament and a subtle modern emphasis to the role of the conscientious steward. But for me, Olivia's steward should always be played by a man, and Olivia by a woman.

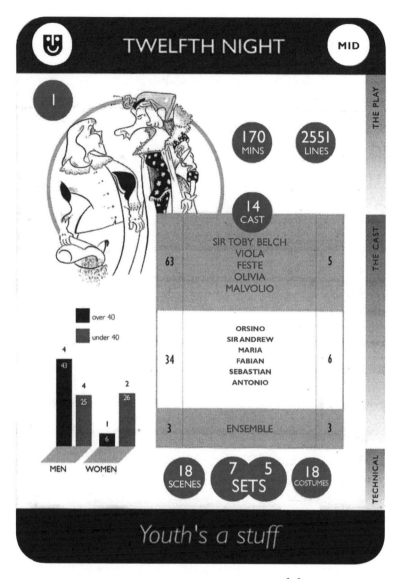

TWELFTH NIGHT

MID

I

170 MINS

2551 LINES

14 CAST

63	SIR TOBY BELCH VIOLA FESTE OLIVIA MALVOLIO	5
34	ORSINO SIR ANDREW MARIA FABIAN SEBASTIAN ANTONIO	6
3	ENSEMBLE	3

over 40
under 40

4
43
4
25
1
6
2
26

MEN   WOMEN

18 SCENES

7 5 SETS

18 COSTUMES

Youth's a stuff

The main requirement of this play is for **older men** with 43% of the lines. The play has an **average** number of scenes with **few** sets and **few** costumes. This play is **recommended**, particularly early on in a Shakespearean involvement or career.

VIOLA Dorothy Tutin   **OLIVIA** Geraldine McEwan

23

MACBETH

MACBETH Ian McKellen **LADY MACBETH** Judi Dench

MACBETH
The fiend that lies like truth

Macbeth murders his King to gain a crown that might have been his without the murder, if he had believed what the witches foretold, and not acted on his Lady's urgings.

Returning from victory over rebels against Duncan's Scottish crown the generals Macbeth and Banquo are met by witches who foretell that, among other honours, Macbeth shall be King and Banquo father to kings. Ross greets Macbeth as Thane of Cawdor, which the witches had prophesied.

Hearing of these prophesies Lady Macbeth urges Macbeth to kill the King who arrives at Macbeth's castle to celebrate the victory. After the banquet Macbeth murders Duncan, killing Duncan's guards to cast suspicion on them or Duncan's sons, Malcolm and Donalbane, who flee. Macbeth is elected Duncan's successor, not without the misgivings of Macduff and Banquo.

Banquo is now dangerous and Macbeth has him murdered, though Banquo's son Fleance is not killed as intended (and lives to found a later line of kings). Macduff goes to England to join up with Malcolm and an English army to oust Macbeth who, in the meantime, has revisited the witches who appear to guarantee his continuing reign. He has Lady Macduff and her children murdered.

The sleepwalking Lady Macbeth apparently confesses her guilt in Duncan's murder to a Doctor who conveys the news of her behaviour to Macbeth. Macbeth, now beset by the invasion, continues to believe he is immune from his enemies but dies at the hands of Macduff who restores the crown of Scotland to Malcolm.

If one of the decisions in *Hamlet* is where to set the interval, in *Macbeth* the decision is whether to have one at all, so swift is the action, so inexorable Macbeth's fate once he has decided to accept the equivocal prophesies of the witches.

Some scholars believe that the version of *Macbeth* we have is based on a shortened version prepared, maybe, for some special occasion. I am not so sure. Had there been a longer version I am sure the editors of the First Folio could have found or remembered it – both presumably acted in the play in 1606 when it was first performed. The play we have was, however, almost certainly added to by other hands. The bloody Sergeant has been thought non-Shakespearean but I think he is authentic enough. Hecate on the other hand seems a spurious interpolation that adds nothing except to focus the satanism of the witches on a classical rather than a Christian precedent.

I am suggesting a cast of 18. Of the doubled/multiple roles I would like to mention three. The role of Seyton, Macbeth's companion, has only four lines, but by adding the roles of the messengers, and the role of the 3rd Murderer he can be (and often is) given a looming presence throughout. The Scottish Doctor who watches the sleepwalking scene (he actually has more lines in that scene than the Queen, as does even the waiting gentlewoman) and reports to Macbeth, making profound points about the mind and bad con-science, is a role in which I made my professional debut. It is one of the great small parts ("There are no small parts in Shakespeare, only small actors") in Shakespeare. I doubled this with Duncan, a double that I recommend here (to which I would also add the Old Man and Old Siward). On my professional debut a boy in the front row, who was clearly not engaged by the action, greeted my appearance as the Doctor, in dark light, muffled, with the immortal line: "I thought that bugger was dead," which means at least he was awake to the end of the first act.

Another part that makes a huge impact, Lady Macduff, is also a very short one and I would suggest that one of the witches might double up with Lady Macduff to augment the actress's role and, incidentally, make an interesting comment on "Birth strangled babe" in view of what is to come.

As always, there are plenty of degrees of freedom in choosing which parts might best be doubled, which depends on the availability and aptitudes of actors in each production. My scheme simply suggests one possible solution with the overall objective of increasing the attractiveness of being in the play and reducing the time spent waiting and watching in rehearsal.

Attendants are necessary for striking and setting, e.g., the banquet, and can also be the waiters and soldiers. The main cast will need to fill out, e.g. again, the banquet, with actors playing Macduff, Malcolm, Duncan, the Sergeant, etc., seen only from behind, and in a different costume.

Set requirements are not great, though the idea of battlements might need some construction, or a permanent set with different levels. Most interiors are straightforward: the banquet scene needs a table, and a throne would probably help the idea of Macbeth's obsession (Kurosawa called his version of the play *Throne of Blood*).

This play is a prime example of Shakespeare's genius when it comes to lighting. Remember his plays were usually performed in broad daylight. Most scenes are set at a specific time, if only by inference. In Act II Scene 1 ("How goes the night boy?"), lighting is defined at once; it's dark and (in the next lines) we learn that there is no moonlight. While teaching this line at a school I learned a great lesson not only about light but also about small parts in Shakespeare. The lad playing the servant was understandably miffed that I had assigned him a role with no words, which got us into examining why the role is needed. Well, there is the order that Macbeth gives him, to alert Lady Macbeth to his coming, and to cause the bell to ring that summons Duncan "either to heaven or to hell". That helped; but what clinched the matter was when I asked him what happened as he left the stage. It took a few moments for the penny to drop… "The stage gets darker," he said at last. This prepares us wonderfully for the next line: "Is this a dagger which I see before me?", the darkness heightening Macbeth's state of mind at the last moment of his innocence, the darkness in Shakespeare's day (though we can do it today with a simple lighting cue) being achieved only through the imagination by a servant, with a torch, leaving the stage.

I shall come to sound cues in a moment, but I should spend a moment on costumes. What is emphatically wrong is for the thanes to be dressed in Sir Walter Scott tartans, though the use of kilts, trews and furs would be fine. A modern *Macbeth* (Shakespeare's Globe tried this with disappointing results) seems to add nothing, though a Zulu *Macbeth* was a sensation with its costume and dance in the '70s. The witches can legitimately be left to the designer's imagination even if the hints in the text (withered hags, choppy fingers, beards) are sometimes ignored.

The first of my cruxes is sound, and specifically whether there was a storm during the murder of Duncan, or whether it was so quiet that "Macbeth hath murdered sleep" is imagined or heard by Macbeth. Well, Kurosawa's squeak of Lady Macbeth's kimono as she walks up and down the chamber as the deed is done, and virtually all other productions I have seen, make noiselessness the feature of this scene, and I agree with that. So, the evidence of the Old Man (if the part is not to be cut) might be a comment on the aftermath of the killing or a prelude for the scene with the Porter. The director must decide what is right for his or her production given the conflicting evidence.

The second crux is the equivocation of the fiend. How satanic are the witches? Is Macbeth a victim of Satan or of his own ambitions: is Lady Macbeth, the fiendlike Queen, responsible for her husband's crimes? Equivocation is easy to explain. Throughout Shakespeare, prophecy is always fulfilled and misunderstood by the character who receives it. For example, the prophecy about High Dunsinane wood advancing on Macbeth's castle: the trees do indeed advance on the castle because they have been cut down by Malcolm's powers. Macbeth had taken the witches literally: the imaginative small print was beyond him. Is it equivocation of the fiend? Well, the point of Malcolm's exile is that it takes place at the court of the Christian Saint, King Edward the Confessor, who is described as having miraculous powers. The white of England's flag in this play suggests Christian saintliness; the dark of Macbeth's castle and conscience is echoed by the "secret black and midnight hags" who are agents of evil or the fiend.

The Englishness of Edward is seen in the context of a Scottish court in Jacobean London at the time of the play. Banquo derives from the house of Steward, or Stuart, and is thus the ancestor of James I, which makes the vision of Banquo's descendants ruling Scotland, and England, further evidence of the truth of the witches' prophecies. Incidentally I suggest that Fleance should be the first of the figures in the 3rd Apparition. This might be said to be a good outcome to the prophesies and the crux boils down to how explicitly Christian or satanic scenes of witchcraft and prophesy should be made.

The last crux is how to portray Macbeth's relationship with Lady Macbeth, to decide whether theirs is a marriage of love or of political convenience, and whether they wish or had wishes for children, and who is ultimately responsible for the murder of Duncan. Lady Macbeth is mentally overwhelmed by the consequences of the murder and she remains a curiously sympathetic victim. In a sense one would have liked other scenes to develop this point. Were there such in a longer version or did Shakespeare leave it to us to decide? I will offer one point: if Macbeth "hath murdered sleep", is it not ironical that Lady Macbeth reveals her crime to the listening Doctor in her sleep?

Macbeth is a mighty play and invariably leaves a lasting impression wherever it is performed. My earliest experience was seeing Paul Rogers and Ann Todd in the title roles around 1950 at the Old

Vic, Rogers' costume as Macbeth a bright scarlet that commented aptly on his predicament

I am in blood stepp'd so far…

This is one of 20 instances of the word blood in the play.

The theatrical superstition of not saying 'Macbeth' backstage in the theatre to avoid bad luck is still around. My friend the actor and director Michael Burrell thought it had an earlier meaning originating from McCready, the great 18th-century touring actor-manager. Whenever his company was short of money the usual remedy was to put on *Macbeth*, since the play had the strongest box office appeal. To disguise his financial crisis 'The Scottish Play' was used in conversation in case competitors might get to hear of his company's situation, and mount the play themselves.

Our illustration of Ian McKellen and Judi Dench is of a seminal production of the play, by Trevor Nunn, which played in a much smaller space than usual, The Other Place at Stratford and the Young Vic in London. In the modern professional theatre this is bound to be uneconomic, if unsubsidised. The great advantage for the actors is that their performances can be viewed more closely than in a traditional theatre, and is the closest the professional theatre can come to showing close-ups, or near close-ups, of the actors in live performance. In the non-professional theatre, smaller, more intimate spaces are usual, which undoubtedly give its actors and audiences artistic and interpretational advantages, even over the professional theatre, film and television.

Ian McKellen, when preparing his second portrayal of King Lear, chose the smaller of the two theatres at Chichester, where the production was due to open, the Minerva, rather than the great space of the Festival Theatre, for this very advantage, remembering the artistic success of the earlier production of *Macbeth* in small spaces.

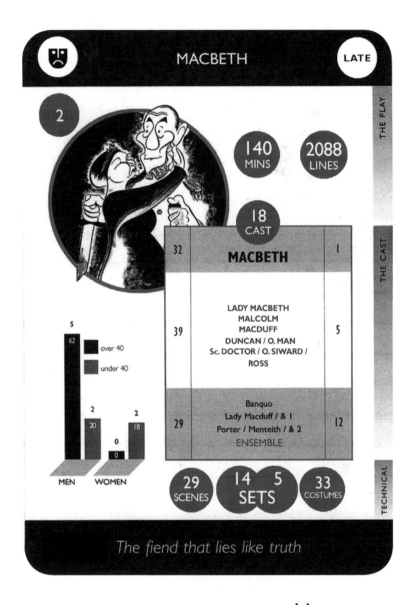

MACBETH

LATE

2

140 MINS

2088 LINES

18 CAST

32	**MACBETH**	1
39	LADY MACBETH MALCOLM MACDUFF DUNCAN / O. MAN Sc. DOCTOR / O. SIWARD / ROSS	5
29	Banquo Lady Macduff / & 1 Porter / Menteith / & 2 ENSEMBLE	12

5

62 — over 40

under 40

2 — 2

20 — 18

0 — 0

0

MEN — WOMEN

29 SCENES

14 SETS 5

33 COSTUMES

The fiend that lies like truth

The main requirement of this play is for older men with 62% of the lines. The play has many scenes with many sets, which can be simplified to relatively few sets, and an average number of costumes. This play is recommended, particularly early on in a Shakespearean involvement or career.

MACBETH Ian McKellen **LADY MACBETH** Judi Dench

ROMEO AND JULIET

ROMEO Laurence Olivier   **JULIET** Peggy Ashcroft

ROMEO AND JULIET
A pair of star-cross'd lovers

In Verona the households of the Capulets and Montagues have again fought each other in a civil brawl. The Prince, Escalus, issues a final warning to the heads of the families.

Romeo, Montague's son, together with Benvolio and Mercutio learn of a feast being held by the Capulets which they gate-crash. Romeo meets Juliet and they instantly fall in love. Later Romeo returns to the Capulet house to exchange vows of love with Juliet. In the morning he confesses his love to Friar Laurence, who agrees to marry them, employing the Capulets' Nurse as intermediary, and they are secretly married shortly afterwards.

Meanwhile Tybalt, a fiery member of the Capulet family, challenges Romeo to a duel but it is Mercutio who falls victim, though Romeo, who flees, is banished to Mantua for his role in the duel. The Nurse arranges for Romeo to spend the marriage night with Juliet.

Lady Capulet tells Juliet that Capulet has arranged that she shall marry Paris. Juliet, distraught, seeks help from Friar Laurence who advises her to take a draught that will appear to kill her but revive her once she has been entombed in the family monument. Romeo is summoned back from Mantua but only hears of Juliet's funeral. Hastening back to Verona he purchases poison in order to commit suicide by the body of Juliet. Paris intercepts Romeo at the tomb and is killed by Romeo who takes the poison and dies. Juliet awakes and kills herself with her dead lover's dagger.

Friar Laurence is left to explain the tragedy to the Prince and the families whom the Prince orders to be reconciled by the tragedy.

Any production of *Romeo and Juliet* needs formidably talented young actors. It is a stars' vehicle but, as usual, a highly competent supporting cast is needed. It is a young actors' play with six of them accounting for 53% of the lines. Its popularity has never been higher and it will always be topical.

One of the cruxes is the speed of the action, to which I shall return. This has implications for the sets, in particular the famous balcony, for if it is to be constructed and dismantled this will inevitably hinder proceedings. If it is to be a permanent feature this will diminish the space for the scenes in the public square. Shakespeare had a permanent balcony in his theatre but asked us to rely on our imaginations too. My own inclination is to do without a balcony unless an elegant design can provide one that does not slow down the action.

The period usually chosen is Renaissance, though famously Baz Luhrmann's film set it in modern times. Despite his brilliant solution to suggest a small arms manufacturer called Sword ("Put up your swords") I incline to using swords not guns for the Tybalt scenes and would suggest that the traditional period best suits the play.

The first crux is the speed of the action. In the Prologue Shakespeare called it "the two hours' traffic of our stage", which is virtually impossible to achieve. The play is 3,000-odd lines long. Today we can expect 1,000 lines to be performed in an hour. So what was Shakespeare thinking of? Well, this line is the first of many references to the speed of events in the play. In real time Romeo meets Juliet, forgets Rosaline, marries Juliet, kills Tybalt, is banished and sent to Mantua, returns to Verona and kills himself in less than a week. Juliet, a mere 13-year-old, calls for time to gallop apace, contracts two marriages, consummates one of them, takes a sleeping draught, wakes and commits suicide in the same short space of time. The imagery is of heat, gunpowder, explosion. Capulet cannot wait to arrange Paris' marriage. The only respite is post-coition when Romeo hears the lark and Juliet the nightingale as the hour of his banishment intrudes on his marriage night.

But, because of the imminent banishment, even this scene has an urgency that catches the overall mood of the play.

But that does not mean gabbling. No audience could stand it. The crux is to judge the balance between speed and comprehension. A couple of examples:

- The action in the square is lethargic, under the hot midday sun, in the scene between the supporters of the Montagues and the Capulets. The otherwise incomprehensible exchanges between Sampson and Gregory must be delivered slowly enough for us to appreciate the wit. The two word "You lie" is the spark that ignites the explosion.
- At the feast there will be music and movement but when the famous sonnet of Romeo and Juliet's first meeting occurs, I would freeze the hubbub to enable us to hear each word.

And if the play runs nearer to three hours than two, a correct understanding of the tempi and the urgencies will make it seem less.

The second crux, lighting, is one over which Shakespeare had no influence but, as I argue elsewhere, his words give us the clue that he was a master of light and shade, moon and starlight and sunlight, indoor and outdoor light, and in this play the ghostly light of the Capulets' vault. We can get the lighting right with modern technology and on-stage lights such as torches.

The contrasts in this play are most marked and we can achieve what Shakespeare could only suggest in the imagination. A midday outdoor performance meets the same practical challenges that faced him. It is a formidable challenge to rely only on the words.

The third crux is the imagery of love – the verse forms, the syntax are all a challenge for a modern actor and for a modern audience. Take the falconry imagery – "tassel-gentle", etc. – Juliet must understand the finer points of hawking to make sense of those lines. The traditional verse forms are reinvented in this play with a young modern energy that still obtains today. This crux, then, is to get the balance right between the old and new, e.g. the cheveril wit of young Mercutio and the old Nurse, full of cheap bawdy jokes and the new seriousness of love: "He jests at scars that never felt a wound." The old ideas of a daughter's duty to a father are challenged. In this case, the father is a testy unstable patriarch for whom old family values come before youth's personal fulfilment. To show the consummation of a hasty marriage is a truly revolutionary idea, even today, and especially when most fathers behave like Capulet. We must not forget to make this clash of cultures as shocking as it was when the play was written.

When presenting my *First Act Shakespeare* to schools, *Romeo and Juliet* was often asked for and the opening Chorus provided a conclusive endorsement of the main idea of this book. The text of the opening Chorus was set on an overhead projector. The cast was chosen. Interestingly, the two cast as Romeo and Juliet had to be corpses since the Chorus gives away the plot at once, and more focus is given to those involved in the warring households. The actor playing the Chorus was then asked to open the show. Invariably the line was given perfectly but with a level delivery. 'No, No,' I said, 'you have to ACT it as:

TWO HOUSEHOLDS	Loud and Gesture to Each
BOTH ALIKE IN DIGNITY	Gesture of Equality between them
IN FAIR VERONA	Gesture embracing whole town.

You have made three key points in two lines, by acting rather than saying them.' It invariably made the point, and the Chorus, and the street quarrel that followed, sprang to life.

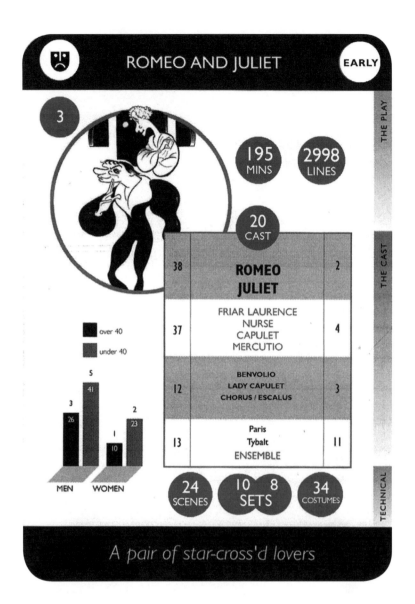

	38	**ROMEO**	2	
		JULIET		
	37	FRIAR LAURENCE NURSE CAPULET MERCUTIO	4	
	12	BENVOLIO LADY CAPULET CHORUS / ESCALUS	3	
	13	Paris Tybalt ENSEMBLE	11	

3

195 MINS

2998 LINES

20 CAST

over 40

under 40

MEN — 5, 41, 3, 26
WOMEN — 1, 10, 2, 23

24 SCENES

10 8 SETS

34 COSTUMES

A pair of star-cross'd lovers

THE PLAY

THE CAST

TECHNICAL

The main requirement of this play is for **younger** men with 41% of the lines. The play has **many** scenes with an **average** number of sets and an **average** number of costumes. This play is **recommended**, particularly early on in a Shakespearean involvement or career.

ROMEO Laurence Olivier   **JULIET** Peggy Ashcroft

THE MERCHANT OF VENICE

SHYLOCK Al Pacino

THE MERCHANT OF VENICE
The villainy you teach me

Bassanio borrows money from Antonio, the merchant, to enable him to woo Portia, a lady of great fortune. Antonio's ventures have over-stretched him and he borrows money from Shylock, who makes it a condition that if the money is not repaid he can demand a pound of flesh from Antonio. Thinking this is a joke, Antonio agrees. Bassanio and his outspoken friend, Gratiano, doubt Shylock's motives.

Portia is enjoined by her father's will to marry the man who solves the test of the three caskets and two princes, of Morocco and Arragon, fail the test by picking the wrong casket.

Jessica, Shylock's daughter, and Young Gobbo, his servant, both plan to leave his service and Jessica elopes to marry Lorenzo, a friend of Bassanio, stealing some money from her father. Antonio's ventures apparently fail and Shylock calls in his bond. Bassanio solves the casket test but before he can arrange his marriage with Portia, Portia and her waiting woman Nerissa decide to travel to Venice to defend Antonio in court, dressing as a lawyer and his clerk. Portia pleads for Shylock to show mercy; he refuses to consider any other return than the pound of flesh. However, by a brilliant cavil, Portia forces Shylock to abandon his case, and he is disgraced and his goods confiscated. Antonio is given power over this fortune and he demands that Shylock becomes a Christian and leave his possessions to Jessica. Bassanio rewards the lawyer with a ring.

Reunited at her home, Portia and Nerissa taunt Bassanio and Gratiano about the rings given to the lawyer and clerk, which had previously been exchanged between them as vows of their own love.

O f all Shakespeare's eponymous heroes, Antonio the Merchant is the least attractive to the actor. Who has ever made his name in this part? The actors playing Shylock, Portia and even Bassanio do far better, critically, in this play than the colourless fool of fortune that Antonio is.

But Shakespeare called it The Merchant of Venice – not The Jew of Venice, not The Three Caskets, not The Learned Doctor, not The Marriage Contracts – to suggest but four possible other titles.

The mercantile thread is very important. A merchant venturer was what we would call an entrepreneur, but a gambler too. He would buy and pay for the crew of a ship – send it on a long voyage to trade and to return unscathed for profits to be realised in the markets. The risk was entirely the merchant's: he was venturing a sizeable investment to enjoy the eventual returns. If the ship was lost or the market for the commodities had collapsed, too bad. It was a high-risk, high-stakes game: the rewards were huge if, and only if, fortune smiled on the 'venture'. Antonio, with six such ventures out at one time was foolishly over-stretched, and, until the last moments of the play when three cargoes came "suddenly to port", he probably deserved catastrophe, but the ethos of the day in fact admired the entrepreneurial spirit; a case of greed being good.

Of Antonio's other qualities – generosity, loyalty, fortitude, perseverance, equanimity – one cannot speak too highly. And these qualities and the extraordinary quandary to which these qualities led him were enough to justify the title.

The Jew of Venice would never do, though the treatment of Jew v. Gentile is in this play broader, more fair-minded and tragic than it is in, say, Marlowe's *Jew of Malta*. *The Merchant of Venice* is a wider play than the story of the caskets, or of the trial scene or, indeed, of marriages and money. So, though not the title of the play, these themes are nonetheless cruxes that must be faced.

The number of settings is few. As always in Shakespeare much of the setting can be understood from the language and context.

Switching is fast between scenes but there is probably a need for some set building, e.g., the courtroom scene, to assist the action.

While there is no sea scene, much of Act I Scene 1 describes the realities of what faces the merchant venturer's ship – water is never far removed from Venice and Belmont, which is situated on a nearby island. Shakespeare makes the sea a dominating feature of the play.

Words create atmosphere; in Act V the setting is the night sky and the Lorenzo/Jessica dialogue (not necessary in the slightest to describe the action) makes this explicit. And music too, "the music of the spheres", played by the house musicians, augments this atmosphere.

The first crux that must be faced is racism: specifically Jew v. Christian, though as well as this central theme of Jewishness, the play touches on several other racial themes. One of Portia's wooers, the Moor, is at pains to say, "mislike me not for my complexion". The servant Young Gobbo has also introduced this multicultural idea by getting a young Moor with child. Portia and Nerissa, even before the Moor arrives on the scene, have fun with other racial stereotypes, a Frenchman, a German, a Neapolitan, a Scotsman (and an Englishman). A later wooer is a Spaniard and even Bassanio is "foreign". The fact is that Elizabethan England was rapidly coming to terms with the variety of foreigners and their accents, and such 'racism' was more good-natured than vicious.

Not so with Jewishness. Barabbas the Jew in *The Jew of Malta* is an engaging character, but totally amoral. There was a famous Jewish plot fresh in Elizabethan minds which helped inflame attitudes against Jews. How vicious should anti-Semitism be in this play? The citizens of Venice in the persons of Salerio and Solanio and Gratiano are thoroughly bigoted and attack Shylock endlessly and gratuitously. The Duke, representing the State, is less censorious but would prefer Christians to thrive. Antonio speaks against Jews for their usury, yet uses the Jew's money when he has little alternative. The servant Gobbo runs away from the Jew, for feeding him too little, and his dilemma is brilliantly expounded in his conscience v. the Devil soliloquy; equating the Jew with the Devil fits Elizabethan sensibility perfectly.

The character of Shylock is multi-dimensional, whereas that of Barabbas in *The Jew of Malta* was not. It is Shylock who introduces the idea of civility into intercourse between Christian and Jew. The slights that Jews receive, not on account of their evilness but of their Jewishness, are memorably challenged: "if you prick us do we not bleed?" In the trial scene, Shylock suggests that slavery, on which Venice relies, is of doubtful morality.

The director is faced with the crux of where to pitch Shylock's Jewishness: at one extreme the courtly and courteous neo-Rothschild that Olivier and Jonathan Miller chose, or Irving's Fagin-like caricature who made the sharpening of the knife on the sole of his shoe a memorable feature of his performance.

One further aspect must be addressed, that of Jessica's crimes against her father and his religion. No doubt Elizabethans, and probably Shakespeare, too, applauded her choosing a Christian future. But she is a flawed creature: the theft of his money, the conspicuous expenditure of her inheritance and her renunciation of her faith are not easily acceptable. The trial scene awards her (and Lorenzo let us not forget) the dowry that Shylock would certainly have refused her had he not been caught out at law.

It is for the trial scene, however, that the play is most remembered and admired. It plays wonderfully in the theatre, making Shylock and Portia two of the most sought-after roles in the canon, for this scene only. The judgement for the director is then where to pitch the conflicts between Jew and Gentile, Father and Daughter, Accused and Prosecutor, to make sense of a text that argues both sides without offering a particular verdict.

The second great crux is money, and within that subject earning it v. inheriting it. Portia's father made his daughter's future as a wife conditional on the three caskets. When Bassanio wins her he wins her wealth as well. She could have remained rich and unmarried; she marries and surrenders her wealth to her husband. Such a contract today would not be commended, as Portia commends it, to the "wisdom" of a father. Bassanio is a penniless gentleman, because he has (like the Merchant) overstretched his finances to keep up the appearance of an eligible gentleman. He causes Antonio to take on new debt to pursue a great inheritrix. The rewards are immense. Bassanio "hazarded all he had" and hit the jackpot – "gained the golden fleece", as Gratiano puts it, whose own fortunes mirrored that of his friend.

Unless you inherit money (the Duke, Portia) you must marry it (Bassanio, Gratiano) or earn it by venturing all (Bassanio, Antonio). To make money out of money (Shylock) or have it fall into your lap (Jessica, Lorenzo) is altogether less admirable for those times.

The third crux stems from the second, which is the letter of the law. The law is supreme and outranks money. Although the law might take the easy option and demand that Shylock renounce his bond for the restitution (and more) of his outgoings, that would create a dangerous precedent for the State. Even mercy, infused by the State, would upset the precedence of the law. Such conditions give rise to the outcome of this trial which might today be summed up by 'Read the small print' – not only in the cavil between flesh and blood, but also the forfeits that the Venetian State demands in such a case as this. Mercy v. Justice is the choice.

Choices such as Mercy v. Justice; Gold v. Silver v. Lead; Jew v. Christian; venture or not; money v. love, dominate this play. The fact that the outcomes of each choice are so fundamentally opposite, and the stakes so high for failure, is what makes this play as rich in thought as it is in sheer entertainment. One last choice, sad v. merry, should also be noted. The first words of both Act I Scene 1 and Act I Scene 2 are of the sadness of both Antonio and Portia. Shylock's rationale for entering into the bond with Antonio is a "merry" one. Young Gobbo is seen as "merry" where her father is not to Jessica. The level to which merriness or sadness should permeate these scenes is a choice the director might make. And after all these momentous choices, with 'ideal' characters like Portia and Bassanio, what are we to make of the transformation from the Act V night, light and music and romance to the crude bawdy of the rings with which the play concludes? Sure choices and a sure-footedness in achieving these choices, are essential for a successful production.

Our illustration is of Al Pacino playing Shylock in a filmed version of this play. This introduces two important contributions to Shakespeare from America: films and stars. Shakespeare is not the preserve of the British and several examples follow, e.g. the filmed version of *Julius Caesar* with Marlon Brando, and theatre performances by Charles Laughton and Paul Robeson. Over and above this are the numerous North American festival performances of his plays including in New York City where Joe Papp mounted a production each year in Central Park. And Sam Wanamaker, another American star, created London's Shakespeare's Globe Theatre, which attracts students from all over the world.

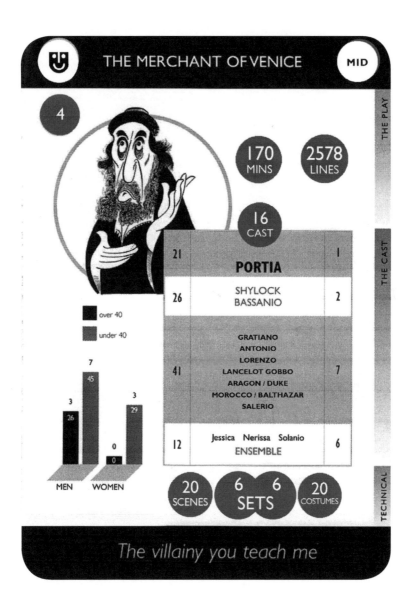

4

170 MINS

2578 LINES

16 CAST

21	**PORTIA**	1
26	SHYLOCK BASSANIO	2
41	GRATIANO ANTONIO LORENZO LANCELOT GOBBO ARAGON / DUKE MOROCCO / BALTHAZAR SALERIO	7
12	Jessica Nerissa Solanio ENSEMBLE	6

over 40

under 40

7
45
3
26
3
29
0
0

MEN   WOMEN

20 SCENES   6 6 SETS   20 COSTUMES

The villainy you teach me

The main requirement of this play is for younger men with 45% of the lines. The play has an average number of scenes with relatively few sets and relatively few costumes. This play is recommended, particularly early on in a Shakespearean involvement or career.

SHYLOCK Al Pacino

HAMLET

HAMLET
Simon Russell Beale Benedict Cumberbatch
Jonathan Pryce David Tennant

HAMLET
Spur my dull revenge

Hamlet, Prince of Denmark, was not elected King on his father's death. His uncle, Claudius, got the throne and to secure the title married Gertrude, the late King's wife. Hamlet encounters the ghost of his father, who reveals that he had been murdered by Claudius.

Ophelia, Polonius' daughter, believed Hamlet was in love with her and now believes him mad. Claudius engages Rosencrantz and Guildenstern, two school friends, to find out the cause of Hamlet's madness. Polonius also arranges a meeting between Ophelia and Hamlet, which he and Claudius overhear. Hamlet reveals to the audience that his madness is a disguise.

Hamlet arranges with some actors to play a scene based on the circumstances of his father's death. The watching Claudius reveals his complicity in the death. Gertrude tries to get the truth of his madness from Hamlet while Polonius overhears their encounter. Hamlet berates his mother and kills Polonius, thinking him to be the King. Hamlet is banished to England.

Ophelia, distraught at Polonius' death, commits suicide. Her brother, Laertes, returns to Denmark to avenge Polonius' death. Hamlet, who has thwarted his own planned death, also returns and confronts Laertes at Ophelia's grave. They fight a duel in which Laertes fatally wounds Hamlet by foul play. Laertes confesses his guilt. Gertrude drinks the poison that Claudius had prepared for Hamlet who now kills him before dying in Horatio's arms.

Horatio is left to pass Hamlet's crown to Fortinbras, an opportunistic prince from Norway.

Though I have never directed or acted in *Hamlet* this was the first play of this exercise that I felt I did not have to read again before drafting these conclusions. I must have seen a dozen or more productions.

I was surprised when, in my research into the popularity of the plays, *Hamlet* rated no higher than fifth. But it has not been done as often as one would expect, possibly on account of the availability of suitable actors to play Hamlet, possibly on account of its length. On economic grounds it requires considerable forces.

Yes, the great actor is indispensable and it is pointless to attempt a production unless a superstar is available. I once had to promote a natural Benvolio into the role of Romeo which did not turn out well. To promote a natural Laertes to a Hamlet would be equally, if not more, disastrous. A Hamlet must be old enough to have the technique to sustain a role of nearly 1,400 lines over nearly four hours with variety, energy and charisma. He must be young enough to establish why his inexperience had disqualified him from the election to the Danish throne when his father died. He is still a student and his behaviour is misunderstood by his mother. Not only should an actor playing Hamlet have achieved success in acting (not the least to sell seats) but he should be a veteran of Shakespearean performance with a role like Orlando already under his belt. I suspect Burbage was 'too old' when he created the role, or had a stunning technique to suggest the inexperience of the young Dane.

In practical terms these days a Hamlet will probably be in his late 20s but should be able to express adolescence convincingly. Hamlet has 35% of the lines of a long play that runs uncut for nearly four hours, a huge undertaking.

I should mention here an important composite role that I am suggesting. There are many ways of achieving such roles and directors will have their own ideas. However, I would like to propose one treble role that, until Greg Hicks did it, I had never seen before but which adds to the texture of the play, and also elevates this particular role to an importance as great as Polonius. The role is Hamlet's 'Father', a loose description of a father figure, and consists of the Ghost, the Player King and the Gravedigger.

The Ghost has been played by the Claudius actor and this is a valid double ("Look upon this picture, and on this") contrasting the two brothers. Jonathan Pryce, memorably and brilliantly, added to his enormous load the role of the Ghost too, in Richard Eyre's great production, as if an inner voice was forcing itself out of his own body. The Player King plays the Father in *The Mousetrap*. Hamlet's first remark is that he is an "old" friend, with his face valanced, i.e. bearded, exactly as his father's "sable-silvered". Not only that, in the Marlowe parody the First Player played the death of yet another father, Priam of Troy. Much of the dialogue of the Gravedigger scene recalls a time when Hamlet was a boy and Yorick bore Hamlet on his back and set the table on a roar. Both the Gravedigger and the Player King can be said to counterpoint Hamlet's relationship with both his real and ghostly father. It is a busy evening for the actor since the Ghost changes to Player King and back to Ghost before emerging as the Gravedigger, but it is a meaty challenge for a senior actor that makes more dramatic sense than another recent double, Polonius and the Gravedigger.

The first crux to consider is whether to cut the play and, if so, by how much. This is a text that can be so sacrosanct that, even in film, it is not cut (Branagh). In the theatre Peter Hall insists we hear the whole play. Cuts are inevitable, however, if one wishes to bring the action to, say, 3 rather than 4 hours.

Hamlet is only ever played with one interval, though two might suit the play better, were time not such a consideration. The modern tendency is to rush through to as far as is the limit of spectator endurance, i.e. to the end of Act III (nearly 2 ½ hours), but certainly to the end of Act III Scene 1 (nearly 2 hours). In either case effort should probably be made to reduce the need for such endurance.

My instinct is to make internal cuts to speed up the action, but not sacrifice scenes or incidents. I have identified about 450 lines that could go without spoiling the overall shape. For example practically every director that cuts, cuts the topical Elizabethan reference to the boy actors and I see no harm in that, but to cut the Reynaldo scene to speed the action is, to my mind, villainous.

The Players' scenes are considerable and the advice to the Players and other passages slow up the action of the play. I feel strongly, as I have argued elsewhere, that the advice to the Players is central to understanding Shakespeare if not, particularly, this play; to cut it is wrong, to shorten it difficult for me to recommend.

On the whole I agree with Polonius that the Player King's speech is too long and I have never understood why Claudius does not get the point of the dumbshow and stop the play before it gets going. The dumbshow makes *The Mousetrap* itself a luxury as far as the speed of action is concerned, and time could be saved with cuts to the play rather than the dumbshow.

Some directors have cut Act I Scene 1 (saving 11 minutes); all I would say is that if wholesale cuts are to be made, I would rather this scene went than the Reynaldo scene or the advice to the Players.

Some roles are often cut completely. The English Ambassador is often dispensed with, a minute saving and, in general, the political scenes (Tribute from Norway, Fortinbras' expedition, Tribute from England, Fortinbras' accession, News of Deaths of Rosencrantz and Guildenstern) are important to the fabric of the play.

The size of the Danish court is another crux. One of the best features of the Russian film version of the play was the size and importance of the court. The prize of kingship, which Claudius has won at the expense of young Hamlet, is a large one. The only way we can achieve this on stage is having attendants and extra courtiers to fill out the stage, which means not cutting the Corneliuses, the Ambassadors and the Reynaldos. There may be other ways to achieve this (soundtrack, filmed backdrops) but it does seem desirable to have as large a court as possible.

The final crux for the actor and his director to address is to decide how mad Hamlet is. I have already mentioned that Hamlet was not elected King on his father's death (though he elects Fortinbras on his death, as if he could). Was the reason his absence at Wittenberg, his qualities (not if Ophelia is to be believed), his inexperience or his madness? This is not the place to analyse all the references, both by Hamlet himself and the others to his condition. As part of the challenge of acting the part, the actor must determine for himself what makes him 'mad' and whether this is feigned or real or a mixture. His different ways of relating to people give him an opportunity to create the necessary variety and the necessary ambiguity in the matter of madness. Remember the Elizabethans had a very different attitude to madness than we do today. A madman was an outcast and unfit to be part of society let alone rule a kingdom. But was Hamlet's ambition to inherit from his father, or simply to revenge his foul murder? That is another necessary question of the play.

It is ironic to note that Claudius was elected to the throne of Denmark with Hamlet, the only son of the dead King, being passed over. And on Claudius' death, it is Hamlet, who is also on the point of death, who determines that "the election falls on Fortinbras", without reference to the elective process in Denmark that had denied him the throne.

Fortinbras, the opportunistic Prince of Norway, who had been the subject of a diplomatic rebuff at the beginning of the play, and had later undertaken a hollow invasion of Poland, now inherits Denmark, on the dying words of Hamlet. Something rotten here, surely?

One of my greatest pleasures was to help my granddaughter Alana prepare for her school production of the play scene in *Hamlet*. It opens with the speech:

> Speak the speech, I pray you, as I pronounced it to you,
> trippingly upon the tongue...

She must have been 12 or 13 at the time, and she managed not only to master the difficult syntax, but to perform it excellently and to retain it to this day. This is a vindication of my recommendation that we should learn as much Shakespeare as possible by heart when we are young, as much for pleasure as performance.

Hamlet repays viewing many times. My first was to see Paul Scofield with Mary Ure at the Oxford Playhouse in a cast which included actors in smaller roles who later became leading players in their own right: Richard Pasco and Harry H. Corbett. The celebrated film with Laurence Olivier and Jean Simmonds retains its freshness and power and remains essential viewing.

One of the most interesting *Hamlet*s of the 10 or 12 I have seen was Ben Whishaw. Whishaw played the role straight out of drama school and his youth made the action of passing him over as King in succession to his father all the more believable. Of the four modern Hamlets in our illustration I have seen three, and all these different interpretations have something particular to remember them by. Over the years I have usually written short reviews in a diary for each of them and I commend this as a useful discipline for every play, identifying both 'the necessary questions of the play to be considered' and points in the production and the performances.

There is one final point I would like to make on the authorship question. One of the candidates offered by Anti Stratfordians as the 'real' author is Christopher Marlowe. The elaborate parody of Marlowe's 'mighty line', the Player King's speech about the Fall of Troy, would hardly have been written by Marlowe, nor would Polonius' put-down: 'This is too long,' which I am inclined to think is fair comment.

I continue to be amazed that *Hamlet* is not at the top of the list in popularity. Maybe future efforts may project it further up the list.

HAMLET

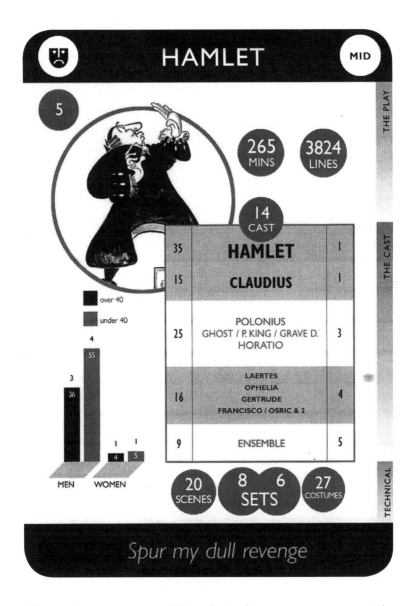

5

265 MINS

3824 LINES

14 CAST

35	**HAMLET**	1
15	**CLAUDIUS**	1
25	POLONIUS GHOST / P. KING / GRAVE D. HORATIO	3
16	LAERTES OPHELIA GERTRUDE FRANCISCO / OSRIC & 2	4
9	ENSEMBLE	5

THE PLAY

THE CAST

TECHNICAL

over 40

under 40

4

55

3

36

1 1

4 5

MEN   WOMEN

20 SCENES

8 6 SETS

27 COSTUMES

Spur my dull revenge

The main requirement of this play is for **younger** men with **55%** of the lines. The play has an **average** number of scenes with relatively **few** sets and an **average** number of costumes. This play is **straightforward**, with a **few** but not insuperable challenges.

HAMLET   David Garrick

53

A MIDSUMMER NIGHT'S DREAM

BOTTOM Charles Laughton

A MIDSUMMER NIGHT'S DREAM
Fierce vexation

Theseus is preparing for his marriage to Hippolyta when Egeus demands his right to arrange his daughter Hermia's marriage to Demetrius. Hermia loves Lysander, and Demetrius is loved by Hermia's friend, Helena. The law of Athens supports Egeus' right. Hermia and Lysander decide to elope. They tell Helena of their plans.

Peter Quince and his friends, including Bottom, plan a play for the Duke's wedding celebration and they rehearse it in the forest.

In the forest Oberon and Titania, King and Queen of the Fairies, quarrel. Oberon instructs Puck to punish Titania by anointing her eyes with a flower which has the power to make her fall in love with whomever she sees when awaking. Puck is also told to anoint Demetrius' eyes for rejecting Helena.

Puck gets the wrong Athenian, so it is Lysander that now pleads with Helena for her love, and Hermia is enraged at what she thinks is a plot. At the rehearsal Puck puts an ass's head on Bottom and it is Bottom that Titania sees on waking. She orders her fairies to attend on him.

Eventually the relenting Oberon orders antidotes to these confusions and Theseus arrives to hear the stories of the lovers. Egeus' objection to Lysander is over-ruled and the three couples see the play of Pyramus and Thisbe performed by Bottom and his friends.

Oberon, Titania and Puck bless the impending nuptials.

It is arguable that Peter Brook's production of *A Midsummer Night's Dream* in the 1970s was definitive. It still casts its shadow on the play. I shall argue that one of Brook's ideas has become a crux that cannot be ignored. But as the rest of that production fades in the memory, the play's greatness re-emerges fresh for new productions that do not need to plagiarise Brook.

A cast of 17 is proposed, though if, for example, the Fairies are played by the other actors (memorably recently by the Mechanicals), 15 would be a workable minimum. There is a remarkable balance of good parts.

The settings are practically nondescript in the sense that the action can take place virtually anywhere, especially in the open air where, since most of the play is set in a wood outside Athens, the midsummer night magic can easily be suggested. The use of fairy lights, sparklers and torches under a dark night sky invariably add to the delights of a production – remember to calculate dusk accurately, since the play is short (2 ¼ hours) and at midsummer night might not fall quickly enough if an early start, say 7.30pm, is chosen. The rooms in Theseus' palace can easily be transposed to the open air while Peter Quince's house needs no more than a workbench and a few tools to suggest it. Costumes are not a problem; the simplest of materials can produce the greatest effect.

The crux that Peter Brook decided was that much of the action is in fact the dreams of Theseus and Hippolyta that occur before their wedding, in which, if you like, their hidden natures are suggested to each other, specifically in the Oberon/Titania subplot. Brook simply cast Theseus and Oberon together and Hippolyta and Titania. Other directors have often adopted this on both economic and theatrical grounds. The play is a DREAM. Add to this that the pedantic and unimaginative Philostrate – the Master of the Revels – becomes the mercurial and mischievous Puck and the point is reinforced. It all works perfectly well – two quick costume changes that can be performed in sight of the audience is all that is necessary, though the surprise of the second change (the last entrance of the fairies) is probably best done offstage. No textual transpositions are needed – no stage business either. Titania's infatuation with Bottom was suggested in one production by Bottom bumping into Hippolyta at the palace as he delivered some of his wares for the nuptials. The actor playing Egeus can also play one of the more taciturn Mechanicals, not so much to add to Brook's point as to give the actor a more rewarding part.

The Dream convention gives virtually unlimited scope to actors and directors to examine these relationships and discover new truths – the second crux. The lovers, through the magic potion, transform themselves for a while to their opposites and suffer the distortion of the dream, while the Mechanicals, in aspiring to be actors, assume responsibility for the imagination – unfortunately they are living more of an artistic nightmare than a dream in the theatre. We all may dream of achieving higher truths, though often the effort is more to be applauded than the achievement.

This play, in fact, is one of Shakespeare's most telling on the subject of the life of the imagination:

> "The lunatic the lover and the poet are of imagination
> All compact."

There is so much in this speech that these lines preface. It is crucial to study it to understand the subplot of this play. The lunatic (touched by the moon) is one example of madness. The lovers, both the quartet and Theseus/Oberon and Hippolyta/Titania, are madly in love. The poet is of course Shakespeare and he seems to be saying that the act of creating a play such as this is a sort of madness. Actors, however good (or however bad, as in the play of Pyramus and Thisbe), depend on the "fine frenzy" of the poet to make their performances of value for their audiences. Shakespeare in this speech makes telling statements about his art, even if this is not strictly necessary to this play.

Not necessary either are the short speeches on the merits of Theseus and Hippolyta's hounds. But is there a better example of the poet's imagination than these wonderful speeches?

The third crux is one that occurs throughout Shakespeare, the harsh reality of the law that no ruler can either override or ignore. In this play Athenian law gives the plot momentum – the flight of the lovers to the wood is to escape that law. Hermia's father, Egeus, insists that his will be preferred to hers simply because the law says it must. Though (happily) such intransigence is rarer today than in the 16th century it is important that modern audiences appreciate this code that affects plays like *A Midsummer Night's Dream* so profoundly.

A Midsummer Night's Dream is an ideal play for the outdoors where the bulk of scenes are set, and especially in midsummer. I have directed it twice and if the closing moments are played at around dusk with the addition of fairy lights and sparklers, there is an enchantment that is quite magical. Once a nearby two-star restaurant was persuaded to keep the band from playing until after the end of the performance, so as not to destroy the magic.

This play ranks sixth in popularity, rather lower than I had expected. It is as perfect as a Mozart opera and will continue to delight audiences for years, whether they believe in fairies or not. It is a dream. Simply that.

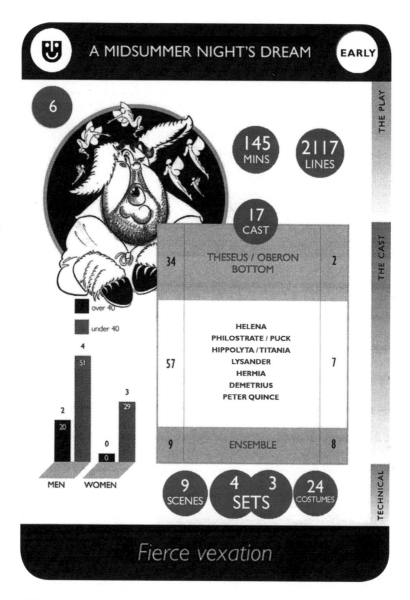

6

145 MINS

2117 LINES

17 CAST

THE PLAY

THE CAST

TECHNICAL

	THESEUS / OBERON BOTTOM	
34		2
57	HELENA PHILOSTRATE / PUCK HIPPOLYTA / TITANIA LYSANDER HERMIA DEMETRIUS PETER QUINCE	7
9	ENSEMBLE	8

over 40

under 40

4

51

3

29

2

20

0

0

MEN   WOMEN

9 SCENES

4 3 SETS

24 COSTUMES

Fierce vexation

The main requirement of this play is for **younger** men with **51%** of the lines. The play has relatively **few** scenes with relatively **few** sets and relatively **few** costumes. This play is **recommended**, particularly early on in a Shakespearean involvement or career.

BOTTOM Charles Laughton

MUCH ADO ABOUT NOTHING

BENEDICK Michael Redgrave   **BEATRICE** Googie Withers

MUCH ADO ABOUT NOTHING
Sigh no more ladies

Don Pedro, Prince of Arragon, and his followers arrive at Leonato's house after a war. One of these, Benedick, appears to be a confirmed bachelor. Beatrice, Leonato's niece, also seems destined not to marry, and they continue a history of sharp talk between them. Another of the followers, Claudio, is in love with Leonato's daughter Hero, and engages Don Pedro to woo her for him at a party. Don John, Don Pedro's brother, tells Claudio that the Prince is wooing Hero for himself.

Leonato and Don Pedro trick Beatrice and Benedick into liking each other more than they say. Borachio, a follower of Don John, arranges a plot in which Hero would appear to be unfaithful to Claudio. Dogberry and Verges on watch overhear Borachio discussing Don John's plot but are unable to prevent the revelation by Claudio of Hero's "unfaithfulness" at the church. Hero faints and Friar Francis announces she is dead. Don John flees. Beatrice compels Benedick to avenge Hero by killing Claudio.

Dogberry reveals the truth about Don John's plot and Claudio begs forgiveness. A second marriage is arranged where Hero reappears and is reunited with Claudio. Beatrice and Benedick announce that they too are to marry. Don John is captured before the final celebrations.

This is a very agreeable play and its (1993) film version was faithful to its spirit. Indeed the dance that concludes it was done memorably on camera with a close-up of the dancers transforming into a bird's-eye view of the whole dance in the villa gardens as the camera was hoisted high above the action. The Arden editor, A. R. Humphreys, notes that this is the one play in the canon that ends with a dance – all has ended well, as one might say, despite the ado caused by Don John and his cronies.

It is a play that holds its popularity well (the seventh of the Seven Stars) and this is mainly due to the characters of Beatrice and Benedick – their roles being star parts for actors who have already achieved much with less mature characters. Spinsterhood, bachelordom and marriage have seldom been better discussed. And Dogberry, who pre-dates Mrs Malaprop by a hundred years and more, is one of Shakespeare's greatest comic creations.

Of all the plays, this is the one in which none of the named speaking roles needs to double up. I suggest but three composite roles to cover the unnamed characters in the text. A cast of 19 can manage this play, and it is one with plenty of good roles that will appeal to actors preferring company plays. The smallest part is Verges, but it is a part that can make a great impact as Dogberry's foil.

The play is set mostly in a garden – even the wedding scene in the church could easily be an open-air affair. The prison scene does not need an elaborate set. This is a play that can adapt to a variety of periods, so the costume designer has scope to make his or her own mark on proceedings.

My first crux, one that applies to many plays, is about the nature of marriage where the bride, previously the property of the father, becomes the property of the husband. Fathers dictate who their daughters shall marry. Even if, as in this play, Leonato the father agrees to his daughter's choice of Claudio (or rather his choice of her), when she is falsely accused he sides with the established view of the day that she has dishonoured him in failing to be married according to his wishes. There is little thought of poor Hero. The case of Leonato's niece Beatrice is also part of the same theme – an ageing spinster with a tongue that puts off suitors is a major embarrassment to her guardian uncles who no doubt wish to have her off their hands. This lends added relish to the scenes with Benedick, in that time is really running out for Beatrice, opportunities for marriages of advantage and honour being few and far between. At the lower end of the scale, the potential union of Margery and Borachio has potentially disastrous consequences for Hero. Remember too that Hero had been wooed by Don Pedro at the masked ball and that Claudio had suspected Don Pedro had done this for himself and not, as it turns out, on Claudio's behalf. Such a marriage would have violated the same code.

The second crux has no particular difficulties except to stage it properly with some variety – that of the action being driven by hearsay. I call the play a play of overhearing. The most obvious examples are the staged conversations about Beatrice and Benedick that they overhear in the orchard, by which they are driven to believe that they are each loved by the other despite what has passed between them in their public utterances. The Margaret and Borachio liaison is staged to prove to the watching Don Pedro that Hero is unfaithful, which Claudio then learns by hearsay. The intentions of Don Pedro at the masked ball are overheard by a servant who reports the hearsay. Dogberry's watch overhears the confession of Borachio. By indirections we find directions out.

The third crux is again straightforward – how to play the Dogberry/Verges scenes, whether to laugh at or laugh with them. On the one hand they are simple buffoons whom sophisticates can deride, but on the other they have a dogged perseverance that actually delivers the vital evidence against Don John's plot that merits admiration. All I will say is that an element of ambiguity in these scenes (there are five short scenes) will add much to the play whereas a black or white choice between the extremes will limit our enjoyment.

Despite its comparative simplicity this is a wonderful play that has several substantial themes well worth exploring.

Kenneth Branagh directed the film I mentioned above, playing Benedick opposite Emma Thompson as Beatrice. Later in the Shakespeare Sampler I include the song 'Sigh No More Ladies' as an example of what a song can add to a play, and the film had a splendid version of this song which defined the mood of the overall production.

I should also add a reference to a marvellous National Theatre production of the play where the warring Benedick (Simon Russell Beale) and Beatrice (Zoë Wanamaker) ended up, fully clothed, in a plunge pool.

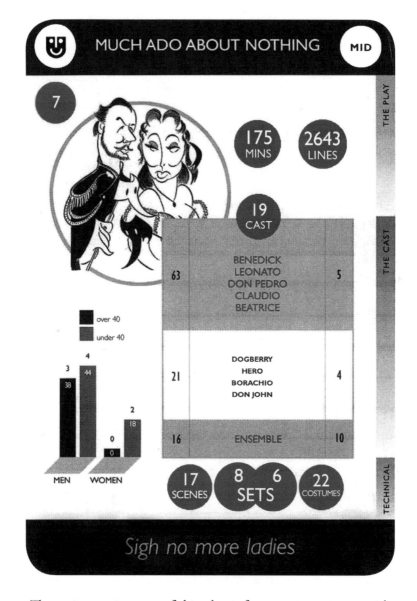

MUCH ADO ABOUT NOTHING

MID

7

175 MINS

2643 LINES

19 CAST

| 63 | BENEDICK
LEONATO
DON PEDRO
CLAUDIO
BEATRICE | 5 |

| 21 | DOGBERRY
HERO
BORACHIO
DON JOHN | 4 |

| 16 | ENSEMBLE | 10 |

over 40

under 40

MEN — 3, 38, 4, 44

WOMEN — 0, 0, 2, 18

17 SCENES

8 6 SETS

22 COSTUMES

Sigh no more ladies

The main requirement of this play is for **younger** men with **44%** of the lines. The play has an **average** number of scenes with relatively **few** sets and relatively **few** costumes. This play is **recommended**, particularly early on in a Shakespearean involvement or career.

BENEDICK Michael Redgrave **BEATRICE** Googie Withers

THE TAMING OF THE SHREW

PETRUCCIO Richard Burton
KATHARINA Elizabeth Taylor

THE TAMING OF THE SHREW
A woman mov'd

Christopher Sly, a drunken tinker, watches a play about the battle of the sexes. Baptista of Padua's daughters are a contrasted pair. Katharina, the shrew, is outspoken and her father will not allow his younger daughter, the demure Bianca, to marry before her elder sister, despite having several suitors, including Lucentio, whose fortune depends on his father Vincentio's approval. Lucentio agrees with his servant Tranio to exchange identities to allow him to become Bianca's tutor and have access to her. Petruccio hears of Katharina's dowry and despite her disdain and contempt for him decides to marry her. He arrives for his wedding in a dishevelled state and, despite her protests, carries his bride off to his house, where, with Grumio and others of his servants, exasperates and humiliates her.

Back in Padua, Lucentio wins the love of Bianca and elopes with her, leaving her other suitor, Hortensio, to marry a rich widow. Tranio finds a double for Vincentio to confirm to Baptista the extent of Lucentio's fortune. Meanwhile Petruccio and Katharina, returning to Padua, meet up with the real Vincentio and all is revealed to Baptista who finally accepts the situation. At the wedding reception for the three couples, Katharina, greatly changed, urges the other new wives to be obedient to their new masters.

For a relatively short play, *The Taming of the Shrew* needs considerable resources: 33 parts are listed. My suggestion is for 15 actors, which is the minimum needed for both the Christopher Sly scenes and the play itself; cutting the former does not reduce this number, given that my suggestion involves Sly playing Grumio and the Lord, Lucentio. Fifteen is already dangerously large in professional (i.e. economic) terms.

As usual, settings are relatively unimportant, though the interiors at Petruccio's country house and at Baptista's need some inventiveness. The Sly scenes are often set in a covered balcony and that is also a design consideration. The main action takes place in and between Padua and Verona.

It is worth mentioning commedia del arte and Jacques Callot when thinking of which period to set the play in. The Italian commedia companies were performing outside Italy from about 1570 onwards. Their plays had stock characters such as Pantalone, usually an old father opposing the marriage of his daughter to the young wooer, often preferring a suitor of his own age with money. The word pantaloon occurs in this play (as it also does in *As You Like It*). The servant-turned-master idea in this play is also a common device of commedia del arte, as it was in Roman comedy. Tranio the servant is both witty and pert, a typical Roman servant. It is no accident that his first line is a Latin quotation. All of this suggests costumes based on Jacques Callot's famous designs, though these would have been designed at around 1620, later than the play which was written in the 1590s. Molière used stock Commedia types but he was writing even later – c.1650. Having loved Callot for years I would certainly opt for designs based on his costumes.

The Taming of the Shrew is a straightforward play with a good story that stands very well on its own. Petruccio and Katharina are roles that top actors are delighted to play. The first crux to be addressed is how feminist to make Katharina, and how chauvinist to make Petruccio, both modern ideas that Shakespeare anticipated. As always in Shakespeare, the choice of either extreme would not be a good idea. The lines and the situations are full of subtle ambiguities that should not suggest an arbitrary choice of one extreme. I suggest that you go for whichever emphasis fits your actors best, have fun in directing it and appreciate that for every choice there is an opposite choice that might have done as well. This all culminates in Katharina's famous Act V speech: your task is to make it both heartfelt and tongue in cheek, and all shades in between.

The second crux – whether or not to include the Christopher Sly scenes – is more difficult. There is little doubt that some of the original Sly scenes have disappeared. Additional scenes involving Sly might have been part of an earlier play by a different author, that Shakespeare adapted or rewrote but, for whatever reason, were dropped or not included in the Folio. Such scenes still exist and if the Sly scenes are included I would suggest using the Epilogue to complete the decision to make the Petruccio–Katharina story a play within a play.

This raises two further points. The Lord in the Induction is remarkably similar to Theseus in *A Midsummer Night's Dream,* who chose a play to eke out the time before his nuptials were consummated. This same Lord also expresses the pleasures of hunting with dogs. In elaborately convincing Sly that he is really a great Lord himself, watching a play, the Lord is adding a further degree of ambiguity; is the play, and especially its outcome, true or imaginary?

Sly is a low-life character who dresses up noble; this is Tranio's situation too. So the actor playing Tranio might also attempt Sly, with the actor playing the aristocratic Lucentio doubling as the Lord in the Induction. The boy/lady could be played by the actress playing the widow. Each company must decide for itself how to handle the Induction and I would not criticise any decision on this crux.

The final crux to be addressed is that of Master and Servant. I have talked about Lucentio and Tranio; a second servant, Biondello, is younger and of a much lower status. As in Victorian and Edwardian households, the relative standings of the servants must be constantly borne in mind. Petruccio has an enormous retinue of servants. At the top are Grumio and Curtis, probably equals, certainly senior to the various 'single job' servants in the country house scene. The Tailor and the Haberdasher are not servants but probably lower in status than Grumio and Curtis.

The Taming of the Shrew has plenty going for it for a modern audience. The central conceit has hardly ever been more apposite, and the comedy at several levels is deft and witty. This is a play to have fun with.

On my retirement from business I commissioned a painting from Ronnie Copas entitled *The Poet and the Painter* to contain a defining moment from each of the 37 plays of Shakespeare. The incident from this play is an example of a bit of stage business in an RSC production with Vanessa Redgrave and Derek Godfrey which followed the line:

> Why does the world report that Kate doth limp?

Petruccio, sitting on a stool at a table, is wooing Katharina, who is called the Shrew on account of her reputation for plain-speaking. Though she has been storming round the room, Petruccio pretends to take no notice. Katharina, enraged, kicks the stool from under Petruccio. He, however, stays perfectly motionless, in sitting attitude, as Katharina limps aside. The line is a perfect put-down.

This, a brilliant illumination of the text, underlines my contention that Shakespeare is best experienced by acting it, and is better seen in performance than read.

And what better performances than those given by Richard Burton, Elizabeth Taylor and Michael Hordern in Franco Zeffirelli's film celebrated in our illustration? It is an outstanding version of the play.

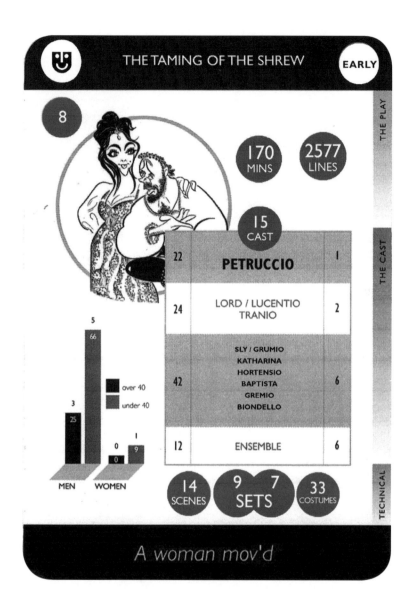

8

170 MINS

2577 LINES

15 CAST

22	PETRUCCIO	1
24	LORD / LUCENTIO TRANIO	2
42	SLY / GRUMIO KATHARINA HORTENSIO BAPTISTA GREMIO BIONDELLO	6
12	ENSEMBLE	6

5

66

over 40

under 40

3

25

0

0

0

1

9

MEN WOMEN

14 SCENES

9 SETS **7**

33 COSTUMES

A woman mov'd

The main requirement of this play is for younger men with 66% of the lines. The play has relatively few scenes with an average number of sets and an average number of costumes. This play is recommended, particularly early on in a Shakespearean involvement or career.

PETRUCCIO Richard Burton
KATHARINA Elizabeth Taylor

ANTONY AND CLEOPATRA

CLEOPATRA Helen Mirren

ANTONY AND CLEOPATRA
Such a mutual pair

Antony, one of the triumvirs ruling the Roman Empire, and Cleopatra, Queen of Egypt, are lovers. Antony is recalled to Rome from Egypt by Octavius to deal with Pompey's revolt. In Rome Antony is encouraged to marry Octavia, Octavius' sister, following the death of his wife, the news of which infuriates Cleopatra. Pompey's revolt seems quashed and Antony returns to Egypt, but Octavius reopens hostilities with Pompey. News reaches Antony that Octavius is preparing to attack him in Egypt and the recall of Octavia to Rome in an attempted reconciliation does nothing to diminish Octavius' resolve.

Enobarbus, Antony's officer, advises Antony in vain not to fight at sea and the flight of Cleopatra's vessels at Actium results in a defeat. Enobarbus deserts Antony who, none the less, generously treats him by sending his treasure after him. Enobarbus, consumed with grief and guilt, dies. After making some gains in a land battle Antony again suffers a decisive defeat at sea.

Cleopatra, charged with betrayal by Antony, sends word back to him that she has killed herself in her burial monument. On the news Antony tries to kill himself and is carried, grievously wounded, to the monument where he dies in Cleopatra's arms.

Octavius tries to persuade Cleopatra to come to Rome but, knowing she will be humiliated, despite Octavius' promises, she kills herself, but not before her loyal maids, Charmian and Iras, predecease her.

This great play demands great resources of a company. The difficulties are usually accepted if it means offering a great actress the chance to play Cleopatra and a great actor Antony.

The first difficulty is the size of cast, which has economic consequences for the professionals – though this is an opportunity for a non-professional company. Shakespeare identified 34 roles by name, a further eight messengers, several of whom have important scenes. The story embraces Eastern and Western Roman Empires, and an impression of appropriately sized courts and armies is highly desirable. By cutting, transposing, doubling, trebling and quadrupling roles a cast of 24 (20 men, 4 women) is suggested.

The second difficulty is the proliferation of scenes – 42 – and the time taken simply to change scenes. The action switches between Rome and Egypt, with diversions to Pompey's boat and one scene in Syria. If this were not enough, the final scenes take place in Cleopatra's monument where the body of Antony is raised from floor level to a higher level – never easy to do, and certainly not quickly. The design challenge is obviously to differentiate between Egypt and Rome and to limit sets to basic settings where decor – cushions, drapes and easily installable props – is to be preferred to building. And costumes too – about 80 may be required, which is a big logistical challenge.

The period seems non-negotiable to me, with its attendant requirement for armour, swords, spears, shields and all the Roman army paraphernalia. And an Egyptian court would not be short of great art.

These economic and logistical challenges are partially offset by the audience-pulling power of a great actress (or actor, as Mark Rylance showed) as Cleopatra. The part was originally written for a boy and a feature is the lack of any great set-piece speeches. The part is all stops and starts, with darts of activity interspersed with periods of static majesty. There are enough clues in the text to suggest how the role should be played, but "infinite variety" will do for a generalisation. One would probably cast a Cleopatra before an Antony, but

Antony is almost as crucial to get right. It demands an experienced Shakespearean with the charisma of Mark Antony in *Julius Caesar,* and with the world weariness of a great man in eclipse – as Octavius Caesar seeks to become the inheritor of Julius Caesar.

There are magnificent supporting roles, Enobarbus and Pompey to name but two. None of the Egyptian court is without interest. There are three significant messengers, a splendid Clown, each with scenes to steal. It is crucial to get the politics right. This takes its tenor from Octavius, the cool and calculating contender for absolute power who shows warmth and humanity only after his opponent is dead. Pompey, Mark Antony and Cleopatra are stepping stones to Octavius' ruthless advance.

Of equal interest is the way that these high politics impinge on the lives of ordinary people, in particular on three of the messengers.

The language of the love match between Antony and Cleopatra has hardly less ardour than that between Romeo and Juliet. But both Antony and Cleopatra switch moods so many times and with such intensity that the first crux is to achieve and sustain the variety. Enobarbus says that Cleopatra distracts Antony from his soldiership. Antony is forever conscious of his pre-eminent political reputation as a general and yet he loses it, and with it his whole world for Cleopatra, who betrays him in battle.

The second crux is to make the military outcomes clear. The military scale is huge. There are three battles, two at sea, the cele-bration of victory and the dejection of defeat, as well as a campaign in Syria; the demands are enormous. Again the bewildering speed of defeat turning to victory and vice-versa demands constant vigilance to understand what is happening. I note that Shakespeare uses the Marlovian device of "high astounding" verse with a proliferation of proper names to suggest the scale of these military actions and the sweep of geography.

The third crux is the impact of these events on the common man and on the contributions of the common man to these events. I have mentioned the three messengers. The common soldiers and guards are used to tell us the real state of the war – the scene between the guards when "the God Hercules" leaves Antony is such an example. In this play each of the parts usually called extras are given lines and insights that illuminate the whole. Unless you have available a large and enthusiastic 'chorus' of actors, it might be better to consider a less challenging play. It is not too much to say that having such a chorus is as important as having an Antony and a Cleopatra.

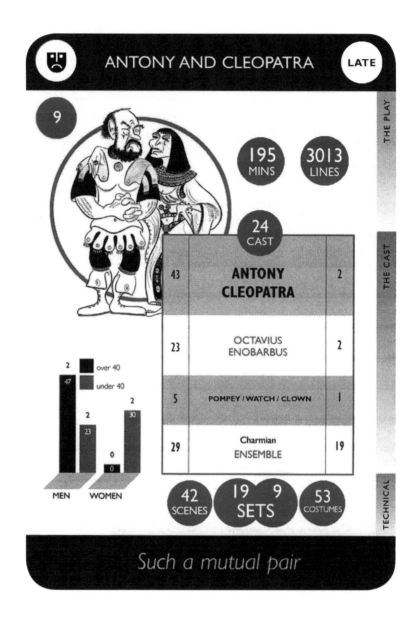

ANTONY AND CLEOPATRA

LATE

9

195 MINS

3013 LINES

24 CAST

43	**ANTONY** **CLEOPATRA**	2
23	OCTAVIUS ENOBARBUS	2
5	POMPEY / WATCH / CLOWN	1
29	Charmian ENSEMBLE	19

2 over 40

47 under 40

2

23

2

0

0

30

2

MEN WOMEN

42 SCENES

19 SETS 9

53 COSTUMES

Such a mutual pair

The main requirement of this play is for older men with 47% of the lines. The play has many scenes with many sets and many costumes. This play is more difficult and probably best left to experienced groups.

ANTONY Richard Johnson **CLEOPATRA** Janet Suzman

OTHELLO

OTHELLO Lenny Henry

OTHELLO
Arise black vengeance

Othello, the Moorish General, marries Desdemona, the daughter of Brabantio, against her father's wishes. Roderigo, a young Venetian, engages Iago, Othello's Ancient, to procure him access to Desdemona. A Turkish invasion of Cyprus prompts the Venetian Senate to send a fleet under Othello to defeat the Turks.

Cassio, Othello's Lieutenant, arrives in Cyprus as does Desdemona, who had been taken there by Iago, who also arranged that Roderigo should continue his pursuit of Desdemona in Cyprus. Othello's arrival in Cyprus coincides with the news of the defeat of the Turks. In a celebration party Cassio becomes drunk and attacks Montano the Governor of Cyprus. Cassio is cashiered by Othello. Emilia, Iago's wife, pleads with Othello for Cassio's reinstatement but Iago arranges it to appear to Othello that this pleading is because Desdemona is Cassio's mistress. A handkerchief, carelessly lost by Othello himself, becomes the evidence to convince Othello of Cassio's guilt and he orders Iago to kill Cassio. Othello confronts Desdemona who cannot understand how she has upset her husband.

Roderigo is now set on by Iago to kill Cassio. Cassio wounds Roderigo but is himself incapacitated by the attack. Othello, believing Cassio to be dead now kills Desdemona only for Emilia to reveal Iago's part in the episode of the handkerchief. Iago arrives and kills Emilia in an attempt to silence her. Othello, appalled that he has killed an innocent Desdemona, wounds Iago, and kills himself as the new powers in Cyprus arrest Iago.

This has been the least popular of the four Great Tragedies (*Hamlet, King Lear, Macbeth, Othello*). Trevor Nunn's 1989 production at Stratford of this play is definitive and my notes reflect my admiration for that production. Points about it include:

- **Ideal casting:** Othello is, for all his qualities, an outsider in Venetian society. Willard White, a distinguished opera singer, not an actor, brought an outsider quality to the play. The other principal roles had distinguished Shakespearean actors, making this contrast particularly memorable.
- **A military setting:** the important roles are of soldiers and their wives.
- **Outstanding understanding of the text:** Iago is one of the hardest roles in the canon – he speaks largely in prose, structured in a tortuous syntax.
- **The use of a small theatre** (as with Nunn's *Macbeth*) intensified what is a deeply personal tragedy by allowing us to *see* it at close range. Contrast this with John Dexter's National Theatre production in which I found Olivier's Othello very mannered. The size of the theatre did not allow the intimacy that seems key to this particular play.

Othello (800+ lines) is not the biggest role – Iago has over a thousand – but is a role that demands an actor of great stature capable of achieving both the music of the lines and the pathos of his predicament. Iago requires an even more experienced Shakespearean.

The Victorians loved the Venetian splendour of the first act, but modern directors seem to prefer to get the Cyprus scenes correct: the military barracks of an army sent to Cyprus for a military conflict is no place for splendour of any sort. Having decided a military setting, the period can be chosen at will; Nunn's was the US Civil War, which fitted as well as anything. There is no real need for lavish sets. (Remember Zeffirelli's disaster at Stratford where the magnificent sets needed over 30 minutes to change.)

The first crux is one that has arisen recently: whether to cast a black actor as Othello, as it is now generally felt that none but black actors should play Othello. But wait a moment – Othello is actually a Moor, more Arab than African or African-American. The parts should go, in my mind, to actors capable of playing them even if they are not of Moorish or Arab parentage. To deny actors of stature the chance to play Othello on the grounds that they are not black seems to me to be wrong.

I am aware that my views are not everyone's. The crux is for each individual production to address this point. But please do so with the play's needs in mind.

I directed a professional version of this play, omitting the first act set in Venice, in London with six actors, which I called *Black and White Sextet*. This title reflected that I had three black actors playing Othello, Emilia and Roderigo, and three white playing Iago, Desdemona and Cassio. (And the pun in *Sextet* was intentional.) Economics dictated that the cast was limited to six, since the venue was The Rosemary Branch, a pub theatre. Even if Shakespeare did not write with actors of different ethnic backgrounds in mind, the casting of a black Emilia strengthened Iago's suspicion that his wife had had an affair with Othello. And having a black Roderigo, played as a rich and foolish princeling enamoured with a white heiress, added to his play, as I believe it did in these instances.

I would like to record my admiration for the cast, led by Ben Onwukwe and Richard Earthy, in proving that the power of Shakespeare need not be diminished by compression.

The second crux is how the relationship between Othello and Desdemona should be played. Desdemona is not an Octavia, meekly submitting to either her father or her husband. Her defence of Cassio is a result of a genuine openness and good nature. She is playful, not politic and it is this very frankness that disastrously misleads Othello as to her suspected guilt. On her deathbed she gives a robust defence to all Othello's accusations and in her dying breath shows defiance, courage and sheer virtue in trying to deflect

Othello's obvious guilt in it. The skill and devilishness of Iago's revenge on Othello for promoting Cassio over him is enough to allow Othello to remain convinced to the end that his motives in killing her are right and reasonable; and this makes the pity of it all the more poignant.

The third crux is to get the military and political ranks understood. Montano is the Governor of Cyprus before Othello arrives. Montano has served under Othello and is therefore junior to him. He remains in service in Cyprus but it is Cassio who is confirmed as Othello's Lieutenant, the rank that Iago had aspired to, which, not getting, is the cause of his determination to bring down Othello. Montano is wounded in the brawl caused by Iago getting Cassio drunk. He is criticised for the brawl by Othello, notwithstanding his recent rank. It is only after Desdemona's death that he regains the governorship and he organises the search for Iago and the confining of Othello to his quarters. Lodovico, on the other hand, as envoy from the Duke of Venice, has a de facto seniority to Othello. Any production must make sense of these different levels of authority.

OTHELLO

LATE

10

210 MINS

3255 LINES

14 CAST

32	**IAGO**	1
25	**OTHELLO**	1
19	DESDEMONA CASSIO	2
14	EMILIA BRABANTIO / GRATIANO RODERIGO	3
10	ENSEMBLE	7

THE PLAY

THE CAST

TECHNICAL

3
68

over 40
under 40

2
13

1
7

12

MEN   WOMEN

15 SCENES   8 SETS   4   24 COSTUMES

Arise black vengeance

The main requirement of this play is for older men with 68% of the lines. The play has relatively few scenes with relatively few sets and relatively few costumes. This play is recommended, particularly early on in a Shakespearean involvement or career.

OTHELLO Paul Robeson

THE WINTER'S TALE

LEONTES Antony Sher

THE WINTER'S TALE
Things dying... things new born

Leontes, King of Sicily, suspects his wife, Hermione, has been unfaith-
ful with Polixenes, King of Bohemia, his boyhood friend. Polixenes,
alerted by Camillo, one of Leontes' courtiers, flees Sicily accompanied
by Camillo. Leontes is thus convinced of Hermione's guilt. Hermione is
committed for trial, and is delivered of a baby in prison. Leontes orders
an old courtier, Antigonus, to abandon the baby in a hostile place, to
which Antigonus reluctantly swears. His wife, Paulina, puts it out that
Hermione died in childbirth, and Leontes repents of his actions too late
when he learns of the death of his only son Mamillius.

On the coast of Bohemia Antigonus sacrifices himself to save the
infant from a bear. An old shepherd and his son find the infant. He
vows to bring her up as his daughter.

After a gap of 16 years Polixenes and the exiled Camillo learn that
Prince Florizel, Polixenes' heir, is in love with Perdita, the shepherd's
daughter. Florizel is ordered not to pursue his love, but escapes Polixenes
to visit Sicily. The shepherd and his son are cozened by Autolycus, a
rogue, into going to Sicily as well, where Leontes has received the young
pair with warmth. Polixenes and Camillo follow. Paulina invites
Leontes and Polixenes to view a statue of Hermione which reveals itself
to be the long-thought-dead Queen and mother of Perdita. The union
of Perdita and Florizel is joyfully welcomed, and Camillo and Paulina
announce they are to marry too.

*T*he Winter's Tale enjoys some popularity, and some notoriety too. "A sea coast in Bohemia," snort the pedants. "Exit pursued by a Bear – oh please!" The pedants are wrong, as I hope I shall prove. And the play, generally considered a comedy, has plenty of dark corners too.

I recommend a relatively large cast of 21 which includes a boy. It has five substantial roles and five or six other fulfilling roles. Its last scene never fails to bring tears to the eyes.

None of the different locations presents great problems in terms of set construction. The prison scene is short and does not need to be realistically constructed. The court of justice and Paulina's house where the statue of Hermione is displayed need some thought but the rest could be set in an indeterminate outdoors, especially since most of the play is set in Sicily where the winters are mild. Winter is the season, however, and the designers (set and lighting) should suggest this and, in particular, be in contrast to the spring setting of the sheep-shearing scene.

I don't think I have ever seen the dance of the 12 satyrs, probably on account of the availability of that number of dancers. But even if this is cut there should be a goodly sprinkling of bodies for this scene.

The real point of the play, and my first crux, is whether "Exit pursued by a Bear" is a sign of Shakespeare in his dotage or, as I believe, the fundamental core of the play.

The scene is a deserted seashore in Bohemia. The sea is rough. Antigonus, an old man, is distracting a bear from devouring the infant he left on the beach. He does so by enticing the bear to follow him, thereby ensuring his own death, rather than that of the child. He is in the act of exiting: he will be pursued by the bear.

Antigonus has just executed the command of his King, Leontes, who suspects his Queen, Hermione, of infidelity. His instructions were to place their infant daughter "in some remote and desert place quite out of our domains". Antigonus is to "leave it (without more mercy) to its own protection and favour of the climate." The infant is Perdita. It is she who, 16 years later, becomes the instrument that restores her mother Hermione to Leontes.

This stage direction is often cited as the most ridiculous in Shakespeare. That's nonsense. It is one of the most pregnant and moving moments in all the plays. It has a crucial point: old age sacrifices itself for youth. This incident is the turning point of *The Winter's Tale,* a seed is planted that will flourish the following spring.

I am usually neutral about the cruxes I suggest. In this case I argue that the point of age sacrificing itself for youth is fundamental.

Antigonus is an example of a good and faithful servant. The notion of faithful service is fully examined in other relationships in this play; Camillo's protection of Polixenes and Florizel; Paulina's of Hermione; the old shepherd's of Perdita. It is common enough in Shakespeare but particularly important in this play. In each case the individual acts in the cause of the greater good, disobeying the strict edicts of authority (poor Antigonus was limited by his oath from simply taking the baby out of the kingdom and arranging for it to be brought up by foster parents). Paulina is particularly forthright in her protection of Hermione while Camillo chooses to serve the innocent Polixenes, exiling himself from his native land. When Polixenes denounces Florizel for engaging himself to a "sheephook" it is Camillo who seeks to mitigate this sentence by engineering Polixenes' return to Sicily where Florizel and Perdita have already been sent. The theme of faithful service is wide and varied, making a crux of how these variations should point up the similarities or stress the differences.

The third crux is how Leontes is to be portrayed. On the one hand we have a tyrant whose behaviour causes, or threatens to cause, several deaths (Antigonus, the Mariners, Mamillius and Hermione), who overrules the decision of Apollo's oracle, justifying his action by falsehood. From the outset, with Polixenes' first words "Nine changes of the watery moon…" Leontes immediately jumps to the conclusion that Hermione's pregnancy began at the very time of Polixenes' arrival in Sicily nine months earlier. For the first half of the play he uses such flimsy circumstance to underline his prejudice, forfeiting our sympathy. Is he then an out-and-out villain who is lucky in his faithful friends, or a good man with fatally flawed judgement? To choose either reading at the expense of the other will be monotonous, so the right mixture of the two, recognising ambiguities, will be crucial for the actor and the director and his or her team to consider. The definitive Leontes has probably not been done, and this remains a challenge for future actors of the role.

As an actor I once played Autolycus, rather badly, I am afraid – I cannot sing for one thing. However, the attempt taught me how to compensate, by miming the words to the singing of a nearby actor with his back to the audience. Not really recommended.

Early in my non-professional career I directed *The Winter's Tale* and *A Midsummer Night's Dream*, each for two performances in the Théâtre Antique in Arles in Southern France. This was an immense undertaking logistically and artistically, and it nearly bankrupted The Tower Theatre, whose productions these were. Playing Shakespeare to a French provincial audience meant the theatre was only about one-quarter full. But it remains a personal happy memory and a small contribution to my knowledge of playing Shakespeare.

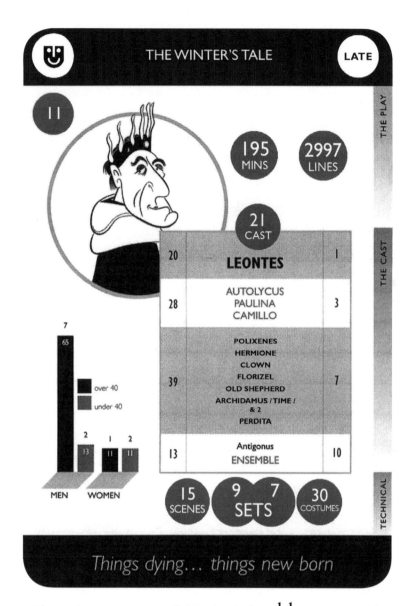

THE PLAY

11

195 MINS

2997 LINES

21 CAST

THE CAST

20	**LEONTES**	1
28	AUTOLYCUS PAULINA CAMILLO	3
39	POLIXENES HERMIONE CLOWN FLORIZEL OLD SHEPHERD ARCHIDAMUS / TIME / & 2 PERDITA	7
13	Antigonus ENSEMBLE	10

7

65

over 40

under 40

2 1 2
13 11 11

MEN   WOMEN

15 SCENES

9 SETS

7

30 COSTUMES

TECHNICAL

Things dying… things new born

The main requirement of this play is for **older men** with **65%** of the lines. The play has relatively **few** scenes with an **average** number of sets and an **average** number of costumes. This play is **straightforward** with a **few** but not insuperable challenges.

LEONTES Eric Porter

KING LEAR

KING LEAR Ian McKellen

KING LEAR
O fool I shall go mad

King Lear divides his kingdom between his three daughters to prepare for retirement, announcing he will spend time with each daughter, together with his retinue. Two daughters, Goneril and Regan, agree to this, but the youngest, Cordelia, refuses to compete with her sisters in flattering the King. The King of France agrees to marry Cordelia. The Earl of Kent tries to persuade the King to reverse Cordelia's disgrace and is also banished. The Earl of Gloucester's son, Edgar, is betrayed by his bastard brother Edmund and is forced to flee, disguising himself as a madman, Poor Tom.

The behaviour of Lear's retinue angers both Goneril and Regan and they demand that their father dismiss them. Lear's anger begins to turn his mind and he leaves his daughters when a violent storm finds him without cover on a heath, accompanied by his Fool and the disguised Earl of Kent. They encounter Poor Tom in a hovel.

The Duke of Cornwall, husband of Regan, now arrests the Earl of Gloucester for assisting the King. Gloucester's eyes are put out and he is turned out of his castle. Edgar, still disguised, meets his blind father as he is carried towards Dover where a French Army under Cordelia has arrived to restore Lear's fortunes. The army of the English under Edmund take Lear and Cordelia prisoner and Edmund orders their deaths. Edgar now issues a challenge to fight Edmund and defeats him. Edmund, dying, admits his treachery. Goneril poisons Regan and takes her own life. Orders are given to rescue Lear and Cordelia but the messenger is too late to prevent Cordelia's death and Lear dies with his dead daughter in his arms.

This mighty play is often done, the main role being a (usually) unavoidable challenge for senior actors. The Peter Brook/Paul Scofield 1962 RSC production (later filmed) continues to cast its shadow over revivals. I have been lucky enough to see a dozen subsequent productions, none without merit but none entirely able to eclipse this seminal production.

It should be noted that Gloucester, Kent and, probably, the Fool are also senior actors, at least highly experienced actors. The role of Cordelia, famous though it is, is very small. Of the other young parts Edgar's is by far the most difficult to make sense of (because he is playing 'mad' for so much of it) and is a formidable challenge for the young actor. Edmund, Goneril and Regan are much more straightforward. The daughters, for example, are not and should not be played as entirely evil.

One of the key points that Brook made was that the hundred knights who were chosen by Lear to accompany him were in fact an impossible burden on Goneril's and Regan's households – the sympathy that is felt for the daughters' action is thus stressed if a bigger number than the usual handful of attendant knights are engaged. The seventeen identified actors should ideally be enhanced by six or eight other bodies who can make this point.

The crucial challenge is how to stage the storm scene (which actually takes place in three different locations) and the need for the lines actually to be heard above the "pother" of the storm. Brook did this by having the thunder sheets visible to the audience; and unshaken – their gentle swinging was enough for us to imagine the storm and hear the words. Lear (or, rather, the actor) should not have to compete with the realism of a recorded storm, or of actual rain, or wind machines when he is declaiming the great speeches. Let him roar, by all means, but do not destroy the words with loud sound effects.

The period is ancient Britain – again Brook did not specify this, having his designer dress the cast in sombre leather in browns, blacks, dull purples, etc. in a style quite non-explicit in terms of century.

Lear's gradual descent into madness and his ultimate self-knowledge is the main crux. It is all there to be discovered in the text by the actor. The signposts might be:

- Lear commits an act of political and personal folly; as Kent notes "… be Kent unmannerly when Lear is mad".
- The riotous knights are a symptom of Lear's folly.
- The Fool, who is wise, instructs the King who is a fool, and is himself foolish enough to follow his master when his daughter throws him out.

Notice that the Fool's input dies away as Lear assumes folly. No more need for him and he "goes to bed at noon". Notice, too, the quartet of madness in the storm scene – Lear and the Fool make two, but Edgar feigns madness for his safety and Kent, also feigning, "foolishly" echoes the Fool's comments, making sense only to the audience.

The second crux is the subplot. Lear has daughters, some evil, one not; Gloucester has a bastard son who allies himself with the evil daughters, and a son who is the ultimate redeemer. Father and Daughters: Father and Sons might be a subtitle to emphasise the parallels between the two plots. Gloucester loses his eyes (note the proliferation of images concerned with eyes, sight and lack thereof) and Lear loses his reason. Both Lear and Gloucester achieve cathartic self-knowledge after their tragedies. The scene between them near Dover is one of the greatest in the entire canon. Of course, it can be left to Shakespeare to suggest these linkages, but a company new to Shakespeare should have a view about how parallel these scenes are, and whether the resonances between them are designed or fortuitous.

I have never seen Gloucester's imagined fall from the cliff top to the beach, with Edgar using two identities to explain his role, done convincingly. I believe that Gloucester should be violently pushed forward before the fall, violently enough for him to lose the breath out of his body as he hits the beach (as he thinks) as he hits the floor (in reality). Such violence (technically, not actually perpetrated) would help us understand his state of mind before and after the fall. The purpose of the scene is to allow Gloucester to come to self-knowledge, to make some sense from his appalling suffering.

The last crux is syntax – making sense of a very involved plot, not the least where the action is taking place and how the various characters come to be there. The sequences of letters and messengers riding between locations is complicated, and, particularly if cuts are made, can become confused. The general drift of the story is easy enough to follow without agonising too much about the detail. But a careful reading of the syntax and the plot involving the journeys and messages will add to your success.

On a personal note, well after writing these words, I came to play King Lear in 2015 in a production that played in a small theatre in London and in a garden theatre in Paris. Ian McKellen, who had already played Lear for the RSC worldwide, and was to play the part again, was at my first night in London. "Well," he said at the end to Sheila my wife, who sat next to him, "he need never act again." I took that as the ultimate compliment and confirmation that ACTing Shakespeare is the best way to experience his genius.

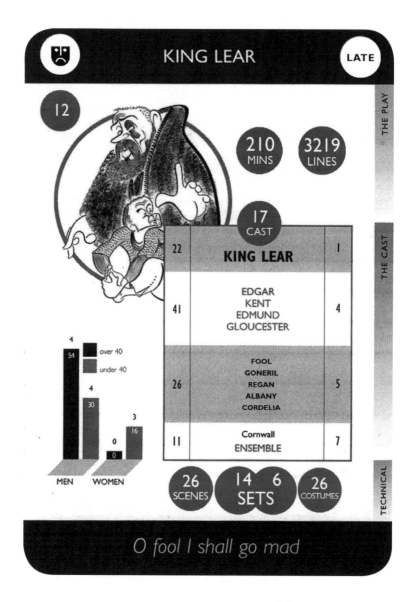

KING LEAR

LATE

12

210 MINS

3219 LINES

17 CAST

22	**KING LEAR**	1
41	EDGAR KENT EDMUND GLOUCESTER	4
26	FOOL GONERIL REGAN ALBANY CORDELIA	5
11	Cornwall ENSEMBLE	7

over 40

under 40

4

54

4

30

0

0

3

16

0

MEN   WOMEN

26 SCENES

14 6 SETS

26 COSTUMES

O fool I shall go mad

The main requirement of this play is for **older men** with **54%** of the lines. The play has **many** scenes with **many** sets which can be simplified to an **average** number of sets and an **average** number of costumes. This play is more **difficult**, and probably best left to experienced groups.

KING LEAR Paul Scofield   **FOOL** Alec McCowen

AS YOU LIKE IT

ROSALIND Vanessa Redgrave
JACQUES Max Adrian

AS YOU LIKE IT
Most loving mere folly

Duke Senior has been banished by his brother Frederick who has usurped his Dukedom. At a tournament Rosalind, his daughter, had fallen in love with Orlando who defeated the Duke's champion wrestler. She too is banished. Disguised as a boy, and accompanied by Frederick's daughter, Celia, and a clown, Touchstone, she now makes for the Forest of Arden to join her father. Orlando, treated badly by his brother, Oliver, also leaves the court, with his old servant Adam. Orlando and Adam stumble on Duke Senior's retreat in the forest where they are welcomed. One of this court is Jacques, a melancholy philosopher, and he meets up with Touchstone in the forest to his great approval. Touchstone debates with Corin, a shepherd, on the advantages of town life over country life.

Phebe, who has spurned the advances of Silvius, falls under the spell of Rosalind's alter ego, Ganymede. Rosalind finds verses of love to her from the besotted Orlando. Ganymede persuades Orlando to woo him, in Rosalind's place, rather than desecrate the forest further. Touchstone becomes enamoured with a country girl, Audrey.

Orlando rescues Oliver from a lion and the brothers are reconciled. Celia is enthralled by Oliver.

Gradually the true identities emerge and a quadruple wedding is arranged, Phebe agreeing to take Silvius after all. The two brothers marry Rosalind and Celia, and Touchstone Audrey. Restored to his Dukedom, Duke Senior leaves the forest, but Jacques and Frederick decide to remain in the forest in a life of contemplation.

This popular play is often revived, and it is not difficult to understand why. It is a comedy with a small cast, several wonderful roles and easy to mount since it has relatively few demands of set and costumes. The Seven Ages of Man is possibly the most famous speech in Shakespeare and in Rosalind there is one of the greatest parts for an actress. I missed Peggy Ashcroft but was lucky enough to see Vanessa Redgrave. Such a performance is unforgettable and reason enough for reviving the play again and again.

I suggest that as few as 16 actors can perform this play. I suggest that one actor plays both dukes (there will be a few quick changes) as a way of pointing up the differences between two systems of rule – the despotic and the indulgent – and providing an actor with a richer role. The size of cast is important in most productions from the economic point of view and this play is one of the relatively few that can be successfully performed professionally on this account. And there is no need for expensive sets – most of the play is set in the open air in the Forest of Arden. The few interior scenes can be played outside. The costume demands are slight.

The first crux is town v. country. It is not necessary to take sides in this particular debate, but it should be understood that many of the characters are operating outside their own preferred milieu. The court of Duke Senior which includes Jacques, Amiens and several Lords is in exile from the town, and despite the occasional idyllic condition of the country, they are subject to the winter wind. Rosalind, Celia, Orlando and Touchstone are also exiled and Touchstone in his scene with Corin specifically compares the two ways of life in a way that does not entirely convince that he is in his element in exile. The characters from the country are simple if not simpletons, but there is a gentle mocking of their ignorance and simplicity. Jacques' decision not to return to court, but to seek out the newly converted duke in a life of rural contemplation does not really convince. Shakespeare was a countryman who chose the town. This play is perhaps his own contribution to the debate as to whether he personally was right.

I consider Touchstone and Jacques crucial to this debate. Touchstone's set piece on country life ("the copulation of cattle") and on court life ("the lie seven times removed") are wonderfully apt. Jacques' Seven Ages of Man and the Anatomy of his Melancholy are splendid variations on this theme. These two evidently hit it off together in the forest. Questions of folly and wisdom are brilliantly contrasted and these two unforgettable characters add their own magic to the great themes of the play.

The second crux is music. Many plays have an important musical content. In this play there are no fewer than five staged performances of songs that enhance the story if not actually driving it forward. Of these "Under the Greenwood Tree" and "Blow Blow Thou Winter Wind" make the very point about the harshness of forest life I referred to in the first crux. The other three are more commentaries on romantic love. Amiens, who is usually given the majority of these songs, and the two pages, must be accomplished singers underlining Jacques' poor efforts at singing. The suggestion by the Arden editor and others that Amiens also performs the role of Hymen recognises that the best singer should be given most of the songs.

The third crux is to understand the four variations of romantic love, viz: Rosalind and Orlando; Celia and Oliver; Touchstone and Audrey; Silvius and Phebe; not to forget the variations of country love of Phebe and Ganymede and William and Audrey. It is given to the relatively less important role of Silvius to make perhaps the profoundest points on the subject in his contribution to the great hymn to love in the last act:

> It is to be made of sighs and tears…
> It is to be made of faith and service…
> It is to be all made of fantasy,
> And made of passion, and all made of wishes;

All adoration, duty, and observance,
All humbleness, all patience, and impatience,
All purity, all trial, all obeisance.

The variations of each of these relationships are handled as Mozart might do later in opera. The lyrical and the prosaic, the improbable and the ill-starred each have something to delight us and to teach us.

There are no fewer than five examples from *As You Like It* in the Sampler later in this book, which concentrates on Shakespeare's own thoughts rather than those of his characters. I recommend these, both for close study and learning by heart. This play is much more than a superficial comedy and introduces us to the deeper, even darker themes of the great tragedies. And, as an introduction to later greatness, I would mention seeing Kenneth Branagh as Touchstone, a key character involved in these Shakespearean thoughts, which presaged many of Branagh's own future Shakespearean achievements.

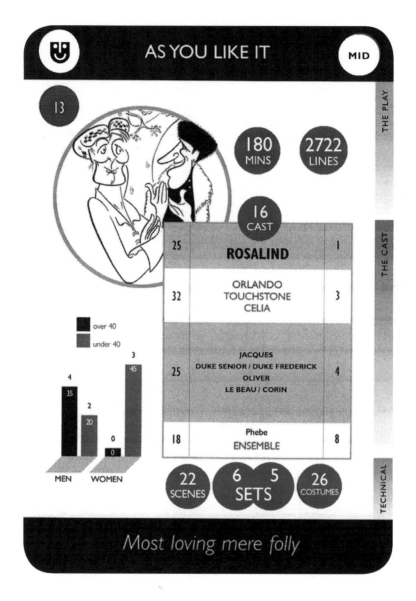

13

180 MINS

2722 LINES

16 CAST

25	**ROSALIND**	1
32	ORLANDO TOUCHSTONE CELIA	3
25	JACQUES DUKE SENIOR / DUKE FREDERICK OLIVER LE BEAU / CORIN	4
18	Phebe ENSEMBLE	8

over 40
under 40

3
45
4
35
2
20
0
0

MEN   WOMEN

22 SCENES

6 5 SETS

26 COSTUMES

Most loving mere folly

The main requirement of this play is for younger women with 45% of the lines. The play has an average number of scenes with relatively few sets and an average number of costumes. This play is recommended, particularly early on in a Shakespearean involvement or career.

ROSALIND Vanessa Redgrave
JACQUES Max Adrian

THE COMEDY OF ERRORS

ANTIPHOLUS Ian Richardson
ADRIANA Diana Rigg
ANTIPHOLUS Alec McCowen

THE COMEDY OF ERRORS
Which the natural man?

A merchant from Syracuse, Egeon, searching for his wife and sons, lost at sea, arrives in Ephesus where, because of a strict law against all Syracusans, he is arrested and condemned to die. The Duke allows him a respite of one day to raise money to pay his fine.

One of the sons, Antipholus, arrives in Ephesus with his servant Dromio, where the other son, also called Antipholus, has married Adriana and is also served by his servant, the identical twin to Dromio. Adriana, her sister Luciana, Balthazar, a merchant, and Angelo, a gold merchant, and others are then baffled by the behaviour of the two Antipholuses and the two Dromios as they meet and part on various errands and businesses in the town. Antipholus of Ephesus is thought to be mad and is conjured and confined by Pinch, a schoolmaster. He escapes and runs to the Duke to seek redress. His brother, involved in a street fight about the goldsmith's chain, escapes into a priory where the Abbess, Aemilia, protects him.

Egeon, on his way to execution, recognises one of his sons, and, in the Duke's presence, Aemilia presents the other son. Aemilia is the long-lost wife of Egeon and every confusion is cleared up to general rejoicing, not the least by the two pairs of twins reunited with their other halves. Egeon is pardoned, Luciana marries the spare Antipholus and Adriana is restored to her Antipholus.

This is Shakespeare's shortest play and has the smallest cast. Its humour retains its freshness and it can safely be recommended for any group of actors.

The first crux is whether to have four actors or two as the two sets of twins. In opting for the latter, and adding another 'twin', namely The Duke and Pinch, for reasons I shall come to, a cast of 11 is suggested. I have even managed it with a cast of seven using modern aids like film and old devices like mirrors – but this was to fit a tiny theatre with economy also in mind. The version worked, though not without a certain amount of strain on actors and audience.

It should be noted too that Adriana and Luciana, who are played by different actresses, are sisters who fall in love with a different Antipholus twin. Luciana's dilemma at apparently falling in love with her sister's husband is a wonderful counterpart to the idea of being a twin, and it is an attractive challenge for the actress playing Luciana to portray the act of falling in love with a forbidden lover.

Choosing a single actor to play the Antipholuses and the Dromios gives two satisfying roles where the individual actor can explore the nature of being a twin. There are many ways this can be done, e.g., left handedness and right handedness, which can add to the fun of Shakespeare's design. In Act V each twin has to meet his opposite number and ingenuity is needed. The length of time when they are on stage together is short and the audience is invariably curious to see how the problem is resolved. Film could be used. Mirrors can present two images (the right/left handedness being particularly pertinent); a body double can be used; or some 'magic' involving the priory door can solve the situation.

The RSC famously mounted a production at very short notice – it was preparing a version of *King Lear* when Paul Scofield became ill. The cast of *King Lear* prepared *The Comedy of Errors*, with basic costumes of black leotards, ornamented by sashes and hats, with a minimum of rehearsal and to such acclaim that they revived the production for several seasons. The shortness of the play and the minimal requirements for set and costume made this possible. The setting is of an open place in front of three houses – one for Antipholus of Ephesus, one for the courtesan and one for the Abbess, so three doors are needed (or one door that serves for each location) and that is about all. Indeed when directing it for an amphitheatre, with the audience at a steep rake to the stage, I had but one door (which happened to be a permanent feature of the theatre) and a long piece of rope.

The rope was used in a variety of ways to illuminate the geography, in particular, that explains the circumstances of the splitting of the twins in Egeon's lengthy exposition. This is virtually incomprehensible without visual aids – and it is my second crux that the exact circumstances of those events should be understood. The rope can become a map of the eastern Mediterranean, as it can also be used later as a device for painting Nell the kitchen maid who makes a set at Dromio of Syracuse and it is also used for the binding of the apparently mad Antipholus. *The Rope* is a play by Plautus, often considered a source author for this play, so it is an appropriate prop or indeed part of the set that is simple and economic to use. Whether a rope is used or not the clarity of what happened at the sea of Epidamnum is absolutely crucial – we have a reprise of this at the end of the play when all becomes clear.

The third crux is to understand the Elizabethan attitude to madness, which is the main idea of the scene with Dr Pinch and the dilemma of Adriana in particular when confronted with a mad husband. Pinch's treatment is to bind him with the rope and keep him in a dark room, a standard treatment in Elizabethan England. Pinch is an obvious mountebank, but the crux is to make him believable at least to the Elizabethan convention. I suggested the Duke plays Pinch – Antipholus explains to the Duke the indignities Pinch has inflicted on him, with particular reference to his looks – this adds an extra dimension to the scene with the Duke reacting to his other self.

Its advantages mean that *The Comedy of Errors* is often revived. It should not be treated as a farce, but as a comedy where each actor must treat each situation, however farcical, with a seriousness that inspires laughter. Antipholus of Ephesus' account of his imprisonment at Pinch's hands is a masterpiece of controlled exasperation, a farcical situation about which he is utterly serious.

The amphitheatre I mentioned earlier was the Minack cliffside theatre in Cornwall. For a later professional production of the play by Robert Gillespie, at the Rosemary Branch pub theatre in London, I produced a script whereby the cast could be cut to the (barely) economic minimum. With the use of mirrors, and filmed interludes whereby the actors could act against their doubled and trebled parts, we managed to achieve a successful version of this delightful play.

I should add my favourite line of the play when Diana Rigg, as Adriana, confronts her husband Antipholus and his new-found twin:

Which of you did dine with me today?

Delicious.

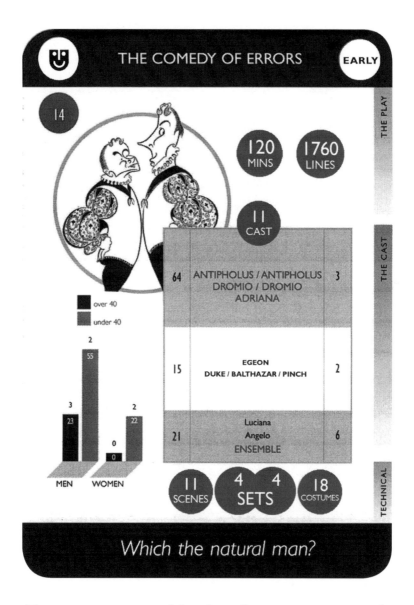

THE COMEDY OF ERRORS

EARLY

14

120 MINS

1760 LINES

11 CAST

64	ANTIPHOLUS / ANTIPHOLUS DROMIO / DROMIO ADRIANA	3
15	EGEON DUKE / BALTHAZAR / PINCH	2
21	Luciana Angelo ENSEMBLE	6

over 40
under 40

2
55
3
23
2
22
0
0

MEN   WOMEN

11 SCENES   4 4 SETS   18 COSTUMES

Which the natural man?

The main requirement of this play is for younger men with 55% of the lines. The play has relatively few scenes with relatively few sets and relatively few costumes. This play is recommended, particularly early on in a Shakespearean involvement or career.

ANTIPHOLUS Alec McCowen
ANTIPHOLUS Ian Richardson

JULIUS CAESAR

BRUTUS James Mason
CASSIUS John Gielgud
MARK ANTONY Marlon Brando

JULIUS CAESAR
The evil that men do

Julius Caesar, having triumphed over Pompey, appears set to assume the kingship of Rome. Cassius mobilises Casca and others to persuade Brutus to prevent this, if necessary by assassination. Brutus agrees after misgivings and keeps his wife Portia in the dark as to his intentions.

Alerted by unnatural events of the previous night and his wife Calpurnia's dream, Caesar declines to go to the Capitol on the day his murder is planned. Decius Brutus, another of the conspirators, inter-prets the dream and persuades Caesar to go. There Caesar refuses the suit of Metellus Cimber and as he does so Casca strikes the first blow, followed by all the conspirators including Brutus.

In the aftermath Mark Antony, Caesar's favourite, negotiates for permission to speak to the citizens in a funeral oration. Brutus agrees though Cassius urges Brutus not to allow this. After his own oration, Brutus leaves Antony in the Forum to incite the crowd to side with him in opposition to Brutus and Cassius, who flee. The poet Cinna is lynched by the mob, being mistaken for another conspirator Cinna.

Antony joins forces with Octavius, Julius Caesar's nephew, and meets up with the conspirators at Philippi. Cassius is again thwarted over the right military tactics by Brutus. Brutus has his way but not without a bitter personal quarrel. The visitation of the Ghost of Caesar does not deflect Brutus from engaging Antony's forces. He learns of Portia's death shortly before the battle. Antony's army prevails and Cassius and Brutus both lose their lives.

*J*ulius Caesar has a huge cast and breathtaking action which takes a bare 2 ½ hours. The story is simple: Julius Caesar, at the height of his reign, is murdered and his murderers receive their retribution. Though he dies in Act II, Julius Caesar exerts his influence throughout so that the title of the play is *Julius Caesar* despite the character having fewer than 6% of the lines.

It is the size of cast that means that professional productions are relatively seldom performed. For non-professional companies the situation is comparable; it is not always easy to attract lots of actors to play the smaller roles. For schools, however, these disadvantages are advantages and my first full-length Shakespeare role was in this play at school. If actors are available for the smaller parts there is plenty of worthwhile action for all, and the excitement of the Forum scene is quite special.

There are 48 identified parts and I suggest a cast of 23. The major roles are few: Brutus, Cassius and Mark Antony, in that order, account for over 60% of the lines. As the play is political there is little in these roles that is not absolutely clear in the text. Julius Caesar is not a play of nuance, subplot or ambiguity. Each of the three main parts is a gift to a good actor and relatively simple to play.

The setting is a challenge for the designer insofar as the Capitol, and to a lesser extent the Forum, and Caesar's House, should give some impression of the grandeur that was Rome. The most potent of the other scenes – Brutus' orchard, the tent for the quarrel scene – are much simpler to achieve. I cannot really understand the value of any other costumes than Roman; but the Elizabethans did it in modern dress and I suppose we could do that too, though the togas and plumed helmets seem to me to augment this play.

A modern production at the Barbican Theatre in London had two interesting points: modern dress and a huge crowd of non-professional actors. You will by now be familiar with my views on professionalism and non-professionalism – I am sure that there will be more mixed casts of this nature in future. The modern dress was seen to be no hindrance to the production, but here I tend to the more traditional solution.

The cruxes are more technical than interpretative: how to make the story that Shakespeare tells clear to a modern audience. The murder at the Capitol and the speeches in the Forum are made in front of a huge crowd of onlookers. The challenge is to orchestrate the crowd reactions to the speeches of Brutus and Mark Antony, from the applause to the denunciation of Brutus and from suspicion of Antony to adoration.

There are several ways of doing this. These include having numbers of the cast in the auditorium, possibly augmented by a soundtrack, possibly backed by actors on stage, or even a screened backdrop. It is the variety of response that is essential; the scene is dynamic as far as the crowd is concerned, and the actor playing Mark Antony needs a clear development of interruption to his oration.

Handling the mob is also crucial in the marvellous little scene where the wretched poet called Cinna is murdered by the mob because he is unlucky enough to have the same name as one of the conspirators.

The Battle of Philippi is another challenge under this crux though most of the fighting, as always in Shakespeare, occurs offstage, making sound effects, lighting and stage decoration (helmets, spears, banners, processions) the key challenge.

The second crux is to get the right balance in Brutus' character; murderer or patriot? It should be noted that as far as military matters are concerned and indeed all political decisions (kill Antony or let him speak) Brutus is always wrong and Cassius is always right and Cassius is always overruled by the moral superiority of Brutus. It is important to establish this moral superiority and to suppress it when the decision is made to murder Caesar, who is at his most vulnerable when he considers himself most secure.

Understanding the supernatural is the third crux, which includes interventions by the soothsayer and the Ghost of Caesar. The supernatural is introduced in the scene of Cicero's conversion. For all his worldly achievement Julius Caesar is helpless when Calpurnia's intuition is overturned by Decius Brutus' interpretation of her dream. Despite the dream, the auguries and the soothsayer, he is finally persuaded to go to his fate. Notably, too, Cinna the Poet had a dream presaging a feast with Caesar before he too ventured out after the murder.

I played Cassius at my school production of *Julius Caesar* in 1956 when I was 18, in a cloak hired from the Shakespeare Memorial Theatre at Stratford with the label inscribed 'John Gielgud'. Our illustration shows the main characters of the film version of 1953, directed by Joseph Mankiewicz, including Gielgud in the role of Cassius. I have always loved the story of Gielgud's playing of the speech 'For once upon a raw and gusty day', which he did in one take. Sensing the speech was a bit too long, and worrying about the syntax of:

> I, as Aeneas, our great ancestor,
> Did from the flames of Troy upon his shoulder
> The old Anchises bear, so from the waves of Tiber
> Did I the tired Caesar

Mankiewicz suggested that Gielgud should cut it, to which Gielgud agreed. However, in each subsequent take, the lines remained in place. Gielgud apologised each time, but eventually the lines remained.

The other main performances by James Mason and Marlon Brando, two great film stars, add to the lustre of this play, and the filmed version remains a Shakespearean masterpiece to this day.

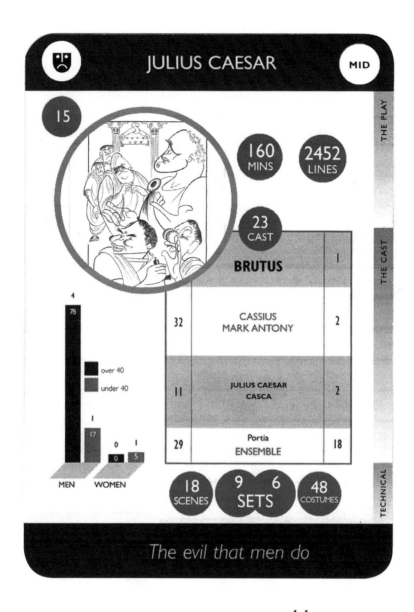

JULIUS CAESAR

MID

15

160 MINS

2452 LINES

23 CAST

	BRUTUS	1
32	CASSIUS MARK ANTONY	2
11	JULIUS CAESAR CASCA	2
29	Portia ENSEMBLE	18

THE PLAY

THE CAST

TECHNICAL

4
78
over 40
under 40
1
17
0   1
0   5
MEN   WOMEN

18 SCENES

9 6 SETS

48 COSTUMES

The evil that men do

The main requirement of this play is for **older men** with **78%** of the lines. The play has an **average** number of scenes with an **average** number of sets and **many** costumes. This play is **recommended**, particularly early on in a Shakespearean involvement or career.

BRUTUS James Mason   **CASSIUS** John Gielgud
MARK ANTONY Marlon Brando

THE TEMPEST

PROSPERO Derek Jacobi

THE TEMPEST
This rough magic

Prospero, exiled Duke of Milan, uses his magical powers to create a tempest with the assistance of Ariel, a spirit. The tempest wrecks the vessel of Alonso, King of Naples, his son Ferdinand and Prospero's brother Antonio, who had exiled Prospero from his dukedom.

Prospero tells his daughter Miranda how they came to the island by the treachery of Antonio, but helped by Gonzalo, a faithful Lord.

Miranda sees Ferdinand near her father's cell. He is given menial tasks by Prospero but the young pair fall in love, apparently against Prospero's will.

Caliban, Prospero's servant, a savage and deformed slave believes himself to be the true ruler of the island until Prospero's arrival and the strength of his magic enslaved him. Caliban finds Stephano and Trinculo, two of the servants of Alonso, and sharing some liquor, gets drunk and plots to kill Prospero. Alonso, Gonzalo, Antonio and Sebastian (Alonso's brother) find themselves miraculously saved and start looking for Ferdinand. Sebastian and Antonio plot to kill Alonso and Gonzalo but are prevented by Ariel's intervention.

A magical banquet is offered to the King and his companions. A masque of spirits appears to Ferdinand. Ariel foils Caliban's plot and brings everyone to Prospero's cell for the final resolution after Prospero has renounced his powers.

Miranda and Ferdinand are blessed by Prospero and by Alonso. Prospero forgives his enemies and regains his dukedom. Caliban is pardoned and Ariel is freed.

*T*he *Tempest* (which stands first in the Folio) is often taken as Shakespeare's own farewell to his writing (though *Henry VIII* was to follow). It is high in popularity, it is attractively short and needs only a cast of 17. The three settings present no real problems unless a full-scale boat is chosen for the storm scene, an idea that is both impractical and unnecessary.

This is the first crux, whether to make the storm real or imaginary. We learn later that it is a storm of the mind, that is an imaginary storm where the ship and the sailors are saved (compare with the poor souls who perish in a sea storm in *The Winter's Tale)*, where the son of the King is not drowned, and the very garments of the King and his nobles are not so much as dampened.

One practical reason for making the storm imaginary is to make the lines audible to the audience. The boatswain has pertinent things to say about the nobles endangering the ship through their interference and panic, and Gonzalo has wonderful things to say about both the boatswain and the wished-for dry land that sound effects and general realistic noises of men in peril often make inaudible. One way is a convention when the din is made to cease while lines are spoken. The dramatic impact of a storm made as realistic as possible must be set against the sense of the lines. Incidentally, I suggest an appearance by the drunken duo, Stephano and Trinculo, in this scene, and also suggest that Ferdinand be seen diving overboard and watched by Sebastian to prefigure later episodes. I even suggest that Miranda might in some way catch sight of Ferdinand as he swims by – she might be the figurehead on the prow of the vessel set there by Ariel perhaps as the storm is created in Prospero's mind.

The second crux is about Rule – virtually every character aspires to be King either of the island or of Naples or of Milan. At the lowest level Caliban resents the usurpation of Prospero and recruits Stephano and Trinculo to help him overthrow Prospero, the latter electing themselves the King and Viceroy of the island. Sebastian and Antonio plot the death of Alonso to succeed to the thrones of Naples and Milan; Ariel longs for freedom from servitude as does Ferdinand, who believes himself to be the King of Naples, having seen his own father lost. Even Gonzalo, the faithful courtier, outlines his ideas for Utopia where kings and rulers no longer exist. Antonio's usurpation of Prospero endangered the lives of Prospero and Miranda. Finally Miranda subjects herself to the rule of a husband who is but the third human, counting herself, that she has seen. The Tempest threatened death. The survivors yearn for power. And Prospero, who has it, has once declined power, is to regain it, yet will renounce it once more.

The third crux is the convention of magical powers as the invisibility of the spirits, which include Ariel as the 'meaner spirits' that perform Prospero's magic. At the time of writing this, I have just performed Prospero in the open air in a production that, I feel, successfully solved this point. Prospero used a staff, his books and a stone to create the magic. The stone became the opening thunder clap; the island itself, the home of the elves, the auspicious star as the symbol of the rough magic that Prospero finally abjures. Ariel is invisible to all but Prospero, but is never touched by Prospero until the final moment when he is released to freedom with a kiss. The masquers become the avenging hounds and the providers of the banquet – the convention of the mask itself establishing that they too are invisible to the mortals. The crux is to adopt such conventions, or to adopt any improvement on these ideas to make the essential points.

I cannot help adding that I am convinced that Shakespeare is putting his own thoughts into Prospero – certainly in the great speech "Our revels now are ended"; but even more emphatically in the epilogue where he (Prospero) asks for the audience's indulgence to set him free from his own artistic labours and achievements.

*The Tempe*st has several personal memories for me. My first experience of seeing a Shakespeare play was on a school outing when I must have been about 11 to see *The Tempest* in the outside Regent's Park Theatre. I remember that the star was the theatre's director,

Robert Atkins, but have never been able to remember whether he played Prospero, the main part, or Caliban, which may have been the part that offered more theatricality. I do remember that we were sat in deckchairs, and that Prospero had an exceedingly long opening scene which is my sole memory of the play.

Much later I got to play Prospero in the Tower Theatre's annual Shakespeare production that played in both London and Paris. The Paris production takes place in the open air, in the Jardin Shakespeare in the Pré Catelan of the Bois du Boulogne, a venue that Penny and Laurence Tuerk had arranged, primarily for an expatriate and schools audience. Our production was directed by Penny Tuerk who had played Prospero herself in a school production. She told me she played mainly male roles at her all-girls school. I on the other hand had played a couple of female roles at my all-boys school. With this experience Penny proved an insightful director and even the occasional prompter in that long first act.

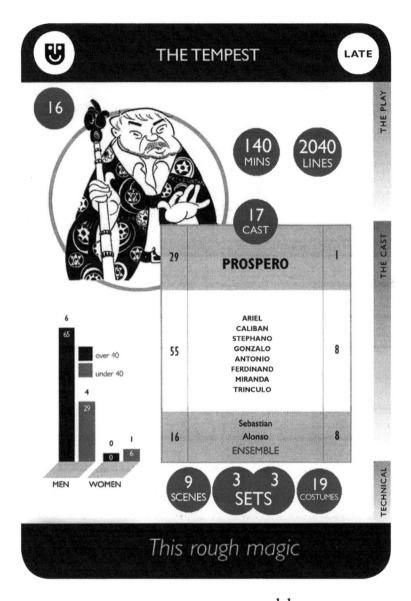

THE TEMPEST

LATE

THE PLAY

16

140 MINS

2040 LINES

17 CAST

29	PROSPERO	1
55	ARIEL CALIBAN STEPHANO GONZALO ANTONIO FERDINAND MIRANDA TRINCULO	8
16	Sebastian Alonso ENSEMBLE	8

THE CAST

6
65
over 40
under 40
4
29
0   1
0   6

MEN   WOMEN

9 SCENES

3 SETS

3

19 COSTUMES

TECHNICAL

This rough magic

The main requirement of this play is for **older men** with **65%** of the lines. The play has relatively **few** scenes with relatively **few** sets and relatively **few** costumes. This play is **straightforward** with a **few** but not insuperable challenges.

PROSPERO Derek Jacobi

THE HISTORY PLAYS

THE HISTORY PLAYS

The next three plays are the three most popular history plays: *Richard II*, *Richard III* and *Henry V*. Before discussing these plays there are some general points I wish to make about the histories.

Shakespeare wrote ten plays about the English kings. Of these an early play, *King John* and a late one, *King Henry VIII,* stand as individual plays without special reference to what has occurred in a previous play. The other eight can be considered as a chronological eight-play cycle, or perhaps two four-play cycles, and have been presented in this way on a number of occasions. They were not written in chronological sequence so the arguments for and against presenting two or more of the plays in sequence are balanced. In the notes to the individual plays I develop these arguments more specifically, and I treat the two parts of *Henry IV* and the three parts of *Henry VI* as sequences, while *Richard II*, *Richard III* and *Henry V* are considered individually.

The four general points are: importance of family; politics of war; heraldry and rank; and period.

Importance of family

When John Barton, the RSC director, was a don at Cambridge he insisted that the actors playing Northumberland, Worcester and Hotspur, in a production of *Henry IV, Part 1*, wore identical wigs – to emphasise that they were all from the same family. In a recent production of the *Henry VI* plays, the actor playing Henry was black, while his uncles and other relations were not. The actor was excellent, but unable to convince that he was a blood relation of his uncles. To have actors of different races and colour play members of the same family is simply wrong. This is not to say that only white Anglo-Saxons can play the histories; of course not. But do not forget the importance of having members of a family resemble each other.

Politics of war

Since we have to rely on our imaginations in battle and war scenes, we must understand the politics of war, if not the details of particular battles. The Elizabethan playwrights use words to take the place of physical action. We may see the occasional hand-to-hand battle. We often hear of superhuman exploits performed offstage. The results of long battles are known quickly and clearly, which is against usual experience in these matters. Battle scenes in the histories can hardly be cut. We need to concentrate on the politics of the build-ups and the outcomes to the battles, but not the particular details of the battles themselves.

Heraldry and rank

The formality of rank and order in the courts cannot be ignored. Heraldry is the dictionary of this formality. I recommend C. W. Scott-Giles's book *Shakespeare's Heraldry.* Note that heraldry was in its infancy in the reign of King John, and in the reign of Henry VIII distinction was communicated more by clothes than visible coats of arms. But coats of arms and the symbolism of the emblems are dominant from Richard II to Richard III. Mistakes in protocol and precedent and getting the heraldry wrong should be avoided. A duke outranks a marquis, and a marquis an earl. Lords outrank barons and barons, knights. The on-stage behaviour of these characters should reflect their various ranks.

Period

A crux for all the history plays is whether the setting should be: contemporary of the events of the play; Elizabethan; or some other later period.

Henry V has recently been effectively staged in modern settings, making the general point that war is bloody and degrading and that the English soldiers are more desperate and degraded than the French in that play. I see little point in setting any of the histories in Queen Elizabeth's reign and would probably choose the first option, which cannot be criticised. I am certain that the histories, which have dropped out of general favour recently, will become popular again, and may well receive revelatory productions in other settings.

Doubling

Since the histories are usually large cast plays this is a convenient place to restate a policy for composite roles. In suggesting the composite parts for many of the actors I am attempting to:

- give each actor as wide a variety of roles as possible;
- suggest roles that can be done without too many quick changes;
- keep overall numbers down.

Of course, directors should take these as suggestions only. What will be found if composite roles are contemplated, however, is that the number of actors needed will be near enough to my suggested figures. There may be more felicitous solutions than mine and a director should always consider other possibilities but I doubt whether the overall cast numbers will be very different from mine, however the parts are divided.

KING RICHARD II

KING RICHARD II John Gielgud

KING RICHARD II
A brittle glory

The Duke of Gloucester has been murdered and Mowbray is accused by Bolingbroke of having committed it. King Richard II commands that the dispute is settled by combat, but he stops the contest. Mowbray is banished for life and Bolingbroke for six years, a sentence reduced through John of Gaunt, his father's, pleading. John of Gaunt dies and Richard seizes the Lancaster property to pay for a war in Ireland to which he goes.

News of this seizure reaches Bolingbroke who, assisted by Northumberland and an army, returns to England to regain his inheritance, and is met by his uncle Edmund of York who is Regent in the King's absence. York is powerless to prevent Bolingbroke capturing and executing two of Richard's followers.

The King arrives back from Ireland too late, for a Welsh army has dispersed thinking him dead. He takes refuge at Flint Castle where he confronts Bolingbroke. He agrees to restore Bolingbroke's lands, which satisfies his claim. However, this surrender is the first step to deposition which shortly follows, though not unopposed by the Bishop of Carlisle and Aumerle, the son of the Regent. Richard takes his leave of his Queen as he is sent to the Tower and later to Pomfret where he is murdered by Exton. Aumerle's rebellion is reported to the new King, Henry IV, by the Duke of York, and Bolingbroke pardons his cousin. Exton announces the death of the King but Henry banishes him, announcing his own pilgrimage to the Holy Land.

This seems to be the most popular of the history plays, giving the actor playing Richard a magnificent role that can make or establish a young reputation. The play also offers Bolingbroke, York and Gaunt tremendous supporting parts. As a power struggle it still has relevance today. It is full of great spectacle and wonderful language.

The settings include the need for a high place on the walls of Flint Castle from which Richard finally descends to confront the invading Bolingbroke. There are other scenes that need suitable sets: the Lists at Coventry, the Garden and the Prison, among others. Few companies have the resources to create (and change) substantial sets, and these are not needed. But a sense of place is important and the designer in this play has plenty of challenges.

The first crux is how effete to play the role of Richard. Richard's early history, not shown in this play, is of a courageous young man, thrust into kingship early by the untimely death of his father, the Black Prince, who had survived the threats of the Peasants' Revolt. By the start of this play he has become complacent, and is in the thrall of questionable advisers. He shows disastrous political judgement in seizing John of Gaunt's possessions to finance a war in Ireland. His handling of the Mowbray/Bolingbroke quarrel is inept – Shakespeare suggests how he might have done this better in an identical situation that Bolingbroke faced and solved later in the play (the Aumerle rebellion). Richard's judgement is arbitrary and his relations with his father's brothers poor. His fall is caused by these misjudgements and any decisive action he might have taken is vitiated by his propensity to indulge in his sorrows rather than address them.

The second crux is to recognise the trail of history throughout the eight plays that begin with *Richard II*. Each play stands on its own, but events in them assume further importance in later plays. It is particularly important in this play to understand how each event is to reverberate in the later plays. In this play, too, there is an important aftermath from a recent political event, the assassination of Thomas of Woodstock – one of the King's uncles. We first encounter this in the scene with the Duchess of Gloucester, who otherwise does not appear again. It is one of the most poignant scenes in Shakespeare that prefigures both the ruin of Richard and the desolation that is the consequence of the Wars of the Roses, themselves the result of the dynastic wars that resulted from the conflicting claims of John of Gaunt and Edmund of York, the uncles to Richard who play such key roles in this play. It is the claim to the succession to Richard that their descendants spend so much time disputing.

The role of Harry Percy in *Richard II* is quite small. He emerges again in *Henry IV, Part 1* as the dashing Hotspur, who remembers how Bolingbroke, before he became Henry IV, had patronised him in this play. And his father, Northumberland, the key support to Bolingbroke in this play, also appears in both parts of *Henry IV* where he fails to deliver his support to his son and his allies on two occasions. The general point is that actions in one play have repercussions throughout the whole cycle. Richard's own reputation changes over the period of the later plays and he becomes "that sweet lovely rose" in the memory, rather than the rather ineffectual King of this play.

The third crux is the idea of duality – Shakespeare's introduction of similar but contrasting situations. The Aumerle rebellion which is contrasted with the Mowbray rebellion. The behaviour of the two uncles is another. And whereas Richard could not cope with Bolingbroke's rebellion, Bolingbroke as King deals pragmatically with the treasonous actions of his cousin Aumerle.

One final point I would like to make is more of a personal notion than received wisdom. It strikes me that Lancaster and York would be a great acting challenge to a single actor playing both roles. The death of Gaunt at the end of Act I is disappointing insofar as this major character disappears. His brother the Duke of York is a far less formidable political heavyweight but nonetheless a good and conscientious Regent. Giving these roles to one actor would make a fascinating comparison that underlines the general point I make about families. In addition it would prefigure in a subtle and interesting way the origins and the aftermath of the Wars of the Roses.

Our illustration is of John Gielgud in a pre-war production of the play in which he was a great success, following up with playing the same character in a modern play, *Richard of Bordeaux*, by 'Gordon Daviot', a pseudonym for Elizabeth MacKintosh, which was also successful.

My first experience of the play starred Paul Scofield as Richard and Eric Porter as Bolingbroke in a memorable production by John Gielgud, which rather stressed the capricious nature of the King.

Jeremy Irons played Richard in an RSC production that was set by William Dudley in a garden, pointing up "this blessed plot" of John of Gaunt's great speech. And Ben Whishaw memorably played the King in a TV production more recently.

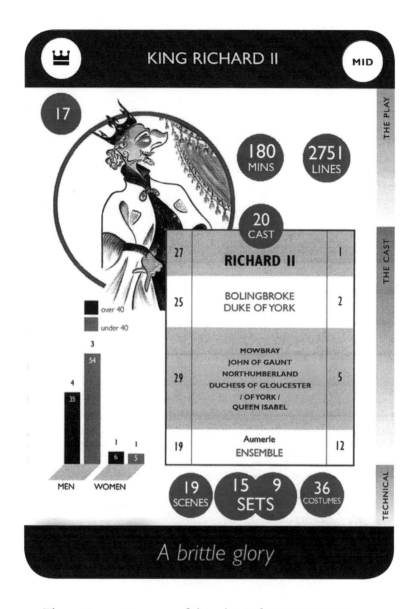
17

180 MINS

2751 LINES

20 CAST

27	**RICHARD II**	1
25	BOLINGBROKE DUKE OF YORK	2
29	MOWBRAY JOHN OF GAUNT NORTHUMBERLAND DUCHESS OF GLOUCESTER / OF YORK / QUEEN ISABEL	5
19	Aumerle ENSEMBLE	12

over 40

under 40

MEN WOMEN

3
54
4
35
1 1
6 5

19 SCENES

15 SETS 9

36 COSTUMES

A brittle glory

The main requirement of this play is for younger men with 54% of the lines. The play has an average number of scenes with many sets which can be simplified to an average number of sets and an average number of costumes. This play is straightforward with a few but not insuperable challenges.

KING RICHARD II John Gielgud

KING RICHARD III

KING RICHARD III Ralph Fiennes

KING RICHARD III
Plots have I laid

With his brother King Edward IV sick, Richard of Gloucester arranges that their brother Clarence is imprisoned. Richard intercepts the funeral procession of the dead King Henry VI to woo Lady Anne, daughter of the late Earl of Warwick.

The newly ennobled kin of Queen Elizabeth are accused by Richard of complicity in the imprisonment and subsequent death of Clarence. On his deathbed the King asks that Richard and the Queen's faction be reconciled. With the support of Buckingham, Richard, now Lord Protector of the young King Edward V and his brother, arranges for them to be taken to the Tower of London.

At a council meeting Lord Hastings is isolated and accused of a plot against Richard and is executed. Richard and Buckingham now enlist the support of the Lord Mayor of London for Richard's claim to be King, inferring the bastardy of the young Princes. He manages to gain enough support to be crowned. He now rejects Buckingham who had expected advancement. Buckingham flees but is captured and executed. The two Princes are murdered. Lady Anne, briefly Queen, dies and Richard now woos a daughter of Edward IV's widow, Queen Elizabeth.

Queen Margaret, the widow of Henry VI, Queen Elizabeth and Richard's mother, the Duchess of York, bewail the loss of their kin. Henry of Richmond, a distant heir of the House of Lancaster, invades England to remove the tyrant King. In the Battle of Bosworth Richard is deserted by Stanley's forces and he dies friendless. Richmond assumes the crown as Henry VII.

This play has retained its popularity from Garrick to Olivier and Sher. There is simply no point in attempting this play unless one has an actor of spectacular ability to play the role, and if one has such an actor the play is almost certain to be a success despite the considerable resources needed.

All the history plays need bodies of attendant lords, soldiers and servants. As well as needing a huge star to play Richard and experienced Shakespeareans to play the other identified leads, there is also a need for at least 16 ensemble players in this play, most of whom play two or three parts. This is a huge challenge for most companies.

By this stage of the Wars of the Roses the dynastic arguments have become quieter; the Yorkist sword has won the day and the Lancastrian claim has descended to a relatively minor figure (who appeared but did not speak in *Henry VI, Part 3*, and who emerges only briefly at the end of this play).

The first crux is how to portray Richard – as murderous Machiavel or a more understated politician. The text certainly endorses the former though the modern idea that Richard is a victim of Sir Thomas More's propaganda has some validity. Whatever approach is adopted, the very length of the part means that a certain variation must be attempted, if only to give the audience much-needed variety. Richard is superior in wit to all other characters and the lines can support virtually any interpretation. He is never dull, in contrast, say, to the wailing ladies who have difficulty in escaping monotony. Led by Queen Margaret, the remarkable widow of Henry VI, these ladies utter a string of complaints and curses (which always seem to become true). It is reminiscent of the witches in *Macbeth*. This suggests that cutting even one of these would destroy the importance of these familial curses working themselves out, hence accepting the need to have the considerable forces listed.

The second crux is to recognise and reflect how to handle the numerous doubling of situations in this play.

- The wooing of Lady Anne by Richard is mirrored by Richard's wooing of Queen Elizabeth for the hand of her daughter.
- Clarence's murder is mirrored by that of the two princes.
- The executions of Hastings' enemies are mirrored by his own execution.
- The prayers of Richard on the eve of battle are counterpointed by those of Richmond.
- The ghosts assail Richard and encourage Richmond.
- The prophesies of Richard's mother and the three queens all come true.

The final crux is to understand the importance of an example of apparently unnecessary characters such as the Scrivener. The part may have been written to cover a costume or scene change but the Scrivener is given a speech of deep insight. He tells us that he has spent the night scrivening, i.e. writing up the verdict on Hastings' trial before the trial has even begun. Once again Shakespeare gives a minor character the chance to make a telling comment on the politics of Richard's court in a surprising and effective way. As always in Shakespeare there are no small parts and one other such character in this play, Tyrrell, is given the lines describing the deaths of the Princes in the Tower, as poignant and ravishing as anything in Shakespeare.

> O thus ... lay the gentle babes,
> ... girdling one another
> Within their alabaster innocent arms:
> Their lips were four red roses on a stalk,
> Which, in their summer beauty kiss'd each other.

Richard III is the culmination of the eight-play cycle beginning with *Richard II*. The character of Richard of Gloucester, afterwards *Richard III*, appears in the two previous plays, *Henry VI, Part 2* (briefly) and *Part 3* where he murders the King and embarks on his mission for power. In a sense, the play of *Richard III* is illuminated by seeing *Henry VI, Part 3* as well, though this is seldom achieved, though a notable soliloquy from the earlier play is sometimes retained as a prologue to the later play.

As would be expected, the culmination of a four-play cycle, *Richard III,* repeats the themes of the previous plays, facing much the same cruxes. And in that culmination it also has the not inconsiderable advantage in the title role of one of Shakespeare's finest and unforgettable characters.

Laurence Olivier's film of *Richard III*, in which he directed and starred, remains a superb account of this play, and my passion for it is shared by my son Owen and younger brother John, with whom I rather overplayed Olivier's opening speech, when he filmed it as we walked the town walls of Chester. It is notable in that no fewer than four knights of the theatre feature in it. Sir Laurence cast Ralph Richardson as Buckingham, John Gielgud as Clarence and Cedric Hardwick as King Edward, all celebrated Shakespeareans. The role of Lady Anne was played by Claire Bloom, whom I had seen play Juliet at the Old Vic in another brilliant performance of Shakespeare.

I should also mention an RSC production of the play in which Antony Sher, also a Shakespearean Knight, played Richard. Played as a hunchbacked spider, on two crutches, he thrillingly launched himself from a standing position midway through the opening speech, his crutches swung over his head, landing like some venomous insect. I purchased many of the costume designs of this production by William Dudley, the award-winning designer, with whom my association goes back many years.

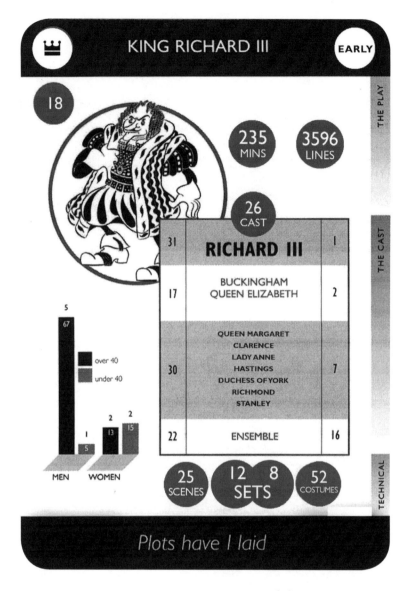

KING RICHARD III

EARLY

18

235 MINS

3596 LINES

26 CAST

31	**RICHARD III**	1
17	BUCKINGHAM QUEEN ELIZABETH	2
30	QUEEN MARGARET CLARENCE LADY ANNE HASTINGS DUCHESS OF YORK RICHMOND STANLEY	7
22	ENSEMBLE	16

5

67

over 40

under 40

2 2

1 13 15

5

MEN   WOMEN

25 SCENES

12 8 SETS

52 COSTUMES

Plots have I laid

The main requirement of this play is for **older men** with **67%** of the lines. The play has **many** scenes with **many** sets, which can be simplified to an **average** number of sets, and **many** costumes. This play is **straightforward** with a **few** but not insuperable challenges.

KING RICHARD III Edmund Kean

KING HENRY V

KING HENRY V Kenneth Branagh

KING HENRY V
Such waste in brief mortality

The Archbishop of Canterbury argues Henry's right, as the newly crowned King of England, to the throne of France. An expedition is assembled to invade France. A conspiracy by the Earl of Cambridge, Lord Scroop and Sir Thomas Grey is discovered and the conspirators executed.

The French court is contemptuous of the English and Henry's demands, conveyed to the French by his uncle, Exeter, are rejected. Henry takes Harfleur but the English army is outnumbered at Agincourt. The French envoy Montjoy is sent back to the French in defiance by Henry.

On the eve of the battle the King, disguised, encounters three soldiers, including Williams, who questions the King's claim and challenges the King should they both survive the battle. Henry encourages his depleted forces, while the French leaders celebrate their superiority, anticipating an easy victory.

In the battle the French are defeated, not without having killed the English baggage boys, which as the Welsh captain Fluellen points out is against the rules of war. Fluellen is deputed to wear Henry's favour and Williams duly challenges him before Henry reveals his identity.

At the defeated French court the Duke of Burgundy pleads for an extended peace between France and England. Henry woos and wins Katharine, the French King's daughter, as his bride and it seems that a period of peace is assured.

In *Henry V* a Chorus is created mainly to 'apologise' to the audience of his day, and to all audiences, for the deficiencies of the stage to portray great themes such as battles, sea voyages, vast crowds of people. Shakespeare could not know it (but I believe he intuitively knew) that all these would be easily achieved in a later age (in film, for example).

The Chorus exhorts us to use our imagination to create these great themes in our minds even though today we do not need to rely on imagination solely with all the modern technical advances at our disposal.

I see no reason why the Chorus should not also act some of the supporting roles. My suggestion for the Chorus to play Ely, Erpingham and Burgundy recognises that these roles need the talents of experienced actors too. The Chorus can move in and out of the main action, explaining and participating, without the need for elaborate costume changes.

Given that *Henry V* involves the French and English at war, it is no surprise that a considerable force of actors is needed: 24 (excluding speaking attendants and soldiers) is a minimum force. The role of the King is massive – over a thousand lines, representing 31% of the play. He is supported by the Chorus, Fluellen and another important composite role of the Archbishop of Canterbury and Charles VI of France, which neatly combines the English and the French sides of the argument. The three traitors could play the three common soldiers (another neat, if convenient, combination). I suggest that the actress playing Mistress Quickly could also appear as Queen Isabel. The rest are more matters of expedience than making any particular comment on the characters themselves.

I am pretty agnostic about the period of the action. This is a play that can be done either as a period piece (as in Olivier's film) or as a modern piece or as a mixture of ancient and modern that was popular in the '90s and may present the best way of dealing with all the problems of bringing such a play to the stage. There is a huge costume need, and the splendour of the French court, for example, should not be stinted.

The first crux, then, is to decide whether the King is Hero or Villain. I suggest this is done by considering the political framework of the play, set by the Archbishop in the first act. Modern experience is that all wars are ultimately bad wars and that a war that lasts a hundred years is a disaster for the nation that starts it. Yet Shakespeare's politics, and that of his age, saw much merit in Henry's justification for war, and throughout this play the virtues of victory, gained through courage, are the ideal human attributes. Today we are not so sure. All I would suggest is that the Archbishop's two scenes should be played deadly seriously. Robert Helpmann's clowning as the Bishop of Ely in Olivier's film, and its effect on Felix Aylmer's Archbishop, which was otherwise brilliantly played is to my mind unfortunate. Olivier, as director, was probably making the point that the whole reason for going to war was ridiculous to a contemporary audience – and he set this scene in an Elizabethan theatre before opting for the realism of war and battle later in the film. The Archbishop's later speech is a remarkable exposition of the Elizabethan political code and repays study for this and indeed for all the history plays. But remember, too, the political motivation of the Church in all this: it was seen that the war would deflect attention that would otherwise be paid to church wealth, and an investment in the war, which Canterbury promises, is well worth it if the rest of Church wealth is left alone for another generation of churchmen.

The realities of war are best summed up in the Harfleur scene when Henry spells out what will happen if the citizens resist – a real domestic horror that Henry would have no compunction about inflicting on the town. In battle, before Harfleur, or with his soldiers, or in his St Crispin's Day speech, Henry reveals the more admirable side of the politics of war, and there is no doubt that in Shakespeare's time (and mine!) these were truly heroic qualities. But Shakespeare understood well enough the ultimate consequences of these actions.

And the politics of dynasty, and dynastic marriages, is of course the seed for the Wars of the Roses, a domestic consequence of what started out as a claim on the Kingdom of France.

The main argument is France v. England, "Whose very shores look pale for envy of each other's happiness," as it is described elsewhere. Allied to this are the regional differences within and outside England: Welsh, Scots, Irish and London clashes of accent and character, not to mention the classical fustian rodomontade of Pistol. Whereas these latter must be done with differentiated accents, the French characters must be handled differently. In the main the French parts are written in standard English – the convention being that when they are among themselves any difference of accent should only be exceptionally introduced, since they are in fact speaking 'French' to each other. In the scenes between the countries, accented English might be attempted to make the point that trying to speak a foreign tongue is less fluent than speaking one's own. The point is inescapable in the two French scenes when Henry speaks French with an English accent. There is no reason, however, why Charles VI, or the Dauphin, should not speak 'perfect' English, and if this makes for better theatre so be it.

Of course the scenes involving Kate and Alice, which are written in French, are wonderfully entertaining, and the bawdiness of the humour utterly delightful and typically English. The four regional accents of the Captains will pose no problems (Shakespeare's spelling is a problem, though). Of more importance to decide than the Welshness of his accent is how funny Fluellen (Llewellyn) should be, whether he is a figure of fun or, as the King says:

> Though it appears a little out of fashion
> There is much care and valour in this Welshman.

The accent is thick, but the character is not. Any humour will come from the situation rather than by mangling the English language with stage Welsh. There may be the odd swipe at the Welsh, but so there is against the Scots, the Irish and the French. Of far more importance with regard to the French is to get their grandeur, or their effeteness, accurately portrayed. They are not fools either, though a gentle mocking of all the nations underlies Shakespeare's English design. This play is far more than a comedy of national manners.

Fluellen's key contribution is not to force Pistol to eat a leek but his insistence on the rules of war, the proper way of behaving according to ancient militarists. He is almost tiresomely pedantic on this point but the actions of the killing of the prisoners by Henry, or the slaughter of the boys guarding the baggage train by the French, need to be considered in the light of these rules. Both themes, rules and language, come together in the Boy's description of Pistol's valour:

> For Pistol he hath a killing tongue and a quiet sword; by the means whereof he breaks words and keeps whole weapons.

The rules of war abhor such. But yet, but yet; is this not to be preferred to unpolicied slaughter? As usual Shakespeare gives us a moral choice and any production should recognise such ambiguity. Was Henry justified in killing the prisoners? He issued the order before he learned of the baggage boys.

The wartime film of *Henry V,* which Laurence Olivier both directed and starred in, was made partly to boost morale, but also to act as a seminal bridge between the worlds of theatre and film. It opened with the Chorus, in a theatrical setting, discussing the limitations of the theatre, "this wooden O" and calling on our "imaginary forces" to do justice to the mighty themes of the play.

Olivier gradually moved the action from the theatre to the realism of film with all its components, including crowd scenes, armies, battles, tracking shots and close-ups, augmented with a thrilling orchestral soundtrack by England's foremost composer of the day. The illustration of Kenneth Branagh as Henry V echoes this development more recently. In the production of the play, with Branagh in the title role and directed by Adrian Noble, the battles were staged realistically, showing all the degrading elements of war.

Some later stage productions of the play adopted such unheroic readings (and Branagh also made a film to complete the transition from 'imaginary forces' to filmic 'realism', though he retained the Chorus of Derek Jacobi, not the least to keep the power of Shakespeare's words). The speech of the Chorus describing the scene before the Battle of Agincourt is included in the Sampler section of this book both as a supreme example of the power of imagination, and a passage well worth learning by heart.

The Tower Theatre, where much of my non-professional work has been done, moved to new premises in 2018, and its first production by John McSpadyen was of *Henry V.* Penny Tuerk, to whose memory this book is dedicated, spoke the first words as the Chorus:

> O for a muse of fire, that would ascend
> The brightest heaven of invention

The imagination meets reality.

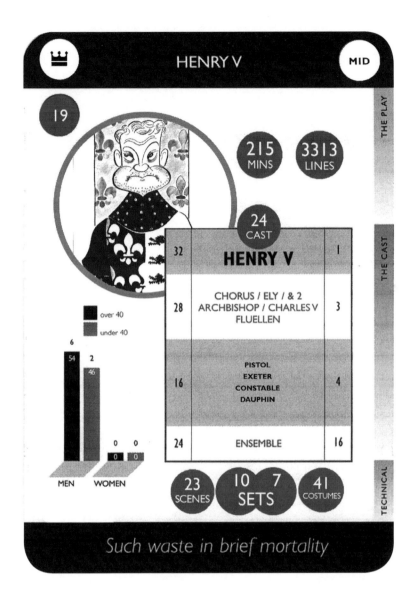

The main requirement of this play is for **older men** with 54% of the lines. The play has an **average** number of scenes with an **average** number of sets and **many** costumes. This play is **straightforward** with a **few** but not insuperable challenges.

KING HENRY V   Kenneth Branagh

THE MERRY WIVES OF WINDSOR

FALSTAFF Simon Callow

THE MERRY WIVES OF WINDSOR
Serve God and leave your desires

Justice Shallow's nephew, Slender, is a suitor to Anne Page. He has the blessing of Master Page, but Anne's mother prefers that she should marry the French doctor Caius. A third suitor, Fenton, a young gentleman, is supported by Mistress Quickly, Caius' housekeeper.

Falstaff is living at Windsor and has used up all his money. He dismisses his servants, Pistol, Nym and Bardolph. He writes identical letters to Mistress Page and Mistress Ford suggesting an assignation. The ladies compare the letters and decide on revenge. Pistol has in the meantime alerted Ford and Page of Falstaff's intentions. Falstaff meets Ford who assumes the name Master Brook for the purpose. Brook asks Falstaff to act as his go-between to Mistress Ford. Falstaff tells Brook of his own plans and Ford then decides to catch him in the middle of his proposed assignation.

Falstaff meets up with Mistress Ford but is interrupted by Mistress Page warning him of Ford's approach and he is hidden in a linen basket and carted to the laundry place by the river, ending up in the Thames. Ford finds nothing.

A second appointment is made. This time Falstaff escapes in disguise as an old woman.

A third appointment is arranged at night in Windsor Park at Herne's oak, where Slender is planning to elope with Anne Page. The two wives ensure that Falstaff is thoroughly humiliated with the help of the Host of the Garter Inn. Fenton gets Anne and marries her. The Pages finally accept their daughter's choice.

This play was written, it was famously said, at the request of Queen Elizabeth I to show Sir John Falstaff in love. To my mind it is a disappointment.

Falstaff is one of Shakespeare's most inspired creations and practically all that can be said of him has already been said in the two parts of *Henry IV* and in *Henry V* where his death is movingly reported by Mistress Quickly. Falstaff in love, is much different from the man in the Histories.

The actors in the Histories who played Falstaff, Pistol, Mistress Quickly, the Page, Bardolph and Nym probably retained their parts in this play. Shallow is a far cry from Shallow in *Henry IV, Part 2*. If the original Shallow retained his part in this he would have been a very disappointed man.

In this play William Page and Robin, Falstaff's Page, could be doubled, and I would recommend this same actor plays Anne Page too – there are no practical difficulties. No real difficulties arise in doubling Nym (yet again a thankless role) with Rugby; Pistol (a disappointing role per se, but in this double a splendid challenge) with Dr Caius; and Fenton with Simple. Fenton is one of the least interesting heroes in Shakespeare and the actor would welcome the chance to add a cameo to his main role.

There are two scenes that probably need a substantial set: Ford's House and Herne's oak. The rest are simply achieved and the play is no problem to stage.

The period is resolutely of its time and completely bourgeois. This is the first crux that a director might consider, the differing ranks of the characters and how these affect behaviour.

Windsor is not the court – it is the country. The characters are not sophisticated and are largely one-dimensional. They are probably viewed by the author with more ridicule than affection. In this play the highest in rank, Falstaff, is completely broke while the richest, Ford, has the finesse of a parvenu. The parson and the country justice will expect due deference to their rank, but the doctor, being a foreigner, might not. Fenton is a gentleman and a desirable son-in-law for at least one of the bourgeois wives.

However debased, Falstaff is the highest rank in Windsor, and is the hero, however flawed. He has wonderful scenes, even if he is not an entirely admirable knight of the realm. The Herne's oak scene has a vigour, even a viciousness, that fable and fantasy provide – it is for directors to choose how far down the path of pain to go. Remember they all go off to the pub at the end, so perhaps the humiliation should be more gentle than hurtful. It is as if the bourgeoisie forgives the errant knight despite his treatment of them.

The second crux is to get the various accents of the lower ranks right. The Frenchman and the Welshman are racial stereotypes to be enjoyed and laughed at, particularly for their accents. As well as the Welsh and French accents, there are Gloucestershire, Estuary (Host?), Mummerset, Midlands (Rugby?), Dim, Educated (the Latin Lesson) and others, including German. This extends to variations in the master/servant relationship and especially how badly masters treat their servants. Falstaff fires Bardolph, Nym and Pistol, keeping only the Page. Caius and Rugby, Slender and Simple, and Caius and Quickly are all variations on the relationships between master and servant. In general the action is very fragmented – not dissimilar to modern soap operas.

The third crux is to make clear the role of money, very much the crucial concern of the bourgeoisie, particularly when associated with marriage and the marriage settlement:

- Falstaff has no money, promises more than he can pay, and is constantly looking for direct or indirect payment from his inferiors. Pistol and Nym break faith when he cuts costs by turning them loose. When Brook offers him money he should smell a rat – no such thing as a free breakfast – and his final humiliation is to have to return it.
- Fenton may have money but he is seen as a fortune hunter by the bourgeoisie; the Pages support other candidates for their daughter who they think are better off.

- The Host is robbed by the Germans and, restored by Fenton's money, he agrees to help Fenton to win the girl.
- Bardolph has to earn his money by becoming a tapster.

There is in this play the enduring conflict between means and appetites, and this is the key to much of the comedy.

In the theatre *The Merry Wives of Windsor* usually pleases, as it was intended to do for Queen Elizabeth I. As noted above, my view is that the Falstaff of this play is a much diminished character compared to the *Henry IV* plays.

One really successful production, in which Peter Jeffrey played Falstaff, was in the Bill Alexander production for the RSC. The Merry Wives, played by Lindsey Duncan and Janet Dale, were set in a hairdressing salon for their opening scene, speaking their lines from under hairdryers in a splendid modern setting.

And, of course, the play provided the story for Verdi's great opera *Falstaff*, another fruit of Shakespeare's imagination.

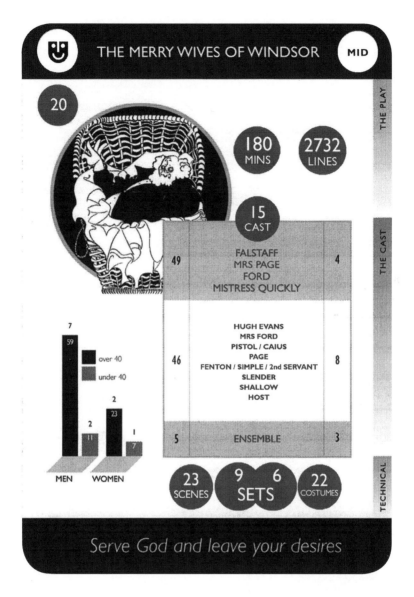

THE MERRY WIVES OF WINDSOR

MID

20

180 MINS

2732 LINES

15 CAST

49	FALSTAFF MRS PAGE FORD MISTRESS QUICKLY	4
46	HUGH EVANS MRS FORD PISTOL / CAIUS PAGE FENTON / SIMPLE / 2nd SERVANT SLENDER SHALLOW HOST	8
5	ENSEMBLE	3

7

59

over 40
under 40

2

2

23

1

7

MEN   WOMEN

23 SCENES

9 6 SETS

22 COSTUMES

Serve God and leave your desires

The main requirement of this play is for **older men** with **59%** of the lines. The play has an **average** number of scenes with an **average** number of sets and relatively **few** costumes. This play is **recommended**, particularly early on in a Shakespearean involvement or career.

FALSTAFF Anthony Quayle

149

CYMBELINE

IACHIMO Henry Irving   **IMOGEN** Ellen Terry

CYMBELINE
You do not meet a man but frowns

Imogen, the daughter of Cymbeline, King of Britain, is in love with Posthumus Leonatus, but he is banished at the Queen's behest so that her son Cloten might marry her.

In Rome, Posthumus is challenged by Iachimo who claims that he can seduce Imogen. So confident is Posthumus in her fidelity that he enables Iachimo to get access to her. By gaining access to her bedchamber by hiding in a trunk, he is able to observe her sleeping and gain enough circumstantial evidence to persuade Posthumus that she has been unfaithful. Posthumus writes to his servant, Pisanio, that he must revenge him but Pisanio arranges for Imogen to be disguised as a boy and go to Wales in order to contact Posthumus again. She enters the service of Caius Lucius, General of the Roman Army that has invaded Britain.

In Wales Cloten, disguised as Posthumus, pursues Imogen who has found the cave of Belarius and his two sons, previously banished by Cymbeline. Imogen, or Fidele as these three know her, becomes ill and apparently dies. Cloten is killed in a quarrel and beheaded by Guiderius, one of the sons. When Imogen awakes, and sees Posthumus' clothes on the corpse, she believes the worst. Found by Lucius she becomes his page.

In the battle, Posthumus, who had arrived with the Roman army, changes sides and, with Belarius and the two boys, defeats the Romans. In the battle's aftermath it is revealed that the two boys, Guiderius and Arviragus, are the long lost sons of Cymbeline. Posthumus and Imogen are finally reunited and peace is made with Rome.

"You do not meet a man but frowns…" is the superb opening line of this play. By the end one has had one's full share of frowns; we experience palpable relief when arriving at "Let our crooked smokes climb to their nostrils from our blest altars." That we need the intervention of Jupiter, a soothsayer and a dream to achieve all this can be seen as dramatic inspiration or exhaustion – I hardly know which.

As a vehicle for actors it has one outstanding role – Imogen; one effective role – Cloten, but the rest seem to me to be virtually unactable and I cannot think of any actor who has boosted his reputation in any of them. Take Cymbeline, a fatuous monarch of terrible judgement in almost everything who is, however, constantly referred to as a paragon of kingship, from the day he was knighted by Caesar for his exploits in battle, to his siring not one but (as it turns out) three paragons of princeship. Yet he commits all the following misjudgements: declaring that the upbringing of Posthumus did not fit him to wed Imogen; dooming Imogen to marry Cloten; banishing Posthumus; punishing Imogen for her failure to marry Cloten; committing Britain to a Roman invasion; marrying the wicked Queen and justifying it because she was beautiful; contemplating the revenge ritual murder of Lucius; sentencing Guiderius to death. Only after the intervention of Jupiter does he become statesman-like; though agreeing to resume the tribute to Rome after Lucius is defeated seems another misjudgement. Iachimo has his moment in Imogen's bedchamber, but the rest of his role, especially towards the end, is disappointing. Posthumus has a devilishly difficult syntax to make clear, and is a pasteboard paragon, his one great line, "Hang there like fruit, my soul, Till the tree die," coming too late to alleviate his basic dullness. The Queen is a pantomime villain while Belarius and the two boys are tediously perfect and deferential.

The plot is famously complex and Act V Scene 5 is often seen as a technically brilliant pulling together, in only 500 lines, of all that has gone before. It should be noted that the audience (if it has been awake throughout) knows what has happened and "the fierce abridgement" of the reconciliation is more for the benefit of the characters than the audience. It is almost as if Shakespeare sets himself the most difficult challenge to show he can rise to it. It all relies on mistaken identities, two moles, a Roman invasion, potent drugs both taken and not taken.

It needs experienced Shakespeareans and a cast of 19, rather too many for economic comfort.

The bedchamber (with chest) and the cave need careful design. The period is pre-Norman Britain and it is likely that any other period chosen for the play will present more problems than insights.

The key crux is syntax – the verse is difficult and obscure. The frame of reference includes the sanctity of kingship; the destruction of one's enemies being the height of princely breeding; the honour of the outcast; filial duty v. true love – all familiar enough in Shakespeare but not always easy for a modern audience to grasp, much less believe in. The verse will help the actor explain, but he will need to put in much effort to understand the footnotes himself if he is to illuminate the text for the audience.

Add to this the extraordinary identity muddle of many of the characters; sorting these out clearly is the second crux. Cymbeline's derivation is explained with reference to Cassibelan, Tarantius and Mulmutius, not to mention Augustus Caesar. His sons and their foster father have two names each. Imogen appears as Fidele. The body of Cloten is given the false name of Richard du Champ by Imogen who believes it to belong to Posthumus. We are told of Imogen's mother and Cloten's father, while Posthumus sees in his dream another pair of brothers, his mother and his father who shares his given name Leonatus. The evil Queen does not have a name (though her Lady in Waiting does) and the invading Roman, Caius Lucius, has two. Our comprehension of all these identities is quite severely strained.

The third crux is the dream and Jupiter's appearance – the first decision being whether to stage it at all. In an era when the masque (that courtly extension into the realms of godhead) was becoming fashionable, Shakespeare gives us one of the most elaborate, combining costumes, set and music in the resolution of a literally fantastic story. To make this central to the production is a challenge, particularly in an age that hardly believes in such visions.

I have a feeling there is a director and a cast somewhere that will do for this play what Peter Brook did for *King Lear*, say, which would dissolve my doubts, revealing wonders. I hope so; but mere mortals should treat this play with care.

Cymbeline was the Marlowe Society of Cambridge's choice in my second undergraduate year and was directed by Dadie Rylands, who with Donald Beves had made the Society an important vehicle for young actors to experience Shakespeare (and his contemporaries) at the professional Arts Theatre. I did not audition since my earlier exams had not gone well, but I did receive an invitation to play the deus ex machina, Jupiter, who arrives from the heavens on an eagle, which I declined, even though the cast had considerable strength – Margaret Drabble, Clive Swift, Derek Jacobi and Ian McKellen taking prominent roles. Rylands was renowned for getting the spoken word correct and, at that time, organised the complete recordings of Shakespeare for Argo Records with many of my undergraduate friends taking part.

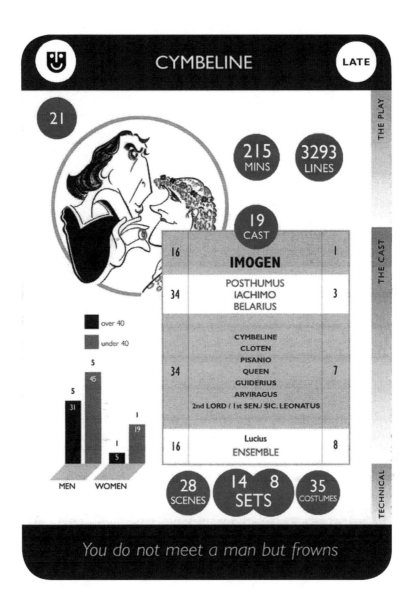

CYMBELINE

LATE

21

215 MINS

3293 LINES

19 CAST

16	**IMOGEN**	1
34	POSTHUMUS IACHIMO BELARIUS	3
34	CYMBELINE CLOTEN PISANIO QUEEN GUIDERIUS ARVIRAGUS 2nd LORD / 1st SEN./ SIC. LEONATUS	7
16	Lucius ENSEMBLE	8

over 40

under 40

MEN: 31, 5
WOMEN: 5, 1, 19, 1
45, 5

28 SCENES

14 8 SETS

35 COSTUMES

You do not meet a man but frowns

The main requirement of this play is for **younger** men with **45%** of the lines. The play has **many** scenes with **many** sets and an **average** number of costumes. This play is more **difficult**, and probably best left to experienced groups.

IACHIMO Henry Irving   **IMOGEN** Ellen Terry

155

KING HENRY IV, PART 1

FALSTAFF Ralph Richardson

KING HENRY IV, PART 1
Do thou stand for my father

'Fathers and Sons' could be a subtitle for the two Henry IV plays.

After a battle Henry Percy, called Hotspur, son of the Earl of Northumberland, has refused to hand over his prisoners to King Henry IV, and after an acrimonious meeting the Percies and the Earl of Worcester enter into an alliance with Glendower and Douglas to wrest the crown from Henry. Lady Percy, Hotspur's wife, counsels against rebellion but Hotspur overrules her.

Henry's son, Prince Hal, spends his time with Sir John Falstaff and his lowborn companions, including Poins. For a variety of reasons, not all commendable, the Prince takes part in a robbery in which Falstaff's cowardice and talent for embellishing truth are established. Back at the tavern Falstaff persuades Hal to rehearse in an impromptu play, his response to the King's command to join his force against the rebels. Henry envies Northumberland his son, yet, just before the campaign Northumberland withdraws his forces from his son on the grounds he is sick. Hal, on the other hand, proves a truer son than his father thinks, by leading the King's forces and by killing Hotspur in single combat at the Battle of Shrewsbury. Falstaff feigns dead on the battlefield and opportunistically claims to have killed Hotspur, who had revived once Hal had left his body on the battlefield. With misgivings Hal allows Falstaff credit for what he claims.

Worcester and the rebels still alive after the battle are executed and Hal is reconciled with the King, who plans further retribution on those rebels who had not been at Shrewsbury.

KING HENRY IV, PART 2

FALSTAFF Orson Welles
PRINCE HAL Keith Baxter
MISTRESS QUICKLY Margaret Rutherford

KING HENRY IV, PART 2
I know thee not old man

The Earl of Northumberland, whose son Hotspur died at Shrewsbury, enters an alliance with Scroop, Archbishop of York against the King. Falstaff is again given a commission to raise soldiers against the rebels and, taking leave of Doll Tearsheet and Mistress Quickly and the Boar's Head Tavern, sets off with Bardolph to visit his old acquaintance Justice Shallow in Gloucestershire where some wretched recruits are enlisted and bribes accepted for others who are released.

The King, exhausted and sick, leaves his forces in the hands of his sons Prince Hal and Prince John of Lancaster. Prince John receives a deputation from the rebels and promises to right their grievances. The rebels disperse their army and are arrested for their pains.

The King hears news of the victory but collapses and is taken to his bed. Prince Hal arrives and, believing his father to be dead, takes the crown. The King revives and accuses Hal of wanting his death. Hal convinces him this is not so and is reconciled before the King dies. The new King shows magnanimity to an old adversary, the Lord Chief Justice.

Back in Gloucestershire Falstaff hears from Pistol of the King's death. Promising advancement to Shallow, and borrowing money against the event, Falstaff confronts the new King and is rejected by him. Lancaster forecasts that the new King will invade France.

Before considering the forces needed for these plays I must start with the first crux: does one choose a single production of either Part 1 or Part 2; or choose to mount productions of both parts played in repertory or, conceivably, to conflate the two parts? There is much to be said for each approach.

Single productions

Part 1 is a complete play in itself, culminating in the Battle of Shrewsbury at which the madcap Prince Hal restores himself in favour with his father. Henry IV had despaired of his son's leaving his dissolute life with Falstaff and the Eastcheap crowd. Henry IV had doubted Hal's fitness to rule, to establish his own dynasty which he had usurped from Richard II. Henry had envied Northumberland whose son, the rebel Hotspur, seemed to have better qualities for rule than Hal. But Hal defeated Hotspur at Shrewsbury. Northumberland's sickness at the crucial moment dooms the rebellion.

Part 2 is also a complete play with a very similar 'line' to it: sick King; further dissipation by Hal; another rebellion; Falstaff seen as a cynical manipulator of Hal's patronage; Hal (and his austere brother John of Lancaster) defeat the rebellion (ingloriously). The King is reconciled to Hal before his death. Falstaff expects (and promises) further patronage from the new King, and is rejected.

It is difficult to choose between the two parts. For my money the rebellion of Part 1 is more interesting and theatrical. So is the tavern scene in Part 1, though Doll Tearsheet adds a huge dimension to the Part 2 tavern scene. Part 2 has the Lord Chief Justice episodes and the Shallow scenes and the great autumnal sweep of Falstaff with Doll, the sick King unable to sleep and the Shallow/Silence discussion on mortality. The part of Hal in Part 2 is less important than in Part 1. The real Falstaff emerges more clearly in Part 2 and the rejection scene is chilling. I would probably opt for Part 2 if I had to choose.

Both parts in repertory

Doing both parts in repertory is, of course, ideal but with twice the amount of rehearsal, and a large cast, this is going to be a big undertaking that needs much time, money and logistical skill to organise. And, look at it from the audience's point of view – do I book for two plays in the same run and find two evenings when I am free, making sure that Part 1 is seen first? Or, do I chance one if I cannot manage both? If I book for one, how do I know it is the 'best'? In recent years the subsidised companies in England do both parts in repertory and that is probably the ideal situation. However, the demands on the actors are formidable; Falstaff, with over 1,200 lines, Prince Hal (800+) and Henry IV (600+) have major challenges of both learning and performing these huge roles. Few actors of the necessary stature are keen to accept such a challenge, at any rate for long runs. And, unless you have an actor capable and willing to accept these roles, not to mention a Hotspur, you cannot contemplate such an undertaking.

Conflation

Which leaves conflation, famously done by Orson Welles in his *Chimes at Midnight*, a solution to many of the problems that I have outlined. My own instinct would be to preserve the 'best' rebellion, Hotspur's, both tavern scenes (but not the Gadshill robbery, merely the aftermath), the Doll and Lord Chief Justice scenes, Shallow and the usurpation scenes.

The main lines of both plays are preserved – Hal's move from degradation to accession, Henry IV's decline from anxiety to death, Falstaff's increasing self-serving corruption, Worcester's decline and fall, the Lord Chief Justice's rehabilitation, Shallow's disappointing harvest.

Any director, any company thinking of doing these plays must rehearse all these arguments anew. My own inclination, if doing both parts in repertory is ruled out on economic or practical grounds, is to do the conflation. As a way of increasing their popularity (low at

22 and 24) any solution is all to the good, for these are wonderful plays, and the character of Falstaff (in these plays, not *The Merry Wives*) is one of the outstanding creations of all time.

So what about resources needed:

	MEN		WOMEN	CHILDREN	
Part 1	18	+	3		= 21
Part 2	19	+	2	+ 1	= 22

As is usual in Shakespeare, only a few women are required. In Part 2 I suggest the double of Lady Percy and Doll – to make one great role out of two good ones (there is just time for the actress to change from one to the other). Today, with so few opportunities for actresses, it would be unusual to make a composite of these parts, but that is both more expensive and less of an acting challenge.

I suggest three other doubles which make good theatrical sense:

- Northumberland, important in that he lets the rebels down not once but twice, disappears from the action early in Part 2; a failed father. Warwick, the King's confidant, who acts as a kind of spiritual doctor, appears late in Part 2. If one actor plays these father-figure roles he has the challenge of making the contrast between the balance of faithfulness and unfaithfulness.
- Lord Bardolph has one key speech (on the need to have a workable plan before building a house or starting a revolution). Pistol has bravura and presence. Both need substantial acting prowess and suggest a satisfying double.
- Poins is often depicted as a young foil to Prince Hal. It is too much to call him a false friend, but he is generally regarded as a bad influence. John of Lancaster (in both plays) is Hal's austere younger brother who appears to be everything that Hal is not. This is a natural double.

These are company plays with big stars. But all the supporting roles have something to offer the actor, so strength in depth is necessary. The set requirements are not onerous, though the tavern, and to a lesser extent the Jerusalem chamber and the council room will need some thought. The battles are relatively straightforward. Plenty of costumes are required, and the heraldry has been seen as significant.

The second crux is to make what I call the subtitle – Fathers and Sons – clear in all its manifestations:

   a. Henry IV and Prince Hal
   b. Falstaff and Prince Hal
   c. Northumberland and Hotspur
   d. Henry IV and Hotspur
   e. Lord Chief Justice and Prince Hal

I have dealt with (a) already, which is the major unifying theme of both plays which culminates in the reconciliation in Part 2. (b) recognises that Falstaff is the false father to Hal, leading him to stealing, drinking and (probably) whoring where he should be an example to him. And far from providing for the Prince, Falstaff feeds off him. (c) is the minor key to both plays where the paragon Hotspur is let down by his father who then proceeds to let down Hotspur's successors in revolution in Part 2, not so much a false father as an insufficient one. Yet Henry (d) envies Northumberland his son, wishes even that they might have been switched at birth and that his real son is the valiant Hotspur even though that son is actually in rebellion against him. And Hotspur is ultimately swept away. In Part 2 (e) is the counterpoint to (a) where the Lord Chief Justice, who had acted in the guise of the just father, fears for his life when the Prince he had imprisoned is elevated to the crown, but where the new King accepts all the Lord Chief Justice had done, elevating him to the position of New True Father, so to speak, as he casts off his Old False Father, Falstaff. The crux is to bring out

(d) and (e) to complement the more important, and more obvious (a) and (b). A minor challenge is how sympathetic to make Falstaff, and how unsympathetic to make Hal, in Part 1, recognising that these marvellous plays culminate in the necessary, but merciless, rejection of the old man.

The third crux is the politics of the revolution and its impact on the common man. *Richard II* is largely about the nobles, though the gardener is perhaps the best political commentator of that play. In *Henry IV* the common man is involved as never before – the tavern crowd, of course, and the wretched recruits in the Gloucestershire orchard are all affected by the power games of the nobility. War is given a new texture – not just power flyting – rhetoric as cannon balls – but how it affects the recruits – especially those unable, or disinclined to buy out their service by bribing Falstaff and Bardolph.

And remember that Northumberland is that very same ladder that raised Henry IV to the throne, now in rebellion against him, as the great families jostle for power and replay the politics of the previous reign for their own advantage. Bolingbroke/Henry IV has withered to an apprehensive man with a guilty conscience as he confronts his kingdom's revolt, and the failings of his eldest son. Not even the pale and ruthless younger son, Lancaster, is sufficient to encourage him that his dynasty is secure. Like many another politician in trouble he seeks to deflect attention from home matters to the idea that he might make a crusade to the Holy Land, where new fame might await and justify his usurpation.

And the fabric of the plays – I referred to the autumnal mood of Part 2 earlier – fits these great cruxes magnificently: the language, the mixture of classes, the everyday life of tavern and whorehouse. And Falstaff. What a creation, what an achievement. Every generation should meet him and make up its mind about him – and more than once if possible. To mount these plays, for all their difficulties, will repay all the efforts from both sides of the proscenium.

A regret of mine is that I never acted Falstaff, but I have performed extracts of his scenes including a filmed version of the Doll

Tearsheet scene, with Jules Melvin, which was made in a room at the George Inn in Southwark.

These two plays were hugely important to me in my development as a Shakespearean. I mentioned the Marlowe Society in my notes on *Cymbeline*. My first year's Marlowe Production was both parts of *Henry IV* directed by John Barton, then a don but later one of the founders of the Royal Shakespeare Company. I was cast as the Sheriff in Part 1, a tiny role but (remembering there are no small parts in Shakespeare) one that upstages Prince Hal while on-stage. In Part 2 I had the slightly longer part of the Earl of Warwick, the friend and comforter of the dying King, with two or three significant speeches. And watching, for example, Clive Swift as Falstaff as I waited to enter as the Sheriff taught me much about how to play Shakespeare, and especially Falstaff.

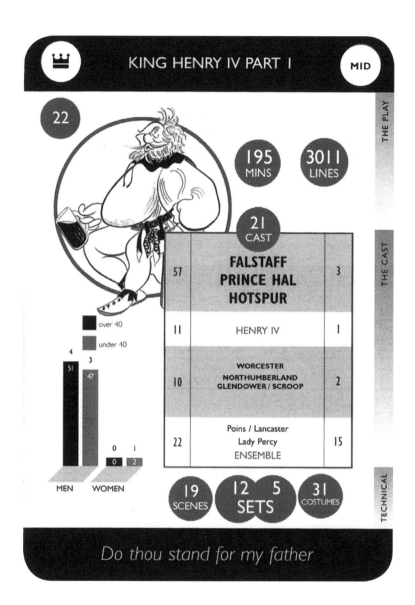

22

195 MINS

3011 LINES

21 CAST

57	FALSTAFF PRINCE HAL HOTSPUR	3
11	HENRY IV	1
10	WORCESTER NORTHUMBERLAND GLENDOWER / SCROOP	2
22	Poins / Lancaster Lady Percy ENSEMBLE	15

over 40
under 40

4
51

3
47

0
0

1
2

MEN   WOMEN

19 SCENES

12 5 SETS

31 COSTUMES

Do thou stand for my father

The main requirement of this play is for **older men** with **51%** of the lines. The play has an **average** number of scenes with **many** sets which can be simplified to a **few** sets and an **average** number of costumes. This play is **straightforward** with a **few** but not insuperable challenges.

FALSTAFF Ralph Richardson

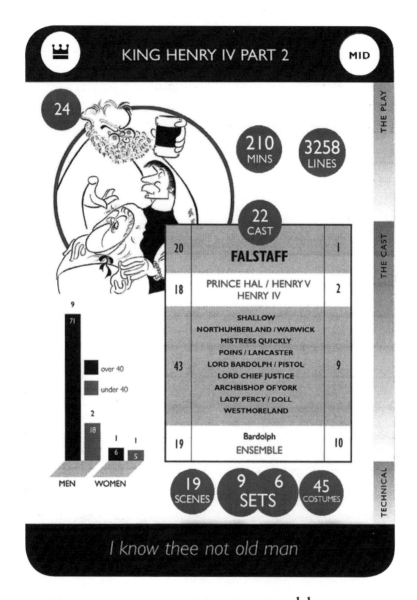

24

210 MINS

3258 LINES

22 CAST

20	**FALSTAFF**	1
18	PRINCE HAL / HENRY V HENRY IV	2
43	SHALLOW NORTHUMBERLAND / WARWICK MISTRESS QUICKLY POINS / LANCASTER LORD BARDOLPH / PISTOL LORD CHIEF JUSTICE ARCHBISHOP OF YORK LADY PERCY / DOLL WESTMORELAND	9
19	Bardolph ENSEMBLE	10

9

71

■ over 40

■ under 40

2

18

1   1
6   5

MEN   WOMEN

19 SCENES

9 SETS

6

45 COSTUMES

I know thee not old man

The main requirement of this play is for **older men** with 71% of the lines. The play has an **average** number of scenes with an **average** number of sets and **many** costumes. This play is **straightforward** with a **few** but not insuperable challenges.

FALSTAFF Orson Welles   **PRINCE HAL** Keith Baxter

MISTRESS QUICKLY Margaret Rutherford

MEASURE FOR MEASURE

ANGELO Emlyn Williams
ISABELLA Margaret Johnston

MEASURE FOR MEASURE
Quite athwart goes all decorum

The Duke of Vienna deputes Angelo to act in his absence, hoping that Angelo will be stricter in his rule than he has been. The Duke disguises himself as a friar to observe what happens.

Claudio has been imprisoned for making Juliet pregnant and Angelo intends to make an example of him. Claudio's sister Isabella, a novice nun, is sent to plead with Angelo, for Claudio's life. Taken with Isabella's beauty Angelo offers to release Claudio if Isabella will sleep with him.

At another tribunal Escalus, Angelo's deputy, hears a case against Pompey, a brothel keeper. Pompey is condemned to serve in prison as an assistant to the executioner due to execute Claudio.

The Duke returns in disguise and suggests to Isabella that she agree to Angelo's proposal, but substitute Mariana, who had been betrothed to Angelo previously. Mariana agrees to the deception.

Angelo, however, reneges his side of the bargain and orders Claudio's death. The Provost of the prison announces the fortuitous death of another inmate, which gives the Friar the chance to supply the dead man's head to Angelo instead of Claudio's.

The return of the Duke is announced. Isabella learns of Claudio's death and seeks redress from the Duke. Angelo denies Isabella's account of the seduction and the Friar is sent for to give his evidence. Mariana now reveals herself and Angelo admits his guilt. The Duke requires he should marry Mariana, and claims Isabella as his own bride. Lucio, a fantastic, who had bad-mouthed the Duke to the Friar is also condemned to marry a prostitute he had debauched.

Sex, politics, religion, and human governance; *Measure for Measure* is a play with all these; no wonder it receives plenty of attention these days. For all that, it is a 'problem' play, one that begs as many questions as it answers. It has perhaps not yet had its definitive production, since the difficulties are great.

A relatively small cast of 14 is required with four major roles including the Duke, whose 822 lines make this one of the longest in the canon. There are seven different settings, of which the prison perhaps will prove the greatest challenge. But there is nothing really difficult for the designer. Recent productions have rather focused on Angelo and Isabella than the Duke and this may be one of the difficulties that make this a problem play.

The first crux is to rationalise the behaviour of the Duke – there are many interpretations of his actions, not all to his credit. It could be argued that he has let a state of immorality arise in Vienna that is to his discredit. His efforts to correct matters find him masquerading as a Friar who imperfectly plays that role too; for example he does not hesitate to broadcast secrets of the confessional, or let the accused (Angelo) try his own action (against Isabella) while keeping Isabella in the dark by lying about Claudio. As the friar, he exasperates Escalus who orders him to prison. It could thus be argued that the Duke is a deficient ruler and a meddler. There is no doubt that the Elizabethans generally and Shakespeare in particular did not hold this view, the divine right of rulers being well understood and accepted. Though he might concede that he has neglected Vienna so that it needs correction, he retains his authority to act, and the actions he chooses to achieve this, though they might appear questionable to another age, would not have been questioned when the play was written. This is an enigmatic character that defies easy classification; the crux is to have a view and portray that view faithfully to the audience.

The second crux is more straightforward: how to manage Angelo's severity and licentiousness. This usually depends on how Isabella is played. Does she lead him on, either consciously or unconsciously, and is his lust for her in any way justified by hopes of a future together? And why is Mariana so ready to forgive Angelo? What human qualities does he retain that she wishes to retain him "rather than my son should be unlawfully born". To play him as severe, precise, formal and without any sense of humour or kindness makes his lust for Isabella inexplicable. The same dilemma faces Isabella, who chooses that her brother should lose his life rather than she lose her virginity. She is a complex character: the tempter or the tempted.

The third crux is perhaps easier to achieve – a true and believable account of the low life of Vienna, or of Elizabethan London as it so obviously is. Pompey, Elbow, Barnardine, Abhorson and Lucio are low-life characters with differing levels of veniality. There is cynicism and humour and rich entertainment in these characters and their situations. The common theme is man's law v. God's law. None of the men is godlike, and while the women have godlike qualities they are at the mercy of the darker side of men's lusts and predilections. It is a heady mixture that lends itself to a wide range of interpretation. It should also be noted that the only real loser is Lucio, ostensibly for bad-mouthing the Duke, but actually for having committed the same sin as Claudio and Angelo (getting a woman with child) who are both let off scot-free. For many, Lucio is a breath of fresh air, an attractive contrast to the austere Angelo and the self-centred Claudio. His fate seems hard while the rest seem to thrive despite shortcomings.

Since writing the above I saw two different productions of the play – a splendid version by Theatre de Complicité with a dark and brooding Duke (David Troughton) set in a vast modern prison – and Mark Rylance (playing the Duke) in his farewell production at Shakespeare's Globe Theatre, where the Duke was a bumbling friar, out of touch with ordinary people, making ad hoc decisions, even in mid-sentence, when the absurdity of his plans becomes apparent.

The point of mentioning this is that both productions kept largely young audiences enthralled and entertained. No problem, then.

I recently heard this question on a television quiz show:

In which country is *Measure for Measure* set?

The answer is Austria, for the play is set entirely in Vienna. The contestant got it wrong as, I suspect, would most general knowledge specialists. Shakespeare's locations are extraordinarily varied, with scenes set in 20 different modern countries, and over 50 individual locations. While Britain (including England, Scotland and Wales) leads with 14, Italy comes second with 11 including 9 individual locations. One of the arguments used by the Anti Stratfordians in the authorship question is that the author 'must' have visited Italy in particular to have been able to write about all these various locations. The counter argument is, of course, that Shakespeare's sources for his stories are largely among the classical authors and he merely copied his play locations from them. And while *Measure for Measure* is set in Vienna, it is a play as much about London in Shakespeare's day as reflecting an Italian (not to say German) original or an earlier English play. In just the same way the Illyria of *Twelfth Night* is nothing to do with Croatia, nor the Arden of *As You Like It* with a forest in Belgium, nor the coast of Bohemia in *The Winter's Tale*, sea coast or not, with the modern Czech Republic.

As in much else, Shakespeare relied on the imaginations of his audience rather than the pedantic exactness of a particular detail. And a further argument against the Anti Stratfordians is that whereas, they say, the Stratfordian could not possibly have understood and written about the political, legal and aristocratic worlds from his own experience, I say what aristocrat could have such a knowledge of low life in the prisons and brothels of Vienna … I should say London.

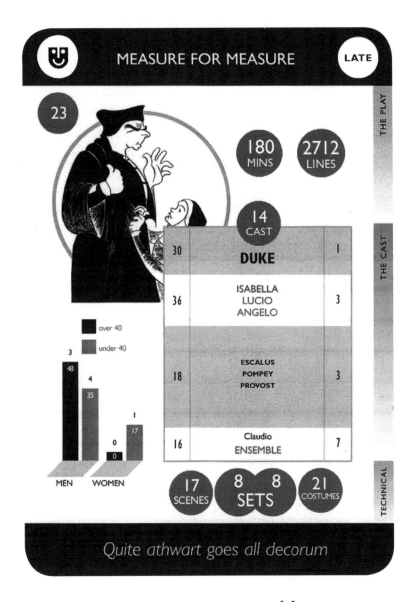

MEASURE FOR MEASURE

LATE

23

180 MINS

2712 LINES

14 CAST

30	**DUKE**	1
36	ISABELLA LUCIO ANGELO	3
18	ESCALUS POMPEY PROVOST	3
16	Claudio ENSEMBLE	7

over 40

under 40

3

48

4

35

1

17

0

0

0

MEN

WOMEN

17 SCENES

8 8 SETS

21 COSTUMES

Quite athwart goes all decorum

The main requirement of this play is for **older men** with **48%** of the lines. The play has an **average** number of scenes with relatively **few** sets and relatively **few** costumes. This play is more **difficult**, and probably best left to experienced groups.

ANGELO Emlyn Williams

ISABELLA Margaret Johnston

LOVE'S LABOUR'S LOST

BEROWNE David Tennant

LOVE'S LABOUR'S LOST
Feast of languages

The King of Navarre and his companions, Berowne, Longaville and Dumain resolve to devote themselves to improving studies and fore-swear female company for one year.

Don Armado is in love with a dairy maid Jacquenetta, and Costard is employed as their go-between. His page, Moth, shows himself to be a classical scholar on 'Love'.

Boyet, a French Lord, accompanies the Princess of France and her companions, Rosaline, Katharine and Maria to the court of Navarre. The King and his Lords fall in love with the ladies and Berowne intercepts Costard and gives him a letter to deliver to Rosaline. Costard mixes this letter up with one from Don Armado to Jacquenetta.

The King and his friends bewail the recent edict, confessing that they are in love, and are overheard by each other. Realising that they have broken their vows, they attempt to disguise themselves and approach the ladies again. Boyet foils this plan and the ladies switch identities.

Armado asks the schoolmaster Holofernes and the curate Nathaniel to arrange and perform a pageant of the Nine Worthies, which is not kindly received by the noble audience. Marcade arrives with news of the death of the King of France, and the mood becomes sombre. The Princess postpones all talk of marriage for one year.

This is a play of language, so do not think of attempting it without an experienced cast of verse speakers, who should revel but not indulge in the profusion of wonderful phrases and verse forms. It is not a play of action but of mood.

The final scene of over 900 lines has 15 different characters. Since there are only 19 identified roles, doubling of roles is kept to a minimum. Maria can play Jacquenetta since the latter does not appear in the final scene. Similarly Dull can reappear without problem as Marcade.

The play takes place entirely in the open air without any need for scene changes (apart from the play within the play). From the practical points of view the play is one of the easiest to stage.

The main crux is language, covering a wide variety of situations. I would especially note the need to understand the elaborate constructions of such situations as:

- the four courtly 'odes' composed and performed by the four men when they think they are alone;
- the "great feast of languages" where they have "stolen the scraps" – the wonderful pedantries of Holofernes and Sir Nathaniel;
- Moth's precocious learning as a foil to Armado's broken English;
- the dissertation on remuneration by Costard;
- the advice of Berowne: "Honest plain words best pierce the ear of grief";
- the play of the Nine Worthies.

Shakespeare provides his own glosses on all these in the course of the play and though often arcane and obscure it is not difficult even today to make sense of even the most challenging of them.

The second crux is to differentiate between age and youth, especially in their ideas of romantic love. The King of Navarre and the Princess of France are both young. While the King gets his courtiers to forswear love for learning, all four subsequently fall under the spell of the "wanton, wimpled purblind boy Dan Cupid", which is reciprocated, though not obviously, by the Princess and her ladies. Set against this is the hopeless old worldly passion of Armado for the country wench Jacquenetta that he cannot resist even if he knows it is a hopeless infatuation. There is a definite contrast between spring and autumn in all these relationships, and the impending period of mourning at the end of the play adds an element of melancholy that has even been seen as a prelude to the catastrophe of the First World War. I doubt if the text stretches the feeling of autumn quite that far, but it is valid to accentuate the differences by implying some impending catastrophe.

An important point in this context is how Armado should be played. Shakespeare intended him as an eccentric foreigner to laugh at. Armado is a Spaniard (his name reminds us of the recent Armada). His maltreatment of the English language was intended to raise English laughter. Yet Shakespeare makes Armado a gentle-flawed individual whose guiding humour is a very English sort of melancholy. When such as Armado speak English they do so with a charm that is very appealing to the English. A figure of fun has become respected and even loved. The pedant, Holofernes, also earns our respect when his play of the Nine Worthies disintegrates in performance in front of the censorious young aristocrats.

And it is the play of the Nine Worthies that is the last crux. As with Pyramus and Thisbe the watching intelligentsia give it short shrift. There is no Theseus in this play to put their efforts into perspective and it is left to Holofernes to restore amends with his rebuke to the unruly audience:

This is not generous, not gentle not humble.

Shakespeare, the thorough professional, sides with Theseus and Holofernes on behalf of the amateur – not with disdain but with an understanding that acting, especially acting Shakespeare, is for each one of us. "Nothing can be amiss when humbleness and duty tender it." Along with Hamlet's advice to the players, and Pyramus and Thisbe, this play is decisive in proving that the author of these plays was a man of the theatre, not a nobleman or any of the other occupations of the usual list of claimants. The play of the Nine Worthies ends with the marvellous song and Armado's equivocal last lines, where Shakespeare recognises that the actors and the audience, by the end of the play, must go different ways. But while we are together in a theatre our imaginations and their efforts can result in moments of lasting magic. As in this play.

A musical version of the play by Clive Swift – *Love's Labours* – was created for an undergraduate production with several of my contemporaries who went on to great things in the theatre. I would have loved to have been involved but my audition, alas, was a disaster and I managed only to admire the production in the theatre.

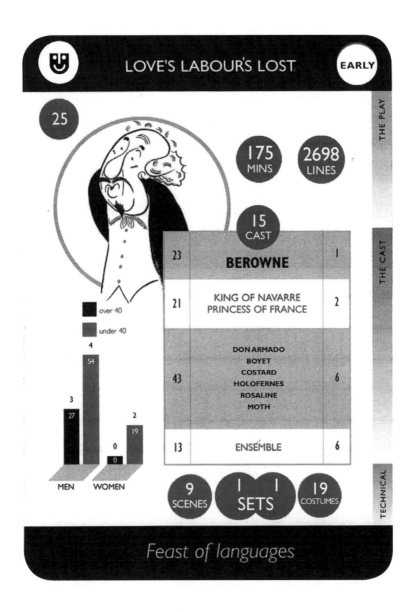

THE PLAY

25

175 MINS

2698 LINES

15 CAST

23	**BEROWNE**	1
21	KING OF NAVARRE PRINCESS OF FRANCE	2
43	DON ARMADO BOYET COSTARD HOLOFERNES ROSALINE MOTH	6
13	ENSEMBLE	6

THE CAST

TECHNICAL

over 40

under 40

4
54
3
27
0
0

2
19

MEN   WOMEN

9 SCENES

1 1 SETS

19 COSTUMES

Feast of languages

The main requirement of this play is for **younger** men with **54%** of the lines. The play has relatively **few** scenes with relatively **few** sets and relatively **few** costumes. This play is more **difficult**, and probably best left to experienced groups.

DON ARMADO Michael Hordern

CORIOLANUS

CORIOLANUS Laurence Olivier
VOLUMNIA Edith Evans
VIRGILIA Mary Ure

CORIOLANUS
You common cry of curs

The people of Rome, led by their tribunes Sicinius and Brutus, are in revolt against the patricians. Caius Martius, an arrogant patrician, treats the tribunes with disdain and Menenius' efforts to pacify the mob are not successful.

The Volscians under Tullus Aufidius attack Rome but are defeated by forces led by Cominius at the City of the Corioles, in which Caius Martius distinguishes himself and is awarded the title of honour of Coriolanus.

On his return to Rome Coriolanus stands for election to the consulship and, though he is elected, his arrogance reopens the enmity of the tribunes. The tribunes then change the minds of the people of Rome which excites the rage of Coriolanus and after a violent confrontation he is banished from Rome.

Coriolanus now allies himself with Tullus Aufidius and the Volscians as they march on Rome. This panics the citizens who cause emissaries to be sent to Coriolanus. These included his mother Volumnia and his wife Virgilia and Menenius. Coriolanus finally relents and Rome is to be spared. Volumnia is received back in Rome with rejoicing.

Tullus Aufidius arranges to have Coriolanus killed for betraying the Volscians. He thus becomes a victim who has been honest to himself but to neither his homeland nor his enemies.

Coriolanus is rather a monotonous hero – patrician, inflexible and lacking humour. Set against him is a wide variety of common men who portray the many tones and shades of opinion and action of plebeian Rome. There are about 40 different (unnamed) characters representing the common citizen in this play. These roles, together with Brutus and Sicinius, those articulate tribunes of the people, account for a third of the drama – a rich variety of roles that makes *Coriolanus* remarkable. This play builds on Mark Antony's swaying of the mob in Julius Caesar, to create action that is uncannily close to how a modern democracy works – the right of an individual to hold an opinion, even if it is 'wrong', and to have a say in the running of the State; the art of political spin; the rhetoric and practice of a 'righteous' war; the victory through dirty tricks and peace achieved through a fatal compromise. The opening scenes prefigure modern conflict between the Trade Unions and the Bosses years before this particular opposition was invented.

A cast of 24 is suggested.

Volumnia is one of the handful of substantial roles for a senior actress; Cominius is an important figure and Sicinius and Brutus, the leaders of the people, figures of depth and interest. Menenius is wonderful throughout, the old Senator of shrewd common sense and strong enough to admit to weaknesses even to his enemies. Tullus Aufidius is a fine adversary to Coriolanus, and Coriolanus, though with little variety of character, has the language of patrician arrogance in abundance, and is a role for a great actor to shine in.

There are plenty of scenes, and most of these are set outside, giving little challenge in the matter of erecting domestic interiors. The storming of the city of Corioli by Martius needs thought. There are plenty of other military settings but the battle scenes are otherwise quite straightforward from the point of view of the set designer.

This play is timeless and could be located in modern, or indeed, any historical time. For my money specific modern settings would fit well enough, but would diminish the universality of the theme. Each production must make its own choice. All I will say is that a 'traditional' setting – obviously Imperial Rome – makes all the general points without being seduced by attractive topical, but partial, modernism.

The first crux is the class struggle: patricians v. plebeians. The fickleness of the mob needs careful orchestration and each change in the mob's affiliations has to be handled convincingly; usually the telling detail (like the will in Julius Caesar) provides the turns of mood, and this needs careful staging. In this play the first complaint is hunger. Are these citizens really starving and oppressed or, as is usual nowadays, well fed and cantankerous? Is this the nature of democracy or demagoguery? The same points apply in Antium where serving men and watchmen show striking individuality in their contributions. Even Aufidius realises that the final outcome depends on what the public thinks. Democracy, however tainted and corrupt, has earned its place in these imperial times. To make that believable is the crux.

The second crux is linked – the magnificent parable of the belly and the other parts of the body given by Menenius to the citizens. The crux is to recognise this speech's imagery and to lay (but not overplay) all the echoes to this speech elsewhere in the play, that gives the play coherence. The language is not easy for us moderns – many times the solution to understanding will come from an appropriate gesture or reference that is consistent with this great speech. Easier said than done.

The last crux is also linked, which is a familiar Shakespearean (I might say Tudor or Jacobean) idea of the military hero, with his code of behaviour and honour. Valour in the field, however hare-brained or foolish, is prized above everything except victory. The scars of the warrior are the signs of worth. Young Martius, in his one line, is determined to follow his father, to prolong the conflicts, and run away until he is old enough to fight. This is why, ultimately, the peace that Volumnia wins is seen by Aufidius as a compromised defeat and reason for assassinating Coriolanus. That peace is the hero's tragedy. Coriolanus rebuffed friends like Cominius who had shed blood with him. His mother, though proud she had borne a soldier, ultimately sacrifices him as he accedes to her idea of peace between the two nations which consigns him to his fate. Peace becomes a fatal compromise for the military hero.

Tyrone Guthrie, the great director, towards the end of his career staged an important production of *Coriolanus* as the opening play for the new Belgrade Theatre in Coventry. He assembled a wonderful cast with John Neville in the title role and Leo McKern as Menenius, and gave a young actor, Ian McKellen, the important role of Tullus Aufidius. McKellen later played Coriolanus at the National Theatre.

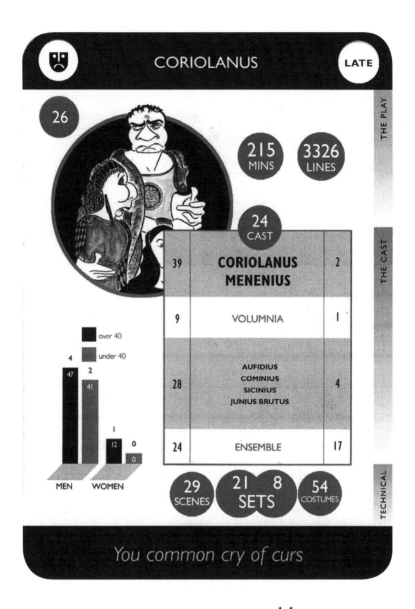

CORIOLANUS

LATE

26

215 MINS

3326 LINES

24 CAST

39	**CORIOLANUS** **MENENIUS**	2
9	VOLUMNIA	1
28	AUFIDIUS COMINIUS SICINIUS JUNIUS BRUTUS	4
24	ENSEMBLE	17

over 40
under 40

MEN   WOMEN

4   2
47   41
1   0
12   0

29 SCENES

21 8 SETS

54 COSTUMES

You common cry of curs

The main requirement of this play is for **older men** with **47%** of the lines. The play has **many** scenes with **many** sets and **many** costumes. This play is more **difficult**, and probably best left to experienced groups.

CORIOLANUS Laurence Olivier

VOLUMNIA Edith Evans

VIRGILIA Mary Ure

TROILUS AND CRESSIDA

CRESSIDA Dorothy Tutin
TROILUS Ian Holm

TROILUS AND CRESSIDA
Wars and lechery

The Trojan war is in stalemate. The Greeks are told by Ulysses that Achilles, their champion, who is refusing to fight, is setting a bad example to the entire army. A coarse commentator, Thersites, and a buffoon, Ajax, are sorry examples of the Greek army. Ulysses counsels a return to the old values, exemplified by the veteran commander Nestor, and suggests that Ajax is sent to the Trojan hero, Hector, in single combat to jolt Achilles into action.

In Troy Cressida falls in love with Troilus, a Trojan prince, son of King Priam, encouraged by her Uncle Pandarus. The Greeks send overtures of peace involving the return of Helen but these are rejected despite the forebodings of Cassandra, Priam's daughter.

Cressida's father Calchas has defected to the Greeks. He persuades Agamemnon the Greek commander to exchange his daughter for a captured Trojan, Antenor. Diomedes is sent to arrange this. Troilus is heartbroken to lose his lover, and later Diomedes compounds this by appearing to usurp Troilus' place in her affections.

Hector and Ajax engage in single combat which is inconclusive and Achilles finally decides to fight Hector despite warnings from Cassandra. After killing Patroclus, Achilles' companion, Hector is treacherously slain by Achilles and his soldiers. Troilus fails to kill Diomedes in the same battle and returns to Troy with news of Hector's death. Pandarus is dismissed by the disconsolate Troilus.

M y key advice is to attempt this play only with an experienced cast – a cast that has played plenty of Shakespeare but, more importantly, one that has done Shakespeare together. The greatest production I ever saw was the Hall/Barton version at Stratford in the 1960s, set in a sandpit with a company cast which included Michael Williams, Dorothy Tutin, Max Adrian, Eric Porter, Derek Godfrey, Roy Dotrice, Patrick Allen and others.

The difficulties are mainly in the language. For example, the part of Nestor, the old warrior, is fittingly written in an archaic and abstruse fashion. However, it needs scholarly footnotes in the text for the modern actor to understand both the form and the meaning of the sentences. The young warrior, Troilus, is also given a syntax that is tortured – to the same extent as his soul is by Cressida's unfaithfulness. His early speeches are simple and lyrical like Romeo's but the difficulties of his later speeches challenge a young actor. No actor has ever made his name as Troilus – his griefs are almost inaccessible (except as a generalised experience) and that may be one reason why this might be so. Another is the relative profusion of other attractive, more straightforward roles, though these also have their syntactical challenges. Thersites is an obvious example – the fool turned bitter, full of insights: "Lechery, lechery, still wars and lechery: nothing else holds fashion."

The senior generals Agamemnon and Priam, speak the archaic language of stately war, as complicated as anything the modern politician and general can dream up. And the great master politician Ulysses has in this play four crucial speeches that serve not only for this play but, I dare say, for understanding Shakespeare's own political philosophy.

Two of these are included in the Shakespeare Sampler. They are all written in language that is easy to understand. The thought behind the language, the politics, is as simple, or difficult, to understand as it fits our own particular political philosophies.

The other major character, Pandarus, is very accessible even to a modern audience. I have seen him played as a cabaret MC, a fading entertainer who takes voyeuristic joy in his niece's loss of maiden-head. He finishes up ravaged with syphilis, a remote and lonely figure, once at the centre of the play, now, like Feste, turned away, an ageing entertainer with nothing to fall back on. While having a superb Pandarus can be reason enough for attempting the play, the real challenges belong not to him but to the rest of the company.

This then is a company play, but one that needs at least three and maybe six really experienced Shakespeareans to carry a young Troilus (and, to a lesser extent, a young Cressida who has a far more straightforward role) through the dense text. The rewards are huge but the dangers great.

I am suggesting a cast of 25 actors, including seven Myrmidons for the key scene of the death of Hector. Of course there will be the usual doubling and trebling of roles, and I suggest one composite role of significance: Prologue/Menelaus/Priam/Calchas – which would make an attractive role for a senior actor.

The set demands are not great. I have mentioned the sandpit used in the Hall/Barton production. Palace scenes are few, and ornate decoration and construction really not needed. Much of the action is in the open air, on the battlefield, in front of tents. The central love story needs interiors. Compared with *Antony and Cleopatra*, however, the scene changes are fewer. The period makes most sense if it is set as it is written, i.e. archaic with spears and swords rather than submachine guns, though I did like giving Pandarus a piano with which to weave his cabaret magic. Cuts can be made – the play is long, 3 hours 20 minutes, and as a general rule the denser the syntax the slower it should be played. Provided the actor under-stands the context the audience, given time, can understand the ambiguities and ironies of the text. But only so far; a contradictory general rule is to aim for a two hour traffic and that is the challenge, to get the balance right for a modern audience who will need skilful help in understanding this play.

The conduct of the war is the first crux. A bitter war, over a whore as Thersites reminds us, has been going on for seven years, with no end in sight. Yet most of the play is spent in council, or truces, or tournaments. The theme is honour and reputation against performance in battle. It is only when Achilles disobeys the honour code by killing an unarmed Hector that blood is shed. The Elizabethan audience would have understood this archaic convention. The crux is to make this archaic convention understandable to a modern audience.

In his book *Playing Shakespeare*, John Barton notes the importance of Time. There are ten references to Time as a character in the play. The crux is simply to recognise this and to decide how each character responds to "envious and calumniating Time" in Ulysses' great speech which is included later in the Shakespeare Sampler.

The third crux – love and faithfulness – centres on Cressida and is as much about Cressida's behaviour as anything. How much of a harlot is she, how much a star cross'd lover? She is the tool of men, from her father through Pandarus, Troilus, the generals and Diomedes. Did Diomedes rape her and if so did she consent, as she seemed to, when the generals demanded their kisses? She is an elemental character (her foot speaks), an object of desire, whose weak powers are thoroughly tested. Diomedes ("the sudden Diomed") seizes the opportunity of Cressida's return to the Greeks for his own ends. A long and seemingly endless war gives rise to numerous opportunities for personal and short-lived gratification.

It is a mighty play, but full of peril for the unwary.

While the Stratford production, which I noted above, is the best I have seen, I must record Roger Allam's performance as Ulysses in a later production, a masterpiece of verse-speaking that underlined the importance of these cruxes, especially that of Time.

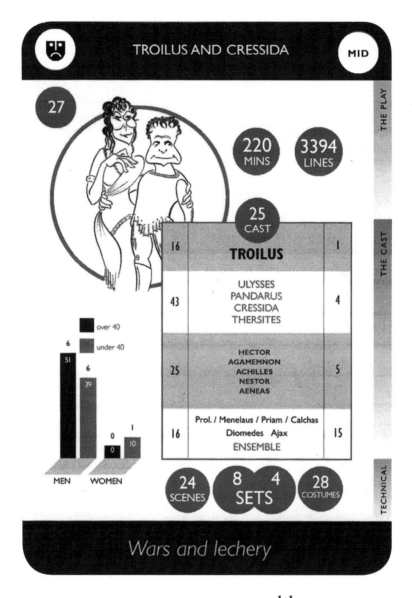

27

220 MINS

3394 LINES

25 CAST

THE PLAY

THE CAST

TECHNICAL

16	**TROILUS**	1
43	ULYSSES PANDARUS CRESSIDA THERSITES	4
25	HECTOR AGAMEMNON ACHILLES NESTOR AENEAS	5
16	Prol. / Menelaus / Priam / Calchas Diomedes Ajax ENSEMBLE	15

over 40

under 40

6   51

6   39

0   1

0   10

MEN   WOMEN

24 SCENES

8   4 SETS

28 COSTUMES

Wars and lechery

The main requirement of this play is for **older men** with **51%** of the lines. The play has **many** scenes with relatively **few** sets and **many** costumes. This play is more **difficult**, and probably best left to experienced groups.

CRESSIDA Dorothy Tutin

TROILUS Ian Holm

191

ALL'S WELL THAT ENDS WELL

COUNTESS OF ROUSSILLON Judi Dench

ALL'S WELL THAT ENDS WELL
All seems well

Bertram, the new count of Roussillon, after his father's death, leaves his mother to find his fortune at the court of the King of France. His mother the Countess finds out that her ward Helena is in love with Bertram and allows Helena to go to Paris both to pursue her love for him but also to attempt to cure the King with medicine given to her by her physician father.

The King is advised by Lafew, a Lord, to let Helena try the cure. This is successful and as a reward the King promises Helena the choice of any young man in his court as her husband. Bertram is chosen but he flees from court to lead the Florentine forces in a war in Italy, vowing that he will only agree to be her husband if she can obtain a ring from him and prove she is pregnant by him.

Bertram is accompanied by the braggadocio, Parolles, and in a trap set for him by the Lords Dumain, Parolles is shown to be the coward he is.

Helena follows Bertram to Florence and finds out that Bertram wants to seduce Diana. A meeting with Diana, and her mother gives her the opportunity to take Diana's place.

The wars now over, the King of France visits the Countess. Bertram and Helena also return to Roussillon. Diana and her mother reveal the bed trick that Helena has successfully played on Bertram, who acknowledges his vow and is reconciled to Helena.

The phrase "all's well that ends well" occurs twice in the play, spoken both times by the heroine Helena. On the second occasion she adds the word "yet" as if some doubt were creeping in. And at the end the King sums up with the slightly more equivocal "All yet seems well". This is no happily ever after comedy. It has a degree of darkness throughout which makes this a fascinating and rewarding play. Yet it is relatively seldom done and ranks low in popularity.

The resources needed are not great compared with most of the plays. A cast of 16 is suggested. There are over 6 roles with over 200 lines and a further 5 (one composite) with over 100. It is a true company play with a range of important characters, none standing out in comparison to the others nor needing stars to be available to play them. Of course, as in a recent production, the presence of Judi Dench to play the Countess adds a great deal. In the second half of the play the Countess has few lines but in this production Judi Dench exerted enormous influence simply through her presence and this added hugely to the story.

There are four locations and seven different scenes in all, none giving especial problems to the designer. I must mention the Vermeer-inspired interiors chosen by Jonathan Miller for his 1980s television production of this play that seemed to fit the Roussillon scenes particularly well. The locations are spread far geographically, and it is important to make evident where each scene is set. The various travels that are made between locations need clear explanation in the various messages and letters. Shakespeare is explicit in the correspondence, i.e. who is writing to whom and why. The audience should be able to recognise the specific messages of the letters as they are sent and received.

The darkness I mentioned has much to do with the sexual politics in which the miraculous cure of the King, Bertram's designs on Diana, and Helena's bed trick are all involved. Add to this Parolles' dissertation on virginity, which is echoed in exactly the same way when Bertram tries to win Diana. The differing social ranks of the characters adds a big dimension to this theme. The first crux is to balance the arguments in each case:

a. Helena's cure of the King is played for high stakes. Because she is of low rank and unqualified she must bet her life against her father's cure in return for the King's promise that she can choose above her rank from among his courtiers. There is the additional hint of impropriety in that Helena is unattended when she ministers to the King.

b. Bertram sets out to deflower Diana partly as a prize for his military victory and on the grounds of pure lust. Despite his eloquence and promises, when questioned by the King about the encounter, he says Diana had approached him and, later, that she was no more than a common courtesan. Bertram's denials of this give him no credit, but one of the points that lends credence to "All yet might be well" is that the encounter with Helena had been a wonderful and memorable experience that might by the end of the play continue into the future.

c. The bed trick is not unique to this play. It depends on the wantonness of the man and the cunning of the woman. It is at once moral and immoral. Again questions of money and rank intrude. Diana is promised money and a good marriage to get her to play her role, and by conceiving as a result of her union with her husband, Helena assures herself of her and her baby's future rank. Dissertations on virginity are relatively common, and play themselves.

The second crux is of military values. It is extraordinary that a raw courtier like Bertram, who defies the King of France to go to the wars, can be entrusted with the generalship of the Duke of Florence's cavalry. However, that is the convention, that military prowess, and especially bravery in battle, is almost automatically awarded to an aristocrat, be he ne'er so young. But Bertram is also devoid of judgement in believing for a long time that the braggart Parolles is a genuinely experienced soldier. The unmasking of Parolles is heavy-handed (and not often very comic in performance). The military virtues and defeats need careful explanation.

The third crux is Mothers and Sons, in this case the Countess and Bertram. Despite the good advice Bertram receives from his mother, his subsequent behaviour makes her disown him and take the part of Helena despite her lack of rank and fortune. She adopts her and supports her in a way that defies political laws and alliances. This is a relationship that has a dominant and decisive effect in this play.

I have not mentioned Lafew and the Clown ("A shrewd knave and an unhappy"), both important roles in this play. They add to the richness of the play, almost as a rerun of Polonius and Feste, to name but two, and make this a dark but illuminating play. It deserves more attention that it, perhaps, has so far achieved.

Despite the fewness of her scenes Judi Dench as the Countess made a powerful impact in a recent production of the play. I like her remark that Shakespeare, for her and many professional actors, is 'the man who pays the rent.'

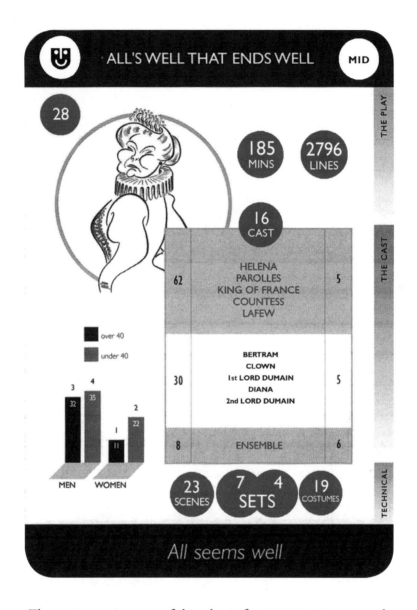

28

185 MINS

2796 LINES

16 CAST

THE PLAY

THE CAST

TECHNICAL

over 40

under 40

62	HELENA PAROLLES KING OF FRANCE COUNTESS LAFEW	5
30	BERTRAM CLOWN 1st LORD DUMAIN DIANA 2nd LORD DUMAIN	5
8	ENSEMBLE	6

3
32

4
35

1
11

2
22

MEN

WOMEN

23 SCENES

7 4 SETS

19 COSTUMES

All seems well

The main requirement of this play is for **younger** men with **35%** of the lines. The play has an **average** number of scenes with relatively **few** sets and relatively **few** costumes. This play is **straightforward** with a **few** but not insuperable challenges.

COUNTESS OF ROUSSILLON Judi Dench

KING HENRY VIII

KING HENRY VIII Richard Griffiths

KING HENRY VIII
Vain pomp and glory of the world

Cardinal Wolsey, Henry VIII's Lord Chancellor, arrests the Duke of Buckingham who is convicted of treason and condemned to death. Queen Katharine of Aragon attempts to intervene but to no avail. She suspects Wolsey of engineering a divorce between her and the King.

Henry meets Anne Bullen and shortly afterwards announces that he is to divorce Katharine and she is summoned to a trial for refusing a divorce. Her defence is to accuse Wolsey but Wolsey is defended by the King who is keen to marry Anne.

Cardinal Campeius, an envoy from Rome, joins Wolsey in trying to get Katharine to accept the divorce. Wolsey's motives in his dealings with Rome are suspected and he is himself accused of treason. On his fall Cranmer, the new Archbishop of Canterbury, marries the King to Anne Bullen.

Wolsey dies repenting his folly and Katharine of Aragon learns of this shortly before her own death. Meanwhile Gardiner, the King's secretary, instigates accusations against Archbishop Cranmer and Cranmer appears before the court to defend himself. With the King's protection Cranmer is reinstated and the Archbishop christens the newly born Princess Elizabeth, predicting a glorious future for her.

*H*enry VIII is different from the other histories. It was written late in Shakespeare's career, possibly with the collaboration of John Fletcher. It covers only a relatively short period of Henry's reign starting with the divorce and death of his first Queen, Katharine of Aragon, and ending with the birth of Elizabeth to his second wife Anne Bullen.

The play needs considerable resources. It is a company play in that the three main parts only have about 10% of the lines each. Henry is the only character who participates throughout as the fortunes of the others rise and fall. Act I concerns the death of Buckingham, Acts 2 and 3 the arraignment of Queen Katharine and the rise and fall of Wolsey who, like the Queen, is dead at the end of Act 4. Act 5 is the arraignment of Cranmer culminating in his encomium for the young Princess Elizabeth. While Henry, Wolsey and Katharine are magnificent parts, none dominates the play in the way that Richard III or Henry V does.

'All is True' is perhaps a helpful subtitle for this play, which smacks throughout of an official, i.e. Elizabethan and Jacobean, version of events that took place seventy-odd years before. Thus Wolsey's political manoeuvrings with Rome are condemned and Anne (Boleyn's) treason is glossed over. The hero of the play is the infant Elizabeth and while Henry VIII is given a proper respect, his misjudgements are not dwelt on. What pervades this play is the official Tudor line. Holinshed's version of events, which is Shakespeare's source, is close to being Sir Thomas More's propaganda. All is True, the Tudors seem to want us to believe.

The demands for sets and costumes arise from the substantial formal ceremonial of Henry's court. The rich paraphernalia of Anne Bullen's coronation needs costumes and splendid ornamentation. The stage directions are unusually specific about what is to be. Shakespeare did not stint in stage show. He even specifies a dream masque for the dying Queen Katharine. All these are challenges for the designers.

So the first crux for directors is to be aware of ceremonial and rank. The positions at the council table for the arraignment of Cranmer are carefully designated, even Cranmer's own empty chair. The King is convinced of Cranmer's innocence by the slights that his accusers gave him – forcing him to wait outside with "poursuivants, pages and footboys" and "boys, grooms and lackeys". The gentlemen give us the new order of precedence at the coronation of the Queen. Wolsey's ambition is to become Pope and when he reveals this to the King his fate is sealed – he is guilty of ambition above his station. Wolsey's low birth but elevated position with "access to the King" infuriates the nobles, whose birth should give them this right, not a butcher's son from Ipswich. The messenger who greets the dying Queen with improper familiarity flouts these rules of ceremony. It should be noted too that minor ranks are also portrayed: the Doctor, the Gentleman Usher, the Gentleman Secretary, the Serjeant at Arms, the Porter, the Crier and even the One Within all have their appointed places in the kingdom.

The second crux is syntax and the place of words in these ceremonies. The syntax is extraordinarily elaborate and difficult to comprehend even if one had the time to reread the lines. It is as if words have been debased by the rituals. The description of the Field of the Cloth of Gold recognises that words can substitute for costume and decoration, but when it comes to the coronation, it is decoration that become dominant. Wolsey retains the great seal because the words of the accusing nobles are less substantial than the seal itself. The words used to describe government and the formality of the court have become tangible as if a dense constitutional lawyer had written them, but the great symbols of State, like the great seal, outweigh the words. When Wolsey muses on his fall, or when Katharine faces her impending death, the language becomes 'Shakespearean' once more; humane and heartfelt and 'true'.

And that suggests the third crux, to what extent a production takes sides. For example, Wolsey's greed and ambition are amply sketched, but may not his concern for Queen Katharine's welfare be sincere, or might not Norfolk (who is later to foist another disastrous

Queen on Henry) and Suffolk be successors to the cynical self-serving nobles of the Plantagenet era? Was Buckingham a traitor or an innocent victim of the politics of the day? Are Rome's motives (in the person of Cardinal Campeius) sinister or benign? Is this the story of three good women – Katharine, Anne, Elizabeth? Is the King corrupt or poorly advised? Were the prophesies that doomed Buckingham true? And what about Cranmer's of Elizabeth? I am not suggesting that a production must have a view, one way or the other, on such issues. There is scope to emphasise the 'official' truths, or their opposites. In such an episodic play where fortunes rise and fall like buckets on a wheel, I suggest an awareness for ambiguity might be appropriate to question the apparent truths that are set out in the text.

I note that *Henry VIII* is seldom staged for whatever reason. But that does not mean it should remain neglected, especially if you can suggest theatrically exciting solutions to these cruxes.

The play can be described as the rise and fall of great ones. In these days of political ambition, sometimes achieved and often dashed, the character of Wolsey in this play expresses it perfectly:

> This is the state of man; today he puts forth
> The tender leaves of hopes, tomorrow blossoms,
> And bears his blushing honours thick upon him:
> The third day comes a frost, a killing frost...

A fuller version of this speech is included in the Shakespeare Sampler.

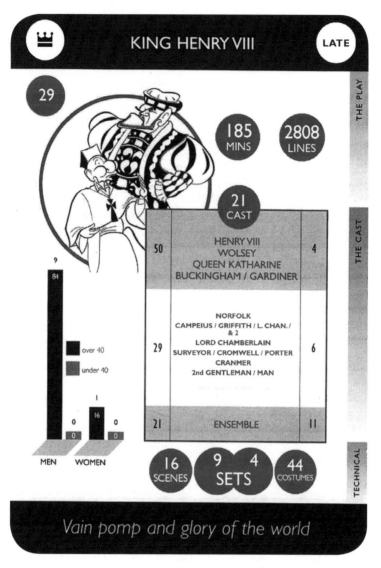

KING HENRY VIII

29

185 MINS

2808 LINES

21 CAST

50	HENRY VIII WOLSEY QUEEN KATHARINE BUCKINGHAM / GARDINER	4
29	NORFOLK CAMPEIUS / GRIFFITH / L. CHAN. / & 2 LORD CHAMBERLAIN SURVEYOR / CROMWELL / PORTER CRANMER 2nd GENTLEMAN / MAN	6
21	ENSEMBLE	11

9

84

■ over 40

■ under 40

1

0 16 0

MEN WOMEN

16 SCENES **9** **4** SETS **44** COSTUMES

THE PLAY

THE CAST

TECHNICAL

Vain pomp and glory of the world

The main requirement of this play is for **older men** with **84%** of the lines. The play has relatively **few** scenes with an **average** number of sets, which can be simplified to a **few** sets, and **many** costumes. This play is more **difficult**, and probably best left to experienced groups.

KING HENRY VIII Harry Andrews
WOLSEY John Gielgud

KING HENRY VI PART 1

DUKE OF YORK Donald Sinden

KING HENRY VI PART 1
Bonfires in France

On the early death of Henry V, the King's uncle Humphrey of Gloucester assumes the Regency and another uncle, the Duke of Bedford, is sent to France to put down uprisings there. The French forces are led by Joan La Pucelle who takes Orleans. Lord Talbot retakes Orleans for the English.

In England the factions of Richard Plantagenet, Duke of York and of the Beaufort supporters of the Lancastrians quarrel in the Temple Gardens and pick the white and red rose as badges of the York and Lancaster claim to the throne. York's own claim was revealed to him by the Earl of Mortimer on his deathbed.

The young Henry VI is crowned in France. La Pucelle captures Rouen but once more Talbot wins it back. However, Talbot's ally, the Duke of Burgundy is persuaded to change sides by Joan and Talbot is denied reinforcements by the rest of the English nobility when he is again attacked and he is killed, dying a hero's death. Joan is finally overcome by the Duke of York and is sentenced and burned at the stake.

Henry sends the Earl of Suffolk to woo Margaret of Anjou on his behalf to cement the peace between England and France. Suffolk falls for Margaret's charms and he sees her as a future ally when she becomes Queen.

KING HENRY VI PART 2

QUEEN MARGARET Peggy Ashcroft

KING HENRY VI PART 2
When I am King

Suffolk brings Margaret to the English court. To secure agreement to her proposed marriage with Henry, Suffolk had accepted some disadvantageous terms and quarrels break out on this issue and on the York claim to the crown. York and Suffolk differ about who should be Regent in France. Cardinal Beaufort increases the opposition to the Protector, Humphrey of Gloucester.

The Protector is implicated when his Duchess is accused of consorting with fraudulent petitioners and of witchcraft. In the aftermath of her disgrace Humphrey is arrested, despite Henry's wishes, and murdered by Suffolk's men. The Earl of Warwick now removes Suffolk from court and, fleeing to France, Suffolk is killed by seamen.

Jack Cade, a populist leader, claims the throne as Mortimer's heir and marches on London. However, after some notable victories Cade is defeated. Cade had been encouraged by the Duke of York to foment rebellion. Returning from an Irish Rebellion, York and his followers seek to remove Somerset from the King's faction and this leads to a decisive battle at St Albans where York, now supported by Warwick, calls on Henry to give up his throne. Somerset is slain and Henry flees to London.

KING HENRY VI PART 3

KING HENRY VI David Warner

KING HENRY VI PART 3
Repurchas'd with the blood of enemies

Richard of York, victor of the Battle of St Albans, compels Henry to surrender the succession to York and his heirs. Henry will be allowed to reign but this concession angers Queen Margaret and Henry's son Prince Edward. The Queen's army arrives and York and his young son Rutland are killed. The Yorkist claim now descends to York's other sons, Edward, George and Richard. Warwick continues to support the House of York and in a further battle the forces of the ineffectual King are defeated. The King again flees while Edward of York plans his coronation as Edward IV.

Henry is caught and sent to the tower while Richard of York, recently created Duke of Gloucester, begins to plot his way to the crown.

Edward IV angers Warwick, who is promoting his marriage with Lady Bona, sister to Louis XI, King of France, when he learns that Edward has married the widowed Lady Grey. Queen Margaret also seeks help from the French King to restore Henry VI to the throne. The insulted Warwick now sides with Queen Margaret, invades England with a French army and restores Henry. Edward's brother, George of Clarence, also switches allegiance. Edward is freed by Richard and assembles new powers and in a series of bloody battles in which Clarence again changes sides, the Yorkists are victorious. Warwick and Henry's heir Prince Edward are killed. Henry is recaptured and murdered by Richard. Margaret is banished to France. Edward's heir is born to Lady Grey, now Queen Elizabeth, and Edward's throne now secured by Richard of Gloucester.

Just as with the two parts of *Henry IV,* the three *Henry VI* plays must be considered together and these could also include *Richard III,* which is the culmination of a four-play cycle that starts with *Henry VI, Part 1.*

The English Shakespeare Company undertook the entire eight-play cycle: *Richard II, Henry IV 1* and *2, Henry V, Henry VI 1, 2* and *3* and *Richard III.* The RSC has also mounted the first four and the second four of these as cycles, though the material of the second four was compressed into three plays which the adapter, John Barton, called *Henry VI, Edward IV* and *Richard III.*

There is no doubt that these plays demand considerable resources. Even with multiple small (and not so small) composite parts the full texts need large casts:

Henry VI, Part 1	27	*excluding attendants*
Henry VI, Part 2	27	
Henry VI, Part 3	23	
Richard II	26	

As a rough guide in the professional (commercial) theatre a cast of more than 17 is likely to prove too expensive. But, among drama students the well-balanced list of interesting characters makes these plays a more attractive proposition. Richard III dominates his play so much that the supporting roles in that play are less interesting as a result. At schools there is unlikely to be an actor of sufficient ability to play Richard, while the other plays lack general appeal for young students, even if casts of above 20 are available. *Henry VI, Part 3* is perhaps the one to choose as best suiting a cast of enthusiastic youngsters needing a stand-alone play, with several excellent parts and no stars. There is plenty of evidence that the three *Henry VI* plays, with or without *Richard III,* are powerful draws if mounted with proper professionalism.

The main demands on designers are the costumes needed, including armour and weapons. Battles are invariably fought offstage, with perhaps one or two hand-to-hand fights on stage. John Barton demonstrated the need for and the power of the conference table in charting the political story, solved by having it hydraulically raised and lowered, rather than carried on and off by attendants. I argue elsewhere that authentic heraldry in banners, surcoats and badges is an obvious and effective way of keeping identities clear.

These plays may have been designed as a cycle once it became clear that the first part was popular, rather like Hollywood block-busters generating lucrative sequels. Remember, these plays were early pieces in Shakespeare's career.

This then is the first crux: single plays or a cycle? The drawing power of the histories generally is low, compared with the comedies and tragedies. A production of a single play like Part 1 is unlikely to be a popular success. In a cycle it may do better but time pressures on the audience may result in playgoers choosing the 'best' plays or the best-received plays, rather than sit through the full cycle. An attractive and famous play like *Richard III*, with its huge star part, is likely to outsell a less attractive play, even *Henry VI, Part 2*, where the important roles are spread out more evenly. Which leads to a subsidiary question – should one conflate, edit and rearrange the *Henry VI* plays, say, to mitigate these problems? The following conflations have been attempted in my experience:

- Alarums and Excursions
- Wars of Roses
- *Henry VI*, *Edward IV* and *Richard III*

I am by instinct both a conflator and an editor. I would be inclined to cut the Talbot scenes and Joan of Arc from Part 1 together with most of the French court. The Duchess of Gloucester scenes in Part 2 are not crucial and some of the battle sequences in Part 3 could be further compressed. The role of Henry VI is not large in any individual play. In a cycle, however, it assumes a major significance.

Margaret of Anjou also develops from quite small beginnings in Part 1 (where she has one small scene) to the second largest part in Part 2, the fifth in Part 3 and the fourth in *Richard III.* Her role would be enhanced by thinking in terms of a cycle rather than a single play.

But am I right? My contemporaries might agree with my choices, but another age might not. And who am I to condemn the Talbot scenes; in Shakespeare's day these were enormously popular, indeed he might be said to have won his reputation with them. That he subsequently bettered the themes of chivalry and conquest in *Henry V* is not to deny that the Talbot scenes might be just as important to a cycle as Warwick the Kingmaker or Jack Cade.

As always in the theatre, in the end it comes down to a judgement about resources and customer appeal.

Other cruxes for the *Henry VI* plays apply to some extent to each part, though *Richard III* needs its own commentary.

The second crux is differentiating the French and the English, not losing sight of the fact that the France of these plays is not the France of today and that the Duke of Burgundy, for example, leads a separate nation and the English are fighting to maintain their control over Aquitaine, Normandy and the other parts of modern France that belonged to the English crown through earlier dynastic marriages. Margaret of Anjou is the daughter of the King of Naples and Jerusalem, a vassal state of France, but a kingdom of little power, nevertheless. Often the French are depicted as buffoons; in Shakespeare's day there was an element of contempt and mockery of the French. In Joan of Arc (la Pucelle) one has to consider how much of a child of the devil she is, and whether she is the whore of the French aristocracy, which Elizabethans might have supposed, or whether she is in fact a patriot with great powers of leadership leading a just rebellion. Margaret begins as yet another bride pawn and finishes up as a patriot warrior for the House of Lancaster, doing the fighting for her militarily inadequate husband, the saint and scholar Henry VI. Later in the cycle the Lady Bona is another such pawn whose rejection by Edward IV causes Warwick to switch sides. The perfect English hero Talbot can be played as a blimpish buffoon, and the English as mere adventurers. Getting the balance right between these two great national rivals needs careful handling.

The third crux is to understand the conventions of marriage. The dynastic marriages were never for love though courtly love that dates back to Eleanor of Aquitaine has its place in these plays too. In particular the wooing of Margaret by Suffolk on Henry's behalf results in a love affair between Margaret and Suffolk, despite the main prize of the dynastic marriage and the assassination of Suffolk. The course of true love never did run smooth.

The great alliances between the Yorkists and Lancastrians occupy all the *Henry VI* plays and the cycles of domination by each side, and defeat, and revenges to those defeats are the main matter of these plays. Within each alliance, allegiances shift (notably Clarence and Warwick) and the long sequence of battles and civil disturbances needs to be made absolutely clear. The symbolism of the roses helps, but it is necessary to clarify the dynastic question (the rival claims of York and Lancaster) where inheritance may be claimed through the female line rather than the strict application of the law of primogeniture. Whether a saintly monarch, or an opportunistic alliance of warriors deserve the crown becomes the question in an age where military glory outranked saintliness and scholarship.

The emergence of popular demagoguery is a particular highlight of these plays – the Jack Cade rebellion is a quite brilliant essay on the power and futility of such movements. Cade outlines his own 'noble' pedigree in the same way as the nobles. When his 'nobility' is questioned by the messenger addressing him with his own name he orders the messenger to be killed. The commoners seize opportunities previously only pursued by the nobility.

The emergence, too, in Part 3 of Richard of Gloucester, later to become Richard III, is a powerful reason for considering *Henry VI, Part 3* as prologue to perhaps the most thrillingly theatrical of all the histories – *Richard III*.

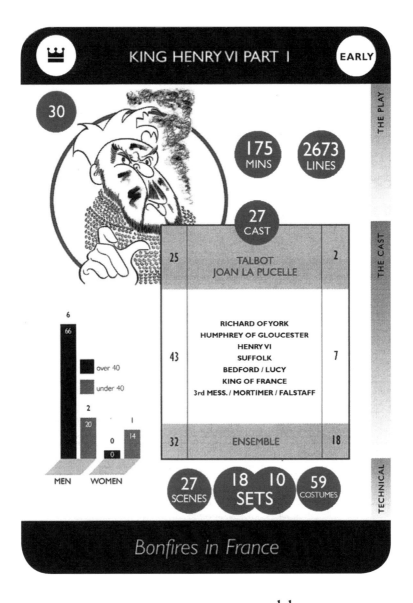

EARLY

30

175 MINS

2673 LINES

27 CAST

THE PLAY

THE CAST

TECHNICAL

25	TALBOT JOAN LA PUCELLE	2
43	RICHARD OF YORK HUMPHREY OF GLOUCESTER HENRY VI SUFFOLK BEDFORD / LUCY KING OF FRANCE 3rd MESS. / MORTIMER / FALSTAFF	7
32	ENSEMBLE	18

6
66
over 40
under 40
2
20
0
0
1
14

MEN   WOMEN

27 SCENES

18 10 SETS

59 COSTUMES

Bonfires in France

The main requirement of this play is for **older men** with **66%** of the lines. The play has **many** scenes with **many** sets and **many** costumes. This play is more **difficult**, and probably best left to experienced groups.

DUKE OF YORK Donald Sinden

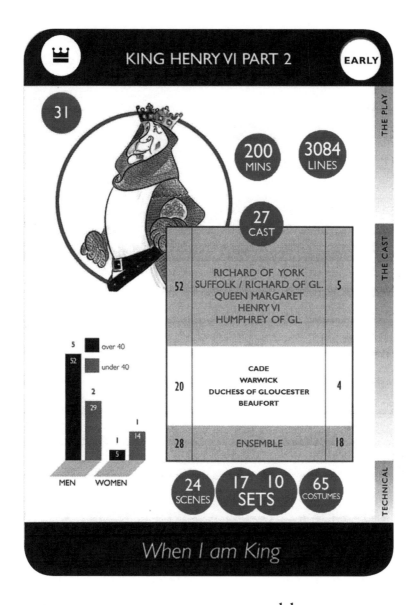

KING HENRY VI PART 2

EARLY

31

200 MINS

3084 LINES

27 CAST

52	RICHARD OF YORK SUFFOLK / RICHARD OF GL. QUEEN MARGARET HENRY VI HUMPHREY OF GL.	5
20	CADE WARWICK DUCHESS OF GLOUCESTER BEAUFORT	4
28	ENSEMBLE	18

5 over 40
52 under 40
2
29
1
1 14
5

MEN   WOMEN

24 SCENES   17 10 SETS   65 COSTUMES

When I am King

The main requirement of this play is for older men with 52% of the lines. The play has many scenes with many sets and many costumes. This play is straightforward with a few but not insuperable challenges.

QUEEN MARGARET Peggy Ashcroft

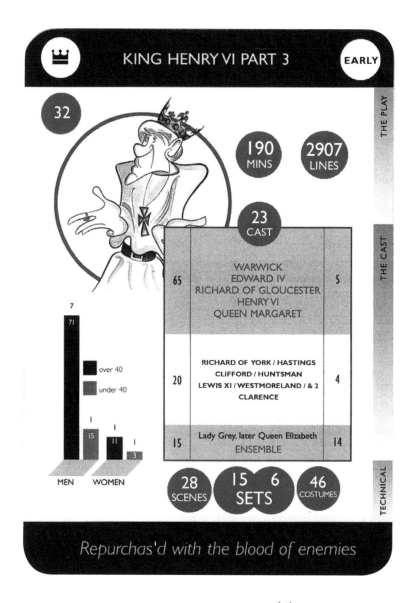

32

190 MINS

2907 LINES

23 CAST

THE PLAY

THE CAST

TECHNICAL

65	WARWICK EDWARD IV RICHARD OF GLOUCESTER HENRY VI QUEEN MARGARET	5
20	RICHARD OF YORK / HASTINGS CLIFFORD / HUNTSMAN LEWIS XI / WESTMORELAND / & 2 CLARENCE	4
15	Lady Grey, later Queen Elizabeth ENSEMBLE	14

7

71

over 40

under 40

1

15

1

11

1

3

MEN

WOMEN

28 SCENES

15 6 SETS

46 COSTUMES

Repurchas'd with the blood of enemies

The main requirement of this play is for older men with 71% of the lines. The play has many scenes with many sets, which can be simplified to an average number of sets, and many costumes. This play is straightforward with a few but not insuperable challenges.

KING HENRY VI David Warner

PERICLES

PERICLES John McEnery

PERICLES
How? A King's daughter?

Pericles, the young Prince of Tyre, woos the daughter of King Antiochus by attempting to solve a riddle which, if solved, will win her as his bride but, if not, will cost him his head. Pericles divines the answer but realising that he is in danger, flees back to Tyre. He leaves Helicanus in charge in Tyre and travels to Tarsus, where he relieves that country from famine, earning the gratitude of Cleon and Dionyza. Returning from Tarsus he is shipwrecked on the coast of Pentapolis. Rescued by fishermen he arrives at Simonides' court where he enters and wins a tournament for the hand of Thaisa, Simonides' daughter.

Leaving Pentapolis with the pregnant Thaisa, he is again in a seastorm in which Thaisa gives birth and dies. Her coffin is cast into the sea (to pacify the sailors and calm the storm) and Pericles, distraught, puts in to Tarsus where the infant (Marina) is left in care of Cleon and Dionyza. The coffin is washed up at Ephesus where Cerimon is able to revive Thaisa.

Sixteen years pass and Dionyza, jealous of Marina's achievements, orders her death, but the would-be murderer, Leonine, is prevented by pirates who take Marina to Mytilene and sell her into a brothel, and into the charge of Boult. Marina eventually persuades Boult into a life of virtue and she becomes a teacher.

Pericles, now old and grieving, arrives in Mytilene where Lysimachus the Governor sends Marina to try to cure his grief. It is revealed that she is Pericles' daughter. Directed by the Goddess Diana in a dream Pericles is sent to Ephesus and there Cerimon reveals that Thaisa has survived.

*P*ericles is one of Shakespeare's greatest plays. But is it his? The hands of Wilkins, Rowley and others have been detected in the early acts but the fishermen's scene, the great sea scenes, the brothel and the final recognition scenes are unquestionably Shakespeare's. It is as if Shakespeare was called on in retirement to rescue a script by one or more lesser lights, and improved it out of all measure. I think it's all by Shakespeare – the Gower scenes for example merely demonstrating that Shakespeare was capable of parody of archaic verse forms.

The story is of how fortune treats Pericles, his triumph in love and his shipwrecks, and who is finally restored to life by his long-lost daughter. Curiously this makes Pericles a less interesting character than what happens to him. Even the array of brilliant characters he meets are somehow more memorable. It is a play that is always enjoyed by its cast. It surprises and delights its audiences who may well wonder why it ranks low in popularity. It takes place in six locations, all bordering the sea, which itself plays a huge role in the fate of the hero.

Though the action is episodic and is written for nearly fifty different characters, the structure gives opportunities for multicasting. Major characters often disappear after a scene or two. And the supporting cast seems to consist of various groups of three: an older wiser head, a strong silent type and a young apprentice; the fishermen, the Pentapolis lords, the sailors, the pirates and so on. These seem to sugget that the main supporting actors can appear and reappear, a bit like a leitmotiv, in all these threesomes. I suggest a speaking cast of 17, of which 9 are of 100 lines or more.

In any fast-moving story scenery must be kept to a minimum. In *Pericles* the six locations are different parts of the Eastern Mediterranean. This gives the designer a challenge to differentiate and allow these changes quickly and stylishly. Antioch is corrupt; Tyre formal; Pentapolis leafy (I put Pentapolis in Greece, recognising it might be a Greek province in North Africa); Tarsus proud but suffering; Mytilene licentious; Ephesus austere. The biggest challenge is the sea: the three great scenes – the first storm, child-birth and the recognition scene – all take place under the influence of Neptune, so the stage should give the impression of the sea's movement. Neptune is finally assuaged by the last scene – it is his feast day and Mytilene has honoured him with his festival so in the scene in the harbour on board ship the sea, previously a threat, is calm. The design challenge is the first crux and here the contention between Neptune and Diana (goddess of childbirth) determines much of the quality of the piece.

The second crux is a major weakness, the ageing of the hero Pericles. It is difficult for a young actor in his thirties, say, to under-stand Pericles' predicament, convinced his daughter is dead, yet finding her on a boat in a distant harbour. And yet an actor in his fifties would be hard put to convince as the young hero. This suggests different actors to play the young Pericles and the older Pericles, a solution attempted at Shakespeare's Globe in 2005.

The third crux is the symbolism and in particular the motifs of the knights described by Thaisa in the tournament scene. These are generally shown as bad heraldry and are dispensed with (even cut) as fast as possible. I believe the motifs, the symbols, are carefully chosen and recur in echoes throughout the play:

- Black Ethiope reaching at the sun (Dangerous aspiration)
- Arm'd knight that's conquered by a lady
  (Gentleness conquers force)
- A wreath of chivalry (Fame of victory)
- Burning torch that's turned upside down
  (Lust consumes itself)
- A hand environed with clouds holding out gold that's
  by the touchstone tried (Faithfulness)
- A wither'd branch that's only green at top (Hope)

This is perhaps the moment to develop my idea that this play is more about the relationships between four fathers and their daughters, of which one is Pericles, than about a single hero called Pericles. The four father/daughter relationships (which could be played by the same actors in each iteration) are:

FALSE FATHER Antiochus and Antiochus' Daughter (Incest)
TRUE FATHER Simonides and Thaisa (Giving in marriage)
FALSE FATHER Boult and Marina (Prostitution)
TRUE FATHER Pericles and Marina (Rebirth)

It is remarkable that Thaisa and Marina have but two lines together which enables (with the aid of a double, perhaps) this fourfold variation to be played. It means that young Pericles does not play the Father Pericles (as I mentioned, the scene on shipboard in Mytilene has never been played convincingly by a young Pericles). Young Pericles is, therefore, the Hero; and Lysimachus, whom we first meet as a brothel customer, but is reformed by Marina's virtue, is the hero of the last scenes.

The same point as for fathers and daughters can be made for the Guardians; there are four male and four female guardians who can be played by the same actors. Despite this, in the following table, as on the play page, I preserve the usual idea that the character called Pericles is played by one actor, and that less concentrated doubling is needed for the play.

Our illustrations depict two brothers, Peter and John McEnery. Peter (in the roundel) had played the role in the traditional way, i.e. performing all the lines of Pericles in the text. John played all the father roles in a pilot film I made, called *Fathers and Daughters*, which followed the pattern I described above and, later, at Shakespeare's Globe Theatre, he did indeed play the old Pericles in the final scenes.

I also played the rebirth scene as an old Pericles with Jules Melvin as Marina in a short programme of Shakespearean scenes for the King's Lynn Festival, which the late Michael Burrell organised under the title 'The Days that we have Seen'.

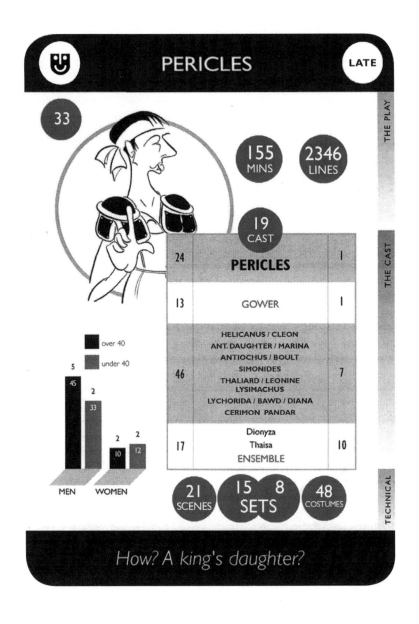

PERICLES

LATE

33

155 MINS

2346 LINES

19 CAST

24	**PERICLES**	1
13	GOWER	1
46	HELICANUS / CLEON ANT. DAUGHTER / MARINA ANTIOCHUS / BOULT SIMONIDES THALIARD / LEONINE LYSIMACHUS LYCHORIDA / BAWD / DIANA CERIMON PANDAR	7
17	Dionyza Thaisa ENSEMBLE	10

over 40

under 40

5

2

45

33

2 2

10 12

MEN WOMEN

21 SCENES

15 8 SETS

48 COSTUMES

How? A king's daughter?

The main requirement of this play is for **older men** with **45%** of the lines. The play has an **average** number of scenes with **many** sets and **many** costumes. This play is **straightforward** with a **few** but not insuperable challenges.

PERICLES Peter McEnery

THE TWO GENTLEMEN OF VERONA

LAUNCE Robert Helpmann

THE TWO GENTLEMEN OF VERONA
One mutual happiness

Valentine takes his leave of Proteus to seek advancement at the court of the Duke of Milan while Proteus stays in Verona to continue his suit to Julia. However, Antonio, Proteus' father, insists that he too goes to Milan where Valentine has fallen in love with the Duke's daughter Silvia. Julia, left in Verona, resolves to assume man's clothes, and follow Proteus to Milan. She is followed by Proteus' servant, Launce, who complains to Speed, Valentine's servant, about his dog, Crab.

Valentine asks Proteus to help him to elope with Silvia, but the changeable Proteus now falls in love with Silvia, and betrays Valentine's plans to the Duke.

The Duke decides that Thurio should marry Silvia and banishes Valentine to Mantua, where he is captured by some outlaws. They are so taken with him that they elect him as their leader.

Julia arrives in Milan and learns of Proteus' perfidy to her and to Valentine. Silvia rejects Proteus and resolves to flee from Milan to find Valentine, asking assistance from Sir Eglamour. Proteus engages Julia, disguised as a page, to aid him in his pursuit of Silvia.

In the forest Silvia is captured by the outlaws and rescued by Proteus who attempts to win her by force, but Valentine comes to her aid. The Duke and Thurio are also captured and in the aftermath Proteus and Julia are reconciled; Valentine is granted Silvia's hand and the outlaws are pardoned.

This play rates low in popularity and, apart from the wonderful Launce and his dog Crab, I can see very little reason for doing it. The best that can be said is that it prefigures characters, themes and situations that Shakespeare developed to advantage in his later plays.

I suggest a cast of 13, of which one is a singer. There are no great crowd scenes, though this makes scenes involving the Duke's entourage implausible since there are seldom more than one or two extras available, making it difficult for the actor playing the Duke to establish any great presence.

Some editors believe that Proteus sings the song 'Who is Silvia?' However, three on-stage musicians are called for and I have assumed that one of these is the (paid) singer.

Settings are not a problem; a court and a forest are to be suggested but neither occupies the stage for long. And neither is the period since the story is essentially timeless.

As the play is quite short there is no real need for cuts, though the scenes featuring chop logic could do with judicious cutting as it is impossible to make (modern) sense of some of the more tendentious passages.

What is crucial, however, is to consider how to navigate the problems of plotting and probability. The Arden editor lists 21 instances of inconsistent plotting. Some of the compression of the last scene, for example, may have been better explained in versions now lost. As the Arden editor puts it:

"It is remarkable that Proteus' rescue of Silvia, his attempt to rape her, Valentine's denunciation of him, Proteus' repentance, Valentine's magnanimous offer of Silvia, Julia's revelation of her identity, the Duke's capture and his acceptance of Valentine as son-in-law, are all fitted into a scene of 170 lines."

Crucial for us is how to present these matters without sending them up as improbable or ridiculous.

Among the 21 instances are confusions of place: Verona, Milan and Padua and the forest between them seem to shift about alarmingly. And why should Milan be reached by ship, when both it and Verona are inland and not connected by a common river?

The second major crux concerns the behaviour of Proteus, whose volte-faces are seemingly wildly improbable. He adopts all these personae:

> In love with Julia; in love with Silvia which though dishonourable and not returned leads to the rape attempt; the exposing of his friend and a sudden repentance.

Proteus is the classic 'changer' and perhaps a modern director might suggest that this is his nature from the outset and that each change, however violent, is less surprising. Valentine has a more constant nature but his almost superhuman forbearance of Proteus, to the extent of offering Silvia to him, is hardly believable and hence a major crux. The characters of Proteus and Valentine may be said to be Changeability and Steadfastness.

The third crux is also making believable two other characters: the Duke and Silvia. The Duke can do no wrong, that's the convention, but there is little humanity in this man – he is a mere cipher of authority who behaves fecklessly – hard to make believable. Silvia is a problem because she is too perfect. Holy, fair and wise ("In that order, gentlemen, if you please," as my headmaster had it), but lacking even a trace of imperfection to set off these wonderful qualities. It's like Browning's Fra Lippo Lippi – the perfect painter, his perfection being ultimately dull. Compared to the cross-dressing Julia, Silvia with her naivety in hiding her emotions for Valentine (and lack of judgement in taking him back?) seems just a passive emblem of perfection. No actor or actress has ever made his or her name as the Duke or as Silvia, and the problem becomes how to attract to these roles actors of enough skill to transcend these problems. They have to compete with Julia, with Proteus and with Launce and his dog.

The outlaws play very well – they are usually given to self-parody that works. The Robin Hood idea is seductive but not given a critical examination, which perhaps it deserves, in this play.

The comedians play well too, though to speed through Speed's lines will confound any actor. Played slowly (so we can see the train of thought) many otherwise improbable lines will actually make sense (same note for the Dromios in *The Comedy of Errors*). Launce cannot fail in any circumstances.

I wonder if this might be the lost play listed by Meres: *Love's Labour's Wonne*. In an otherwise unremarkable speech in Act I Valentine has this on being in love:

> If happy won, perhaps a hapless gain
> If lost why then a grievous labour won.

Could *The Two Gentlemen of Verona* be a subtitle of the 'lost' play?

I mentioned Launce's dog Crab as being a reason for doing the play. Launce describes his parting from his family:

> I think Crab, my dog, be the sourest-natured dog
> that lives: my mother weeping, my father wailing, my
> sister crying, our maid howling, our cat wringing her
> hands, and all our house in a great perplexity, yet did
> not this cruel-hearted cur shed one tear: he is a stone,
> a very pebble stone, and has no more pity in him than
> a dog…

It never fails in the theatre.

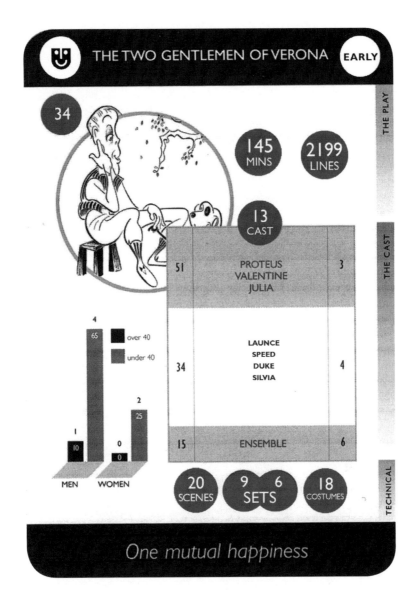

THE TWO GENTLEMEN OF VERONA

EARLY

34

145 MINS

2199 LINES

13 CAST

51	PROTEUS VALENTINE JULIA	3
34	LAUNCE SPEED DUKE SILVIA	4
15	ENSEMBLE	6

over 40
under 40

4

65

2

1

25

10

0

0

MEN   WOMEN

20 SCENES

9 6 SETS

18 COSTUMES

One mutual happiness

The main requirement of this play is for younger men with 65% of the lines. The play has an average number of scenes with an average number of sets and relatively few costumes. This play is straightforward with a few but not insuperable challenges.

LAUNCE Robert Helpmann

TIMON OF ATHENS

TIMON Simon Russell Beale

TIMON OF ATHENS
Pass by and curse thy fill

Timon of Athens is a wealthy nobleman and patron of artists, poets and jewellers. He is known for his lavish entertaining and a large crowd of Lords and senators enjoy his hospitality.

Apemantus, a sour philosopher, is the only outsider to warn Timon of the dangers in such lavish expenditure, and Flavius, his steward, also tells him that he has practically bankrupted himself.

News reaches the lords that creditors are flocking to Timon. When he sends his servants to them for financial assistance, they return excuses not help.

Alcibiades, the Athenian general, has been banished, the same senators that denied Timon having refused his request for mercy for one of his soldiers.

Timon holds one last feast for his acquaintances but rather than the promised banquet he serves dishes of hot water. He leaves Athens to live as a hermit. Digging for roots in the forest he finds gold which enables Alcibiades to pay his army. Timon is then visited by the senators who want him to defend the city against Alcibiades. Apemantus is driven away. Timon dies leaving a bitter epitaph.

This dark play ranks low in popularity but it is full of magnificent lines although much of them are of disgust and loathing. Timon calls himself Misanthropos, a title justified by his friends' reaction to his fall, though the fall had much to do with his lack of judgement in those friends when he was wealthy. It deserves a greater popularity, but its gloomy message has never been great box office.

One of its disadvantages for professional companies is the huge cast it needs. For non-professionals the role of Timon, 800+ lines representing 35% of the play, is likely to be difficult to cast. The energy and variety needed in this role are formidable. There are 18 named parts and no fewer than 35 unnamed parts with lines. By the usual plan of doubling/trebling these I reduce the number of actors to 25. The balance is also a challenge – 1 huge role, 3 or 4 medium roles plus 8 or 10 important ensemble roles give any director plenty of opportunity, but potential hazards too.

It is also a good moment to bring in Trevor Nunn's production of this play (with David Suchet and Barry Foster), which happened to complete the canon for me. This was set in modern dress – Timon's cave being a dumped car in a wood in which a paramilitary organisation had stowed gold, making the soldiers rebels like Timon. The good days of Timon saw him surrounded by confident PAs and dancing girls and it all fitted very well. As is usual in Nunn's productions the text was crystal clear, and Suchet was outstanding as Timon.

So, the setting can be whatever imagination can conceive – the challenge is to differentiate between the opulence and show of the early scenes and the outskirts of civilisation in the later scenes.

The first crux is to distinguish between the social levels of the characters. At the top are the feckless senators with their disastrous judgements. By and large these are not as involved with Timon's extravagance as are the Lords – note how Shakespeare presents four very different excuses for the Lords that fail Timon, each given a rich cameo to make those distinctions. Timon is of that class. He is supported by professionals and artists – his steward might be a modern-day Finance Director despairing of corporate strategy, while a rich variety of artists seek preferment from Timon to make themselves richer and more successful. Apemantus is a philosopher and Alcibiades a soldier who perhaps rank between these and the Lords. The multitude of servants, both Timon's and the Lords', have a status equivalent to PAs rather than waiters at table and are each given significant scenes. The soldiers and the hangers-on bring up the rear. In the anonymity of Lord, Senator, 1st Servant, Messenger, etc., the director must establish an obvious pecking order that is as clear as if he had personalised these parts. The 'business of business' is a phrase to describe how great corporations are run. Few playwrights are as deft as Shakespeare in establishing how money works, the real price of borrowing, the difference between prosperity and bankruptcy. And he is not above parodying his own supreme skill – the Poet is a masterpiece of the poetical poseur, a man who writes for the market and not for immortality. By contrast the Painter seems to be a more genuine article.

The next crux is to get the balance between speed and clarity right. The play is short and moves at a fast pace. Yet in this the handling of the crowds of Lords, Lenders and Servants is crucial. As in a crash of the stock market the dominant qualities displayed are fear and greed, so in this play. The banquet of water is the culmination of these great scenes when the injured think they are about to live the glory days again – expectation and apprehension must be finely balanced.

The third crux is the handling of the Lear-like descent of Timon from the cap of Fortune to a lonely death. I mentioned Apemantus' role in this, the churlish philosopher who points Timon to his own vision of the world, ultimately refusing to join him in a mutual loathing of mankind. His model is the foul-mouthed Thersites but his function is to prefigure the amazing tirades of Timon in Part 2. As I have also hinted these tirades must o'er top Apemantus, but must be done with a variety and structure that develop in tone and bitterness throughout. Here is some of the most difficult syntax in Shakespeare. While his days of fortune are written with an easy elegance, the scenes in the forest emerge from the tangle of thoughts, in no common phrases, using words that are unclear, or sound the same (e.g. hoar and whore) that make precise understanding difficult, though the drift is clear enough. Timon must decline in a progressive argument of disgust in a way that preserves lyricism (some of the late speeches are wonderfully elegiac) and discordance all at once. One could suggest that Timon is a God – beneficence and generosity – who sets mankind some tests which, when mankind fails these tests, brings on a kind of Last Judgement. That may be too strained, after all Timon's judgement in the early scenes is deeply flawed. But the careful unravelling of this particular journey, this descent into despair is crucial, and the mitigating roles of the steward, Alcibiades, even the soldier, must be fitted into this.

Yes, that's it, Timon never experienced the middle of humanity. Does that make him a god, or a fool?

Timon of Athens was the final play in the canon of 37 plays that I saw on stage. Trevor Nunn directed David Suchet as Timon in a modern war setting. Both this production, and that of the Royal National Theatre production of Simon Russell Beale in our illustration, seem particularly relevant today.

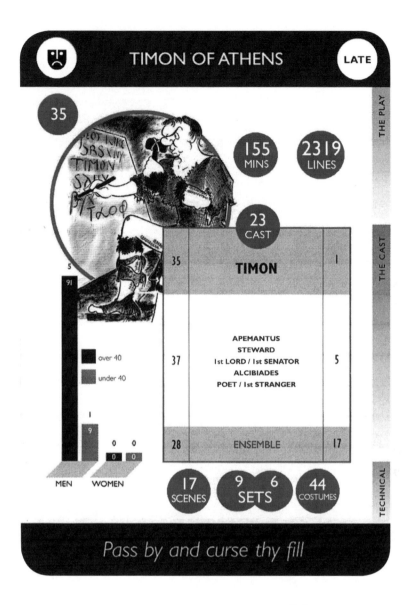

35

155 MINS

2319 LINES

23 CAST

35 **TIMON** 1

APEMANTUS
STEWARD
37 1st LORD / 1st SENATOR 5
ALCIBIADES
POET / 1st STRANGER

28 ENSEMBLE 17

over 40

under 40

5

91

1

9

0 0

0 0

MEN WOMEN

17 SCENES

9 6 SETS

44 COSTUMES

Pass by and curse thy fill

The main requirement of this play is for **older men** with **91%** of the lines. The play has an **average** number of scenes with an **average** number of sets and **many** costumes. This play is more **difficult**, and probably best left to experienced groups.

TIMON Ralph Richardson

KING JOHN

KING JOHN Leonard Rossiter

KING JOHN
The bias of the world

The crown of England is disputed. John is in possession but the King of France supports the claim of young Prince Arthur and his mother Constance.

Philip of Faulconbridge is revealed to be the bastard son of King Richard Coeur-de-Lion. He joins forces with King John to resist the French and their allies, including the Archduke of Austria. Outside Angiers a truce is made when a marriage is arranged between Blanche (King John's niece) and the Dauphin.

The papal envoy Cardinal Pandulph forbids the French King Philip to enter into this alliance, and in the subsequent battle the French are defeated and Prince Arthur is captured. John now orders his keeper, Hubert, to kill Arthur. Hubert demurs. Arthur convinces Hubert to spare him and later escapes but falls to his death from the castle battlements.

The English nobles, under the Earls of Salisbury and Pembroke, believing that Arthur has been murdered, now switch their alliance to the French. John is reconciled with Pandulph. On its way to invade England the French fleet is wrecked and a French Lord, Melun, reveals to Salisbury and Pembroke that the Dauphin is planning their deaths. They rejoin the English and the Dauphin sues for peace.

King John is poisoned and dies leaving an uneasy inheritance for Prince Henry.

*K*ing *John* is an early play and contains more rhymed couplets than Shakespeare's later histories. The structure is formal, full of set-piece rhetoric. Even the doomed Prince Arthur uses ornate verse in the scene with Hubert. Apart from the famous single line:

[kj] Death
[h]   My Lord?
[kj]   A grave
[h]   He shall not live,

the rhetoric approaches Marlowe's in weight and sonority.

What it lacks in action it makes up in excitement, not least the flamboyant brilliance of the Bastard, who is probably the hero of the play. The part is a gift for an emerging young actor. The rest of the nobles are rather a dull lot, though Cardinal Pandulph is a wonderful magnifico of the Church and is a rewarding part for a senior actor. And Constance was a part highly prized by the Victorians – note the dramatic effect of her dishevelled hair which raises the temperature of her complaints. The Bastard has one of the great political soliloquies – commodity and bias. The key to understanding the politics of the histories (and much else, Polonius, for instance, uses exactly the same thinking) is to understand this speech. This argues that *King John* deserves fresh productions and that it deserves better than its current low popularity.

The settings are no real problem – the walls and gates of Angiers are features that probably need a permanent pre-construction – with other scenes played in front of the construction, masked by banners and curtains. The court scenes need some substance, but the rest, including the orchard and the Hubert/Arthur scene can easily be accommodated on an open stage.

My first crux and central to my general point, is Family, this time succession and inheritance. The main contention is a familiar one – should the son of an older brother, or the uncle in possession be the rightful King. The crucial historical figure is Eleanor of Aquitaine, wife of two Kings and mother of two Kings, whose marriage to Henry II had brought half of France to the English crown, and who had claims to the other half through her earlier marriage to the French King. She appears in this play as the upholder of John's right to the English crown, despite being the mother of Geoffrey and the grandmother of the pretender Arthur. And it is she who underwrites Philip the Bastard's paternity, recognising him as the illegitimate son of her son Richard I. Such complex family politics need clear exposition on stage. In addition to Eleanor, there are three other females – Constance (Arthur's mother), Blanche (a granddaughter to Eleanor who becomes a political pawn between France and England), and Lady Faulconbridge (the mother of the Bastard, who reluctantly admits the Bastard's paternity). To add to the confusion, or perhaps to clarify it, I suggest that the actress playing Eleanor should also play Lady Faulconbridge, to point up these matters of family and inheritance.

The second crux is Nations and National Identities. It is important to understand that France is not Aquitaine and that three nations, France, England and Aquitaine, are involved in a great struggle for dominance. The invasion of Louis of France, assisted by yet another bastard (of Henry II), the Earl of Salisbury, against King John is the counterclaim to John's claim on France. Into this the figure of the Count of Limoges/Duke of Austria (an amalgamated character) is also present and one might suggest, albeit mischievously, that at least four different accents might be employed to point up national differences. The behaviour of nations in the play reminds one of lions – dominant males trying to preserve their sovereignty but constantly under threat from younger, or stronger rivals with equal or better familial claims to precedence. Such rivalries are always perilous for the young, like Arthur or Prince Henry who (if played by the same actor) could illustrate both sides of this particular danger – death and inheritance.

As if the political situation were not complicated enough – there is a third strand in this play, the politics of the Church of Rome, in the character of Cardinal Pandulph whose interventions on both sides, in the name of the Pope, but actually following the realities of national power, are decisive.

Pandulph's interventions bring a third political element to this play; Church, Nations and Family. And it is language that is the gunpowder.

Both of our illustrations are of the King despite the biggest part, as identified on the card opposite, being the Bastard. Both Ian McKellen and Ralph Fiennes have played this crucial role memorably, and this character has the great speech on 'Commodity, the bias of the world' as he comments on the shifting politics between the Kings of France and England.

> And this same bias, this commodity,
> This bawd, this broker, this all changing word…

I tried learning this speech for pleasure, not when I was young but middle-aged. I found its complicated syntax hard going, but well worth the effort of remembering it, if only for a short while.

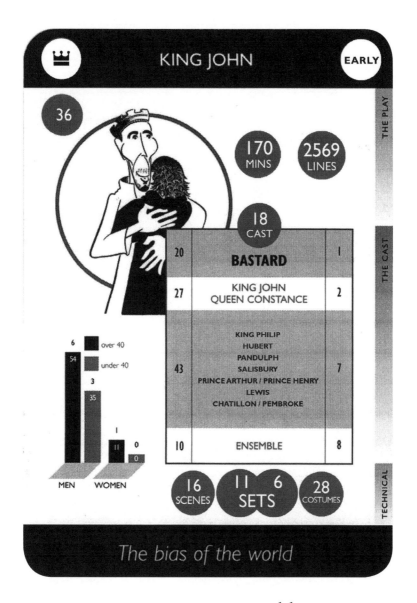

KING JOHN

EARLY

36

170 MINS

2569 LINES

18 CAST

20	**BASTARD**	1
27	KING JOHN QUEEN CONSTANCE	2
43	KING PHILIP HUBERT PANDULPH SALISBURY PRINCE ARTHUR / PRINCE HENRY LEWIS CHATILLON / PEMBROKE	7
10	ENSEMBLE	8

6 over 40

54

3 under 40

35

1

11

0

0

MEN   WOMEN

16 SCENES

11 6 SETS

28 COSTUMES

The bias of the world

The main requirement of this play is for older men with 54% of the lines. The play has relatively few scenes with an average number of sets and an average number of costumes. This play is more difficult, and probably best left to experienced groups.

KING JOHN Guy Henry

241

TITUS ANDRONICUS

TITUS Anthony Hopkins
TAMORA Jessica Lange
SATURNINUS Alan Cumming

TITUS ANDRONICUS
Despiteful and intolerable wrongs

Titus returns to Rome, victorious against the Goths. The people of Rome want Titus to accept the vacant Emperorship but Titus confers the title on Saturninus who asks that Titus' daughter, Lavinia, become his wife. Lavinia is, however, betrothed to Bassianus, Saturninus' brother. Titus is forced to kill his son Mutius when his other sons prevent Saturninus from taking Lavinia by force.

Saturninus then claims Tamora, Queen of the defeated Goths, as his bride. Her two sons, Chiron and Demetrius, are encouraged by the Moor, Aaron, to rape Lavinia. Tamora's sons kill Bassianus when he discovers that she is Aaron's lover. Titus' sons are tricked into the wood by Aaron where they discover Bassianus' body and are condemned to death for his murder. Titus pleads with Saturninus who promises their pardon in exchange for Titus' hand. Titus cuts off his hand, but his sons are not spared.

Marcus, Titus' brother, gradually assumes responsibility for Titus' family as the ravished Lavinia and the apparently unhinged Titus now learn of Tamora's role in these tragedies. Lucius, Titus' oldest and remaining son captures Aaron. Tamora attempts to trap Lucius but Titus prepares a ghastly banquet at which her sons are fed to her and Lavinia is killed by Titus. Titus dies at Saturninus' hand and Lucius revenges his father and is left to become Emperor.

Ranked bottom of my popularity survey, this play is better than that. I saw it at the old St James's Theatre in a magnificent production with Laurence Olivier and Vivien Leigh, and recent productions by Deborah Warner and the film version starring Anthony Hopkins have shown it to be relevant and exciting today. Many editors consider it a prentice piece by Shakespeare, leaning heavily on George Peele. I actually detect more of Marlowe (though I hardly know Peele) with echoes of *The Jew of Malta* and, especially, *Tamburlaine*. The play is short, the action complex and swift, with enough theatricality to warrant considering doing it. At drinks parties it is enough to describe it as a Neo-Senecan shocker. Seriously, though, there are decisions to make as to whether it is a black comedy, a revenge tragedy or a Roman documentary. Sophisticated it is not, but what precocious talent was discovered in 1591.

The cast is relatively small – 11 single parts plus 6 composite parts, of which 5 are of considerable importance. Attendants, to use a stage direction from this play, should be "as many as may be". This is Rome after all. Titus is a wonderful role for a senior actor; Tamora and Aaron are magnificent villains; Marcus (another senior role) has important scenes while the complexity of the Emperor Saturninus raises huge questions as to how to establish imperial nobility in a character so flawed in virtue and judgement. Lavinia is a tiny enough role before the character loses her tongue, but the mute scenes are powerful enough to make this a rewarding role for any young actress.

While the setting is Roman we are back to the debate as to whether one goes for togas, or for Jacobean dress, or for some timeless and neutral setting (as in the film). As with later Jacobean revenge drama great attention must be paid to the spectacle: how one dies, is killed, kills is of the greatest importance. Here we have a ceremonial killing (Alarbus), an arbitrary one (Mutius), a stabbing and an interment in a pit (Bassianus), a rape, the cutting off of hands and ripping out of tongue (Lavinia), a voluntary sacrifice of a limb (Titus), a casual murder (the Nurse), two judicial murders

(Quintus, Marcus), the pie at the banquet of the Queen's sons (Demetrius and Chiron), regicide (Tamora), a revenge stabbing (Titus), an execution (Aaron) and a second regicide (Saturninus). Not all these take place on stage but the variety of casual murders is astonishing and the challenge is to make each memorable and different. Key in all this is the setting; for example the forest in which Bassianus dies and the pit into which he is thrown represent a huge challenge to the designer, not only how to build it but also to remove it for the next scenes since the formal scenes can hardly be set there. And the tomb of Titus' family needs to be substantial enough to underline the importance of the family's sacrifices to Rome. The Act V Masque of Revenge is a challenge too, to pitch it between feigned madness and matter. The designer can help here in establishing who is hoodwinking whom in a difficult scene.

My first crux is making sense of the complexity of the plot and the speed with which it is revealed. Take Act I Scene 1, a scene of only 500 lines which cover 25 facts of the plot. This is astonishing plotting indeed, and the rest of the play rushes headlong to its gory climaxes.

The second crux is black v. white – how evil is Aaron (another Moor but described as coal black in the play, a colour that put its first audience in no doubt that this was a Satanic villain with no redeeming features). And yet his defence of his child begotten on the empress is wonderful: black is truly beautiful. Just as the Jew of Malta was a figure of grotesque villainy, so is Aaron in this play. And yet if Shylock is given redeeming qualities, so is Aaron. Tamora, his co-mate in evil, is also a foreigner, remember, Queen of Goths, savage warriors compared to the effete Romans, yet the Goths arrive at the end, like the US Cavalry, as the expeditionary force with a reforming agenda. Tamora's sons are thugs, but the foreigners are by no means as entirely black (evil) as they can be painted.

The third crux is really a composite one – how to achieve the balance between feigned madness and real madness (Titus) which, of course, occurs in *Hamlet* too – how formal or chaotic the final masque – whether the play is a horror pic or a classical tragedy – are the Roman virtues (as shown by Marcus and Lucius) the dominant themes or the evils of Machiavel – all these contrasts are there and maybe a decision on what is the play's dominant category should be made at a very early stage. All I would note is that sending up such situations is never justified. The true solution will lie some way between the extremes. But it is never easy to find these balances.

Finally I would note a subordinate theme which is remarkable in that the play is about brothers:

> Saturninus and Bassianus
> Titus and Marcus
> Demetrius and Chiron (and Alarbus)
> Lucius and the sons of Titus (and Lavinia)

An attempt should be made to differentiate between these very different sibling relationships.

As a teenager I was lucky enough to see Laurence Olivier on stage in this play, in which his wife Vivien Leigh played Lavinia. It was my earliest experience of Shakespeare on the London stage, though I retain but a few impressions of the production.

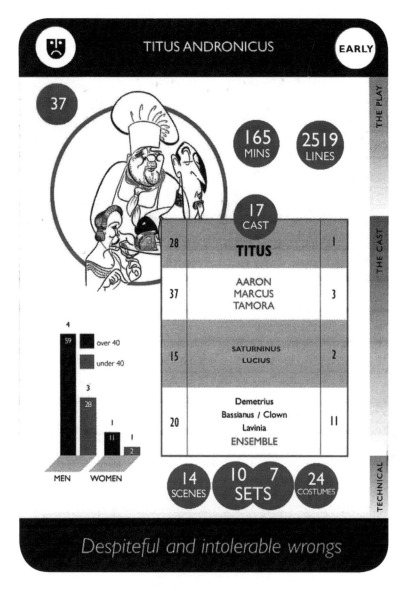

37

165 MINS

2519 LINES

17 CAST

THE CAST

TECHNICAL

28	**TITUS**	1
37	AARON MARCUS TAMORA	3
15	SATURNINUS LUCIUS	2
20	Demetrius Bassianus / Clown Lavinia ENSEMBLE	11

4

59 ■ over 40

■ under 40

3

28

1

11 1

2

MEN   WOMEN

14 SCENES

10 7 SETS

24 COSTUMES

Despiteful and intolerable wrongs

The main requirement of this play is for older men with 59% of the lines. The play has relatively few scenes with an average number of sets and relatively few costumes. This play is more difficult, and probably best left to experienced groups.

TITUS Anthony Hopkins   **TAMORA** Jessica Lang

SATURNIUS Alan Cumming

A S h a k e s p e a r e   S a m p l e r

This book is an invitation to engage in Shakespeare in whatever capacity your powers suggest. My main point of earlier chapters is that only in the theatre can Shakespeare really come alive and the actors (not the readers, not the audiences) of Shakespeare are those that experience and understand Shakespeare most fully. It is notable how often he uses the language of theatrical performance as a metaphor, frequently interrupting a story to expand on the theatrical metaphor. And this language of theatre is another powerful weapon to excite the imagination.

The following pages are intended to give a sample, not only of Shakespeare's finest language, but also of his general view of the human condition, in all its depth and variety. The particular character speaking the words is not as important, in these Sampler pages, as Shakespeare's views of the world and our existence in it; ultimately of the supremacy of the poet and his legacy to us all in the plays he wrote.

An earlier draft of this book was called *The Shakespeare Pack*, which came with two sets of cards, viz:

- Play cards containing details to consider before staging a particular play.
- Quotation cards containing suggested passages for young Shakespeareans to learn by heart.

The play cards are presented throughout the first part of the book, though not now in card form, the only real loss in this edition being the ability to sort cards by given criteria, such as length of performance, relative difficulty, cast requirements and so on, to narrow the choice of play down to a few, or one, that might fit the needs of the group contemplating a production. This can now be done, though less conveniently, by leafing through the pages, relying perhaps on the summary of the requirements for each play to shorten the search.

I have had a fundamental reappraisal of the quotation cards, and have now simplified them into what I now call the Shakespeare Sampler. The problem with the cards was two-fold. First, since there were 37 play cards and 74 sides, easy enough to fill with quotations, but too many quotations for the new Shakespearean to contemplate learning, at least initially. And my suggestion that the cards could be learned on one's commute, or walk, was simply out of date in the new world of personal phones. And many of the new generation have less time than we had to do the actual learning. But, as also suggested earlier, do NOT IGNORE Shakespeare, especially these chosen extracts, to broaden your understanding of Shakespeare.

The *English Sampler* by S. S. Sopwith was a school book I had at the age of sixteen, described as some essential passages of prose and poetry. S. S. Sopwith had little space in his book for Shakespeare, to allow passages by other writers to be included. My selection of essential extracts from Shakespeare, now considerably shortened from the selection on the 37 two-sided cards, can now be described as a Shakespeare Sampler. I believe my Sampler does full justice to Shakespeare's genius in defining the human condition and the importance of his theatre, and will inspire you to learn at least some of them by heart.

While emphatically ruling out success in exams as an objective, I can nevertheless suggest that any Shakespeare that you have memorised will surely enhance any answer you may make in an examination.

The first extract is Jacques' Seven Ages of Man in *As You Like It,* which unites the themes of this book. Through our imaginations and the power of Shakespeare's words, we confront our humanity in a speech that is an extended theatrical metaphor. It is the only extract that I consider mandatory to be learned by heart.

> All the world's a stage,
> And all the men and women merely players:
> They have their exits and their entrances;
> And one man in his time plays many parts,
> His acts being seven ages. At first the infant,
> Mewling and puking in the nurse's arms.
> And then the whining school-boy, with his satchel,
> And shining morning face, creeping like snail
> Unwillingly to school. And then the lover,
> Sighing like furnace, with a woful ballad
> Made to his mistress' eyebrow. Then a soldier,
> Full of strange oaths, and bearded like the pard,
> Jealous in honour, sudden and quick in quarrel,
> Seeking the bubble reputation
> Even in the cannon's mouth. And then the justice,
> In fair round belly with good capon lin'd,
> With eyes severe, and beard of formal cut,
> Full of wise saws and modern instances;
> And so he plays his part. The sixth age shifts
> Into the lean and slipper'd pantaloon,
> With spectacles on nose and pouch on side,
> His youthful hose well sav'd, a world too wide
> For his shrunk shank; and his big manly voice,
> Turning again toward childish treble, pipes
> And whistles in his sound. Last scene of all,
> That ends this strange eventful history,
> Is second childishness and mere oblivion,
> Sans teeth, sans eyes, sans taste, sans everything.

The Natural World

The world is hard to encompass in a short section, but four examples of our world today – country v. town; animals; and the natural environment – may suffice for this Sampler.

Shakespeare was born a country man and spent the main part of his life in the city. I have always loved this exchange from *As You Like It* between the shepherd Corin and the exiled city professional, Touchstone. Corin defines his philosophy:

> I know the more one sickens the worse at ease he is;
> and that he that wants money, means, and content, is
> without three good friends; that the property of rain
> is to wet, and fire to burn; that good pasture makes
> fat sheep, and that a great cause of the night is lack
> of the sun; that he that hath learned no wit by nature
> nor art may complain of good breeding, or comes of a
> very dull kindred…

> Sir I am a true labourer: I earn that I eat, get that I
> wear, owe no man hate, envy no man's happiness, glad
> of other men's good, content with my harm; and the
> greatest of my pride is to see my ewes graze and my
> lambs suck.

Touchstone's retort is typical of the townie:

> That is another simple sin in you, to bring the ewes
> and the rams together, and to offer to get your living
> by the copulation of cattle; to be bawd to a bell-
> wether, and to betray a she-lamb of a twelvemonth
> to a crooked-pated, old cuckoldy ram, out of all
> reasonable match.

If thou be'st not damned for this, the devil himself
will have no shepherds: I cannot see else how thou
shouldst 'scape.

In *A Midsummer Night's Dream* Duke Theseus has several speeches that do not contribute to the story, and one, in particular, that reveals much about the love of countryside pursuits, in this case the sight and sounds of hunting dogs:

> My hounds are bred out of the Spartan kind,
> So flew'd, so sanded; and their heads are hung
> With ears that sweep away the morning dew;
> Crook-knee'd, and dew-lapp'd like Thessalian bulls;
> Slow in pursuit, but match'd in mouth like bells,
> Each under each. A cry more tuneable
> Was never holla'd to, nor cheer'd with horn,
> In Crete, in Sparta, nor in Thessaly:
> Judge, when you hear.

Earlier in the same play Titania berates Oberon for the consequences of their brawls on what today we call the world's natural environment:

> But with thy brawls thou hast disturb'd our sport.
> Therefore the winds, piping to us in vain,
> As in revenge, have suck'd up from the sea
> Contagious fogs; which, falling in the land,
> Have every pelting river made so proud
> That they have overborne their continents;
> The ox hath therefore stretch'd his yoke in vain,
> The ploughman lost his sweat, and the green corn
> Hath rotted ere his youth attain'd a beard:
> The fold stands empty in the drowned field,
> And crows are fatted with the murrion flock;

> The nine men's morris is fill'd up with mud,
> And the quaint mazes in the wanton green
> For lack of tread are undistinguishable:

The delights of the natural world are beautifully expressed by the young Perdita in *The Winter's Tale*:

> Here's flowers for you;
> Hot lavender, mints, savoury, marjoram;
> The marigold, that goes to bed wi' the sun
> And with him rises weeping: these are flowers
> Of middle summer...

The Individual

This section concentrates on Shakespeare's profound knowledge of the human condition, both generally and of individuals. However, as these are passages suggested for learning by heart I have thought to exclude those passages that are specific to an individual character in an individual play. Those passages are to be learned by the actor cast to play that character.

I have chosen passages which describe qualities that are universal, that go beyond the particular story. Any selection is inevitably personal. While there are many other passages that could have been chosen, I hope that the choices I have made will repay study. Brush up your Shakespeare goes the song; much easier when learned young.

These are Miranda's famous lines from *The Tempest* as, for the first time in her life, she beholds the supposedly shipwrecked Lords:

> O, wonder!
> How many goodly creatures are there here!
> How beauteous mankind is! O brave new world,
> That has such people in't!

The irony is that all but one of the Lords she has just encountered are hardly paragons of virtue, and certainly not beauteous.

In contrast to Miranda, Hamlet extols the virtues of the world and the perfection of mankind, at the same time admitting its contrasting imperfection:

> I have of late, – but wherefore I know not, – lost
> all my mirth, foregone all custom of exercises; and
> indeed it goes so heavily with my disposition that
> this goodly frame, the earth, seems to me a sterile
> promontory; this most excellent canopy, the air, look
> you, this brave o'erhanging firmament, this majestical
> roof fretted with golden fire, why, it appears no other
> thing to me but a foul and pestilent congregation of
> vapours. What a piece of work is a man! How noble
> in reason! How infinite in faculty! in form, in moving,
> how express and admirable! in action how like an
> angel! in apprehension how like a god! the beauty of
> the world! the paragon of animals! And yet, to me,
> what is this quintessence of dust? man delights not
> me; no, nor woman neither, though, by your smiling,
> you seem to say so.

Two examples of admirable advice to young men follow, the first in *All's Well That Ends Well* by his mother, the Countess, to Bertram:

> Be thou blest, Bertram; and succeed thy father
> In manners, as in shape! thy blood and virtue
> Contend for empire in thee; and thy goodness
> Share with thy birthright! Love all, trust a few,
> Do wrong to none: be able for thine enemy
> Rather in power than use, and keep thy friend
> Under thy own life's key: be check'd for silence,
> But never tax'd for speech.

The second in *Hamlet* by his father Polonius, to Laertes:

> There, my blessing with thee!
> And these few precepts in thy memory
> Look thou character. Give thy thoughts no tongue,
> Nor any unproportion'd thought his act.
> Be thou familiar, but by no means vulgar;
> Those friends thou hast, and their adoption tried,
> Grapple them to thy soul with hoops of steel;
> But do not dull thy palm with entertainment
> Of each new-hatch'd unfledg'd comrade. Beware
> Of entrance to a quarrel, but, being in,
> Bear 't that th' opposed may beware of thee.
> Give every man thine ear, but few thy voice;
> Take each man's censure, but reserve thy judgement.
> Costly thy habit as thy purse can buy,
> But not express'd in fancy; rich, not gaudy;
> For the apparel oft proclaims the man,
> And they in France of the best rank and station
> Are most select and generous, chief in that.
> Neither a borrower, nor a lender be;
> For loan oft loses both itself and friend,
> And borrowing dulls the edge of husbandry.
> This above all: to thine own self be true,
> And it must follow, as the night the day,
> Thou canst not then be false to any man.
> Farewell, my blessing season this in thee!

The advice often goes unheeded, as the disappointed ladies have it in this song from *Much Ado About Nothing*:

> Sigh no more, ladies, sigh no more,
> Men were deceivers ever;
> One foot in sea, and one on shore,

> To one thing constant never.
> Then sigh not so,
> But let them go,
> And be you blithe and bonny,
> Converting all your sounds of woe
> Into hey nonny, nonny.

True love can be equivocal, as in *Twelfth Night,* where Viola, a girl disguised as Cesario, a page, has the task of wooing Olivia on behalf of her master Orsino, with whom she is secretly in love, as the next extracts beautifully describe:

> If I did love you in my master's flame,
> With such a suffering, such a deadly life,
> In your denial I would find no sense;
> I would not understand it.

> Why, what would you?

> Make me a willow cabin at your gate,
> And call upon my soul within the house;
> Write loyal cantons of contemnèd love,
> And sing them loud even in the dead of night;
> Halloo your name to the reverberate hills,
> And make the babbling gossip of the air
> Cry out, 'Olivia!'

Later, Viola responds to Orsino's question about 'Cesario's' sister…

> And what's her history?

> A blank, my lord. She never told her love,
> But let concealment, like a worm i' the bud,

> Feed on her damask cheek: she pin'd in thought,
> And with a green and yellow melancholy,
> She sat like Patience on a monument,
> Smiling at grief. Was not this love indeed?

Young love is less complicated in another song from the same play, this time by Feste, the clown:

> O mistress mine! where are you roaming?
> O! stay and hear; your true love's coming,
> That can sing both high and low.
> Trip no further, pretty sweeting;
> Journeys end in lovers meeting,
> Every wise man's son doth know.
>
> What is love? 'tis not hereafter;
> Present mirth hath present laughter;
> What's to come is still unsure:
> In delay there lies no plenty;
> Then come kiss me, sweet and twenty,
> Youth's a stuff will not endure.

I must admit a personal interest in this song. It happens I was directing *Twelfth Night* at a time when I met my future wife, Sheila. Shortly after the performances we became engaged and later married. I inscribed her wedding ring with the words "O Mistress Mine", reflecting that mistress has at least three meanings that have fitted our marriage of over fifty years, namely: Mistress is Teacher, Lover and Wife, then as now.

Jacques, the Speaker of 'All the World's a Stage' in *As You Like It*, later describes a range of individuals in the context of his own individual personality. Though certainly not exhaustive it neatly sums up a number of distinctive individual qualities:

I have neither the scholar's melancholy, which is
emulation; nor the musician's, which is fantastical;
nor the courtier's, which is proud; nor the soldier's,
which is ambitious; nor the lawyer's, which is politic;
nor the lady's, which is nice; nor the lover's, which
is all these: but it is a melancholy of mine own,
compounded of many simples, extracted from many
objects, and indeed the sundry contemplation of my
travels, in which my often rumination wraps me in a
most humorous sadness.

Worldly Realities That Confront Us
This section starts with the political environment that is a constant
danger to us all. The argument for an ordered world is best put
by Ulysses explaining in *Troilus and Cressida* why the Greeks have
failed to take Troy:

Troy, yet upon his basis, had been down,
And the great Hector's sword had lack'd a master,
But for these instances.
The speciality of rule hath been neglected: ...
... Degree being vizarded,
The unworthiest shows as fairly in the mask.
The heavens themselves, the planets, and this centre
Observe degree, priority, and place,
Insisture, course, proportion, season, form,
Office, and custom, in all line of order:
And therefore is the glorious planet Sol
In noble eminence enthron'd and spher'd ...
But when the planets
In evil mixture to disorder wander,
What plagues, and what portents, what mutiny,
What raging of the sea, shaking of earth.
Commotion in the winds, frights, changes, horrors,

> Divert and crack, rend and deracinate
> The unity and married calm of states
> Quite from their fixture! O! when degree is shak'd
> Which is the ladder to all high designs,
> The enterprise is sick…

At the opposite end of the political spectrum the rebel Jack Cade exhorts the spirits of revolution with extravagant and uncosted promises in *Henry VI, Part 2*:

> Be brave, then; for your captain is brave, and vows reformation. …
>   There shall be in England seven halfpenny loaves sold for a penny; the three-hooped pot shall have ten hoops; and I will make it felony to drink small beer…
>   All the realm shall be in common, and in Cheapside shall my palfrey go to grass. And when I am King, – as King I will be, – … There shall be no money; all shall eat and drink on my score; … and here, sitting upon London-stone, I charge and command that, of the city's cost, the pissing-conduit run nothing but claret wine this first year of our reign.

During these pronouncements, Dick, one of his followers, exclaims:

> … the first thing we do, let's kill all the lawyers.

And Menenius' parable of the belly in *Coriolanus*, putting the case for Bosses v. the Workers, is a political truism that we may still recognise today:

> There was a time when all the body's members
> Rebell'd against the belly; thus accus'd it:
> That only like a gulf it did remain

I' the midst o' the body, idle and unactive,
Still cupboarding the viand, never bearing
Like labour with the rest, where the other
        instruments
Did see and hear, devise, instruct, walk, feel,
And mutually participate, did minister
Unto the appetite and affection common
Of the whole body. The belly answer'd –,
… 'true is it, my incorporate friends' quoth he
'That I receive the general food at first,
Which you do live upon; and fit it is;
Because I am the store-house and the shop
Of the whole body: but, if you do remember,
I send it through the rivers of your blood,
Even to the court, the heart, to the seat o' the brain;
And, through the cranks and offices of man,
The strongest nerves and small inferior veins
From me receive that natural competency
Whereby they live.'

While on the belly I cannot resist the next sample, Falstaff's dissertation, in *Henry IV, Part 2*, on the merits of sack – a sort of fortified sherry. On one occasion I was planning on directing a conflation of both parts of *Henry IV* for the theatre. To avoid losing this speech, since it might otherwise be cut to save performance time, I planned to use it as a prologue before curtain-up in the nature of an advertisement in the cinema before the main event.

A good sherris sack hath a two-fold operation in it.
It ascends me into the brain; dries me there all the
foolish and dull and curdy vapours which environ
it; makes it apprehensive, quick, forgetive, full of
nimble fiery and delectable shapes, which, delivered
o'er to the voice, the tongue, which is the birth,

becomes excellent wit. The second property of your excellent sherris is, the warming of the blood; which, before cold and settled, left the liver white and pale, which is the badge of pusillanimity and cowardice; but the sherris warms it and makes it course from the inwards to the parts extreme: it illumineth the face, which as a beacon gives warning to all the rest of this little kingdom, man, to arm; and then the vital commoners and inland petty spirits muster me all to their captain, the heart, who, great and puffed up with this retinue, doth any deed of courage; and this valour comes of sherris... If I had a thousand sons, the first humane principle I would teach them should be, to forswear thin potations and to addict themselves to sack.

This speech follows the same idea as the Menenius speech on the belly, showing the effects of circulating, in this case sack, around the body and reaping its benefits. Falstaff contrasts the contribution of sack to Prince Harry making him "very hot and valiant," and to Prince John, his "sober blooded" brother, whose "thin drink doth so overcool their blood," making him a fool and a coward.

The political section ends with what we now call Fake News: the destroyer of enterprises and reputation, which is a prologue in *Henry IV, Part 2*:

> Open your ears; for which of you will stop
> The vent of hearing when loud Rumour speaks?
> I, from the orient to the drooping west,
> Making the wind my post-horse, still unfold
> The acts commenced on this ball of earth:
> Upon my tongues continual slanders ride,
> The which in every language I pronounce,
> Stuffing the ears of men with false reports.

I speak of peace, while covert enmity
Under the smile of safety wounds the world:
… Rumour is a pipe
Blown by surmises, jealousies, conjectures,
And of so easy and so plain a stop
That the blunt monster with uncounted heads,
The still-discordant wavering multitude,
Can play upon it.

In my corporate life I used Iago's words in *Othello* on reputation to justify spending time and money on good relations with the outside world and society as described.

Good name in man and woman, dear my lord,
Is the immediate jewel of their souls:
Who steals my purse steals trash; 'tis something,
        nothing;
'Twas mine, 'tis his, and has been slave to thousands;
But he that filches from me my good name
Robs me of that which not enriches him,
And makes me poor indeed.

The irony here is that Iago, a few pages later, dismisses reputation as so much hot air; but that is a truth (or a falsehood?) best experienced by acting the part.

Falstaff again, in *Henry IV, Part 1*, denounces valour in battle in similar terms:

Honour pricks me on. Yea, but how if honour prick
me off when I come on? how then? Can honour set-to
a leg? no: or an arm? no: or take away the grief of a
wound? no. Honour hath no skill in surgery, then?
no. What is honour? a word. What is in that word
honour? What is that honour? Air. A trim reckoning!

Who hath it? he that died o' Wednesday. Doth he feel
it? no. Doth he hear it? no. 'Tis insensible, then. Yea,
to the dead. But will it not live with the living? no.
Why? detraction will not suffer it. Therefore I'll none
of it. Honour is a mere scutcheon: and so ends my
catechism.

Both Iago and Falstaff speak flawed reason on occasion, and when
it suits them.

It is for us all to pick our way through their arguments and derive
our own truths.

Another song from *As You Like It* expresses the painful reality of
human dealings:

> Blow, blow, thou winter wind,
> Thou art not so unkind
> As man's ingratitude;
> Thy tooth is not so keen,
> Because thou art not seen,
> Although thy breath be rude,
> Heigh-ho! sing, heigh-ho! unto the green holly:
> Most friendship is feigning, most loving mere folly.
> Then heigh-ho! the holly!
> This life is most jolly.

One example of a destroyed reputation comes with Wolsey's lament
for his downfall in *Henry VIII*:

> So farewell to the little good you bear me.
> Farewell a long farewell, to all my greatness!
> This is the state of man: to-day he puts forth
> The tender leaves of hopes; to-morrow blossoms,
> And bears his blushing honours thick upon him;
> The third day comes a frost, a killing frost;

And, when he thinks, good easy man, full surely
His greatness is a-ripening, nips his root,
And then he falls, as I do. I have ventur'd,
Like little wanton boys that swim on bladders,
This many summers in a sea of glory,
But far beyond my depth: my high-blown pride
At length broke under me, and now has left me,
Weary and old with service, to the mercy
Of a rude stream, that must for ever hide me.
Vain pomp and glory of this world, I hate ye:
I feel my heart new open'd. O! how wretched
Is that poor man that hangs on princes' favours!
There is, betwixt that smile we would aspire to,
That sweet aspect of princes, and their ruin,
More pangs and fears than wars or women have;
And when he falls, he falls like Lucifer,
Never to hope again.

I find a deep personal consolation in another of Ulysses' speeches in
Troilus and Cressida in that the only way must be forward:

O! let not virtue seek
Remuneration for the thing it was;
For beauty, wit,
High birth, vigour of bone, desert in service,
Love, friendship, charity, are subjects all
To envious and calumniating time.

Endgame
The King, Henry IV, who had usurped the crown, longs for peaceful
repose in this wonderful passage from *Henry IV, Part 2*:

How many thousand of my poorest subjects
Are at this hour asleep! O sleep! O gentle sleep!

Nature's soft nurse, how have I frighted thee,
That thou no more wilt weigh my eyelids down
And steep my senses in forgetfulness?
Why rather, sleep, liest thou in smoky cribs,
Upon uneasy pallets stretching thee,
And hush'd with buzzing night-flies to thy slumber,
Than in the perfum'd chambers of the great,
Under the canopies of costly state,
And lull'd with sound of sweetest melody?
O thou dull god! Why liest thou with the vile
In loathsome beds, and leav'st the kingly couch
A watch-case or a common 'larum bell?
Wilt thou upon the high and giddy mast
Seal up the ship-boy's eyes, and rock his brains
In cradle of the rude imperious surge,
And in the visitation of the winds,
Who take the ruffian billows by the top,
Curling their monstrous heads, and hanging them
With deaf'ning clamour in the slippery clouds,
That with the hurly death itself awakes?
Canst thou, O partial sleep! give thy repose
To the wet sea-boy in an hour so rude,
And in the calmest and most stillest night,
With all appliances and means to boot,
Deny it to a king? Then, happy low, lie down!
Uneasy lies the head that wears a crown.

He seems to long for death, the final sleep of all, that in the play arrives shortly afterwards.

In the most famous soliloquy of all, Hamlet defines sleep, dreams and death in the context of his own, and life's, calamities:

To be, or not to be: that is the question:
Whether 'tis nobler in the mind to suffer
The slings and arrows of outrageous fortune,
Or to take arms against a sea of troubles,
And by opposing end them? To die: to sleep;
No more; and, by a sleep to say we end
The heart-ache and the thousand natural shocks
That flesh is heir to, 'tis a consummation
Devoutly to be wish'd. To die, to sleep;
To sleep: perchance to dream: ay, there's the rub;
For in that sleep of death what dreams may come
When we have shuffled off this mortal coil,
Must give us pause. There's the respect
That makes calamity of so long life;
For who would bear the whips and scorns of time,
The oppressor's wrong, the proud man's contumely,
The pangs of dispriz'd love, the law's delay,
The insolence of office, and the spurns
That patient merit of the unworthy takes,
When he himself might his quietus make
With a bare bodkin? who would fardels bear,
To grunt and sweat under a weary life,
But that the dread of something after death,
The undiscover'd country from whose bourn
No traveller returns, puzzles the will,
And makes us rather bear those ills we have
Than fly to others that we know not of?
Thus conscience does make cowards of us all;
And thus the native hue of resolution
Is sicklied o'er with the pale cast of thought,
And enterprises of great pith and moment
With this regard their currents turn awry,
And lose the name of action.

Hamlet finally confronts the reality of his situation.

> O God I could be bounded in a nutshell, and count
> myself a king of infinite space, were it not that I have
> bad dreams. Not a whit, we defy augury; there's a
> special providence in the fall of a sparrow. If it be
> now, 'tis not to come; if it be not to come, it will be
> now; if it be not now, yet it will come: the readiness is
> all. Since no man has aught of what he leaves, what is
> 't to leave betimes? Let be.

Equally famously, Hamlet makes salient points about our human
existence, confronting the skull of Yorick, his father's jester:

> Alas! poor Yorick. I knew him, Horatio; a fellow of
> infinite jest, of most excellent fancy; he hath borne me
> on his back a thousand times; and now, how abhorred
> in my imagination it is! My gorge rises at it. Here
> hung those lips that I have kissed I know not how oft.
> Where be your gibes now? Your gambols? Your songs?
> Your flashes of merriment, that were wont to set the
> table on a roar? Not one now, to mock your own
> grinning? Quite chapfallen? Now get you to my lady's
> chamber, and tell her, let her paint an inch thick, to
> this favour she must come; make her laugh at that.

The death of Lady Macbeth prompts Macbeth to reflect on
our mortality.

> She should have died hereafter;
> There would have been a time for such a word.
> To-morrow, and to-morrow, and to-morrow,
> Creeps in this petty pace from day to day,
> To the last syllable of recorded time;
> And all our yesterdays have lighted fools

The way to dusty death. Out, out, brief candle!
Life's but a walking shadow, a poor player
That struts and frets his hour upon the stage,
And then is heard no more; it is a tale
Told by an idiot, full of sound and fury,
Signifying nothing.

Mistress Quickly's account of the death of Falstaff in *Henry V* is touching and poignant, even though he used her badly throughout his life.

Nay, sure, he's not in hell: he's in Arthur's bosom, if ever man went to Arthur's bosom. A' made a finer end and went away an it had been any christom child; a' parted even just between twelve and one, even at the turning o' the tide: for after I saw him fumble with the sheets and play with flowers and smile upon his fingers' ends, I knew there was but one way; for his nose was as sharp as a pen, and a' babbled of green fields.

'How now, Sir John!' quoth I: 'what man! be o' good cheer.'

So a' cried out 'God, God, God!', three or four times: now I, to comfort him, bid him a' should not think of God, I hoped there was no need to trouble himself with any such thoughts yet. So a' bade me lay more clothes on his feet: I put my hand into the bed and felt them, and they were as cold as any stone; then I felt to his knees, and so upward, and upward, and all was as cold as any stone.

Finally in this section on our Endgame, the death, is the lamentation over the dead body of a young boy in *Cymbeline*.

Fear no more the heat o' the sun,
Nor the furious winter's rages;
Thou thy worldly task hast done,
Home art gone, and ta'en thy wages;
Golden lads and girls all must,
As chimney-sweepers, come to dust.

Fear no more the frown o' the great,
Thou art past the tyrant's stroke:
Care no more to clothe and eat;
To thee the reed is as the oak:
The sceptre, learning, physic, must
All follow this, and come to dust.

Fear no more the lightning-flash,
Nor the all-dreaded thunder-stone;
Fear not slander, censure rash;
Thou hast finish'd joy and moan:
All lovers young, all lovers must
Consign to thee, and come to dust.

No exorciser harm thee!
Nor no witchcraft charm thee!
Ghost unlaid forbear thee!
Nothing ill come near thee!
Quiet consummation have;
And renowned be thy grave!

The irony here is that the boy is a girl, and she is not dead.

The Theatre

In Shakespeare's longest play, *Hamlet*, he sets out his precepts for performance in Hamlet's advice to the players. It is not necessary for the story but is crucial for all of us attempting to perform his plays.

Incidentally, this surely clinches the argument over the authorship; the plays were written by a theatre professional, where the theatre is often taken as the metaphor for existence (as Jacques had it) in the Seven Ages of Man.

> Speak the speech, I pray you, as I pronounced it to
> you, trippingly on the tongue; but if you mouth it, as
> many of your players do, I had as lief the town-crier
> spoke my lines. Nor do not saw the air too much with
> your hand, thus; but use all gently: for in the very
> torrent, tempest, and – as I may say – whirlwind of
> passion, you must acquire and beget a temperance,
> that may give it smoothness. O! it offends me to the
> soul to hear a robustious periwig-pated fellow tear
> a passion to tatters, to very rags, to split the ears of
> the groundlings, who for the most part are capable
> of nothing but inexplicable dumb-shows and noise:
> I would have such a fellow whipped for o'er-doing
> Termagant; it out-herods Herod: pray you, avoid it...
> Be not too tame neither, but let your own discretion
> be your tutor: suit the action to the word, the word
> to the action; with this special observance, that you
> o'erstep not the modesty of nature; for anything so
> overdone is from the purpose of playing, whose end,
> both at the first and now, was and is, to hold, as
> 'twere, the mirror up to nature; to show virtue her
> own feature, scorn her own image, and the very age
> and body of the time his form and pressure...
> And let those that play your clowns speak no more
> than is set down for them; for there be of them that
> will themselves laugh, to set on some quantity of
> barren spectators to laugh too, though in the mean
> time some necessary question of the play be then to be
> considered; that's villanous, and shows a most pitiful

> ambition in the fool that uses it.
> Go, make you ready.

In my notes for *Hamlet* I mentioned my coaching of my grand-daughter Alana, cast as Hamlet in the play scene for her school's Shakespeare play. I had great pleasure in coaching her, but it was by acting the role that she made the speech clear to the audience.

In *A Midsummer Night's Dream* Theseus seeks entertainment to celebrate his wedding and asks his master of revels to give him a list of plays to be considered. The final possibility is described thus:

> A play there is my Lord, some ten words, long,
> … But by ten words my Lord, it is too long.

Theseus overrides the objection; and puts the actors' efforts into a more generous perspective:

> I will hear that play;
> For never anything can be amiss,
> When simpleness and duty tender it…

He says they can do nothing in this kind.

> The kinder we, to give them thanks for nothing…
> Where I have come, great clerks have purposed
> To greet me with premeditated welcomes;
> Where I have seen them shiver and look pale,
> Make periods in the midst of sentences,
> Throttle their practis'd accent in their fears,
> And, in conclusion, dumbly have broke off,
> Not paying me a welcome. Trust me, sweet,
> Out of this silence yet I pick'd a welcome;
> And in the modesty of fearful duty
> I read as much as from the rattling tongue
> Of saucy and audacious eloquence.

> Love, therefore, and tongue-tied simplicity
> In least speak most, to my capacity...
> The best in this kind are but shadows,
> and the worst are no worse,
> if imagination amend them.

If imagination amend them – what a comfort to all actors!

Tools Of The Theatre: Words And Music

Next, some samples of the tools of theatre, starting with music.

Theseus' description of hunting dogs earlier includes this description of their music:

> And mark the musical confusion
> Of hounds and echo in conjunction.

The healing power of music is described in *The Tempest*:

> Where should this music be? I's th' air, or th' earth?
> It sounds no more; – and sure, it waits upon
> Some god o' th' island. Sitting on a bank,
> Weeping again the king my father's wrack,
> This music crept by me upon the waters,
> Allaying both their fury, and my passion,
> With its sweet air: thence I have follow'd it, –
> Or it hath drawn me rather, – but 'tis gone.
> No, it begins again.

And in the same play the savage Caliban can also gain solace from music:

> Be not afeard: the isle is full of noises,
> Sounds and sweet airs, that give delight, and hurt not.

Sometimes a thousand twangling instruments
Will hum about mine ears; and sometime voices,
That, if I then had wak'd after long sleep,
Will make me sleep again: and then, in dreaming,
The clouds methought would open and show riches
Ready to drop upon me; that, when I wak'd
– I cried to dream again.

The harmonious conjunction of music in night time is expressed in this passage from *The Merchant of Venice*:

How sweet the moonlight sleeps upon this bank!
Here will we sit, and let the sounds of music
Creep in our ears: soft stillness and the night
Become the touches of sweet harmony.
Sit, Jessica: look, how the floor of heaven
Is thick inlaid with patines of bright gold:
There's not the smallest orb which thou behold'st
But in his motion like an angel sings,
Still quiring to the young-eyed cherubins;
Such harmony is in immortal souls;
But, whilst this muddy vesture of decay
Doth grossly close it in, we cannot hear it.

The next tool of the playwright is, of course, words. With so much that could have been included, I start with the wonderful word play that Shakespeare excelled at. It is from *As You Like It*:

But, for the seventh cause; how did you find the
quarrel on the seventh cause?

Upon a lie seven times removed: … – as thus, sir.

I did dislike the cut of a certain courtier's beard: he

sent me word, if I said his beard was not cut well, he was in the mind it was: this is called 'the retort courteous.' If I sent him word again, it was not well cut, he would send me word, he cut it to please himself: this is called the 'quip modest.' If again, it was not well cut, he disabled my judgment: this is called the 'reply churlish.' If again, it was not well cut, he would answer, I spake not true: this is called the 'reproof valiant:' if again, it was not well cut, he would say, I lie: this is called the 'countercheck quarrelsome': and so to the 'lie circumstantial,' and the 'lie direct.' …

Can you nominate in order now the degrees of the lie?

The first, the 'retort courteous;' the second, the 'quip modest;' the third, the 'reply churlish;' the fourth, the 'reproof valiant;' the fifth, the 'countercheck quarrelsome;' the sixth, the 'lie with circumstance;' the seventh, the 'lie direct.' All these you may avoid but the lie direct; and you may avoid that too, with an 'if.' I knew when seven justices could not take up a quarrel; but when the parties were met themselves, one of them thought but of an 'if,' as 'If you said so, then I said so;' and they shook hands and swore brothers. Your 'if' is the only peace-maker; much virtue in 'if.'

Shakespeare understood low life and the Porter's speech in *Macbeth* (written, I believe, to allow Macbeth sufficient time to change his costume!) has this wonderful description of the effects of drink:

Drink, sir, is a great provoker of three things …
nose-painting, sleep, and urine.

> Lechery, sir, it provokes, and unprovokes; it provokes
> the desire, but it takes away the performance.
>
> Therefore much drink may be said to be an equivoca-
> tor with lechery; it makes him, and it mars him; it sets
> him on, and it takes him off; it persuades him, and
> disheartens him; makes him stand to, and not stand
> to; in conclusion, equivocates him in a sleep, and,
> giving him the lie, leaves him.

Another example of dazzling word play is in *Love's Labour's Lost*
where Sir Nathaniel praises Holofernes the pedantic wordsmith:

> I praise God for you, Sir: your reasons at dinner have
> been sharp and sententious; pleasant without scurril-
> ity ... learned without opinion, and strange without
> heresy.

To which this observation by Moth, the page boy, may justly be
added:

> They have been at a great feast of languages, and
> stolen the scraps.

Later, in the same play, on the news of a bereavement, Berowne
makes the case for simplicity in speech:

> Honest plain words best pierce the ear of grief.

The English language is rightly praised, and to be denied its use is
appalling, as the newly exiled Duke of Norfolk puts it in *Richard II*:

> The language I have learned these forty years
> My native English, now I must forgo:

> And now my tongue's use is to me no more
> Than an unstrung viol or a harp;
> Or like a cunning instrument caged up,
> Or being open, put into his hands
> That knows no touch to tune the harmony…

Words and music, a happy conjunction, in this case, denied.

I must mention another of Shakespeare's theatrical tools, that of imagining light. The disappearance of the servant carrying the torch in the battlement scene in *Macbeth* is an imaginative device to prepare us for "Is this a dagger which I see before me?"

Shakespeare's theatre relied on daylight and he had no access to the technical marvels we have today and yet he understood, imaginatively, the possibilities of all the technical apparatus we use today. In *A Midsummer Night's Dream* Bottom's exhortation to the actor playing Moonshine, at the moment of Pyramus' death, is one such trick of light that is routine today – the slow fade.

> Tongue lose thy light. Moon take thy flight
> Now die, die, die, die, die

Darkness descends as the lantern retreats, and the voice of Pyramus declines to its final gasp.

The Imagination

The Imagination is the essential quality that we must have to appreciate Shakespeare.

Shakespeare worked in and wrote for the theatre and we have considered his principal tools of music and words. But he also needed the imagination of his audience. He calls his art rough magic; and he needs the engagement of our imaginations to create the magic. It is the single most important quality that we must bring to his work.

He uses the words Imagination, Imagining, Imaginary, Imagined on average about twice per play, and relies on us to provide imaginary solutions to the practical limitations of the theatre, for example in battles, crowds, with animals or tricks of light.

In the theatre he can suggest a mob by placing a few actors in the audience and giving them some incendiary words which might, through the incitement of those words, encourage the spectators to join in.

He uses words to evoke what it felt like to be a soldier on the eve of battle, as in this famous description from *Henry V* before the Battle of Agincourt:

> Now entertain conjecture of a time
> When creeping murmur and the poring dark
> Fills the wide vessel of the universe.
> From camp to camp, through the foul womb of night,
> The hum of either army stilly sounds,
> That the fix'd sentinels almost receive
> The secret whispers of each other's watch:
> Fire answers fire, and through their paly flames
> Each battle sees the other's umber'd face:
> Steed threatens steed, in high and boastful neighs
> Piercing the night's dull ear; and from the tents
> The armourers, accomplishing the knights,
> With busy hammers closing rivets up,
> Give dreadful note of preparation.

But there are limits to the power of the imagination, as the banished Duke of Norfolk, in *Richard II,* confronts the realities of his new situation:

> O! who can hold a fire in his hand
> By thinking on the frosty Caucasus?
> Or cloy the hungry edge of appetite
> By bare imagination of a feast?

Or wallow naked in December snow
By thinking on fantastic summer's heat?
O, no! the apprehension of the good
Gives but the greater feeling to the worse:
Fell sorrow's tooth doth never rankle more
Than when he bites, but lanceth not the sore.

Supremacy of the Poet

Recall Theseus' consoling words for actors in *A Midsummer Night's Dream*.

The best in this kind are but shadows
And the worst are no worse, if imagination amend
    them

But Shakespeare realised that the contributions of the actors to his art are limited, and it is to our great benefit that his writing, rather than his acting, outpoints any particular performance and lasts forever.

'The lunatic, the lover and the poet' was an early working title for this book. These three threads – madness, love and poetry – occur time and again in Shakespeare. This is one of those passages that do little to speed the progress of a particular play; Shakespeare includes it as a statement of his own creative philosophy.

Theseus, once again, appears to be speaking for Shakespeare:

Lovers and madmen have such seething brains,
Such shaping fantasies, that apprehend
More than cool reason ever comprehends.
The lunatic, the lover, and the poet,
Are of imagination all compact:
One sees more devils than vast hell can hold,
That is, the madman; the lover, all as frantic,

Sees Helen's beauty in a brow of Egypt:
The poet's eye, in a fine frenzy rolling,
Doth glance from heaven to earth, from earth
        to heaven;
And, as imagination bodies forth
The forms of things unknown, the poet's pen
Turns them to shapes, and gives to airy nothing
A local habitation and a name.
Such tricks hath strong imagination,
That, if it would but apprehend some joy,
It comprehends some bringer of that joy;
Or in the night, imagining some fear,
How easy is a bush suppos'd a bear!

Many feel that Prospero's renunciation of his magic powers in *The Tempest* is Shakespeare's own farewell to the theatre and to his audience. I thought so when playing Prospero some years ago.

Ye elves of hills, brooks, standing lakes, and groves;
And ye, that on the sands with printless foot
Do chase the ebbing Neptune and do fly him
When he comes back; you demi-puppets, that
By moonshine do the green sour ringlets make
Whereof the ewe not bites; and you, whose pastime
Is to make midnight mushrooms; that rejoice
To hear the solemn curfew; by whose aid, –
Weak masters though ye be – I have bedimm'd
The noontide sun, call'd forth the mutinous winds,
And 'twixt the green sea and the azur'd vault
Set roaring war: to the dread-rattling thunder
Have I given fire and rifted Jove's stout oak
With his own bolt: the strong-bas'd promontory
Have I made shake; and by the spurs pluck'd up

The pine and cedar: graves at my command
Have wak'd their sleepers, op'd, and let them forth
By my so potent art. But this rough magic
I here abjure; and, when I have requir'd
Some heavenly music, – which even now I do,–
To work mine end upon their senses that
This airy charm is for, I'll break my staff,
Bury it certain fathoms in the earth,
And, deeper than did ever plummet sound,
I'll drown my book.

And earlier in the play Prospero had included us all as he prepared us for his farewell:

Our revels now are ended. These our actors,
As I foretold you, were all spirits and
Are melted into air, into thin air:
And, like the baseless fabric of this vision,
The cloud-capp'd towers, the gorgeous palaces,
The solemn temples, the great globe itself,
Yea, all which it inherit, shall dissolve
And, like this insubstantial pageant faded,
Leave not a rack behind. We are such stuff
As dreams are made on, and our little life
Is rounded with a sleep

This last speech encapsulates the precepts of this book that acting, and using our imaginations, reveal the riches of the greatest playwright. But it is the poet, not the actor, that is the supreme virtue in giving us all such infinite riches.

Curtain Call

Applause for these infinite riches in Shakespeare's plays is famously expressed by Ben Jonson, Shakespeare's contemporary:

> Soul of the age,
> The applause, delight, the wonder of our stage,
> My Shakespeare rise!

In his encomium of nearly 100 lines, Jonson distinguishes between Shakespeare and other playwrights of the day, and including specifically Marlowe who is sometimes suggested as the real author of the plays. I take this as unequivocal evidence that the Stratfordian is the true author. Jonson would certainly have known the truth and true merit of the

> Sweet swan of Avon

And Shakespeare's editors, his fellow actors John Heminge and Henry Condell, would also have known the truth. Their recommendation to the reader is heartfelt:

> Read him, therefore; and again and again:
> and if then you do not like him, surely you are
> in some manifest danger not to understand him.

I agree, and would only add that the point of this book is to suggest that a better way of understanding Shakespeare is not only to SEE him, or READ him, but:

First

ACT

Shakespeare

Cast Tables

TWELFTH NIGHT

Main Roles	Lines	Ensemble	Lines
SIR TOBY BELCH	360	Captain/Orsino's Servant/Priest	42
VIOLA	326	Curio/1st Officer	20
		Valentine/2nd Officer	18
FESTE	319		
OLIVIA	305		
MALVOLIO	289		
Orsino	211		
Sir Andrew	164		
Maria	154		
Fabian	137		
Sebastian	105		
Antonio	101		

MACBETH

Main Roles	Lines	Ensemble	Lines
		Banquo	98
MACBETH	657	1st Witch/Lady Macduff	98
		Bloody Sergeant/Porter/English Doctor/Menteith	84
Lady Macbeth	221	Lennox	66
Malcolm	188	Angus/1st Murd./Another Lord	58
Macduff	154	2nd Witch/Gentlewoman	54
Duncan/Old Man/Scottish Doctor/ Old Siward	132	3rd Witch	32
		Seyton (= 3rd Murd. = Attendt = Servant = Messenger)	25
Ross	115	Donalbain/Fleance/Lady Mac/Mess/ Young Siward	25
		Macduff's Son/3rd Apparition	24
		2nd Murd./Servant (5^3)	12
		(Other Son)/2nd Apparition	4

ROMEO AND JULIET

Main Roles	Lines	Ensemble	Lines
ROMEO	604	Paris	68
JULIET	530	Sampson/Peter	67
		Gregory/Balthasar	51
FRIAR LAURENCE	337	1st Servant/Friar John	49
		Mont./Cousin/Apothecary	48
NURSE	263	Tybalt	35
CAPULET	260	Abram/3rd Musician/1st Watch	24
MERCUTIO	254	3rd Serv./1st Mus./3rd Watch	14
Benvolio	153	2nd Serv./Tybalt Foll./2nd Mus./2nd Watch	12
Lady Capulet	107	4th Servant/Page	11
Chorus/Escalus	102	Lady Montague	3

THE MERCHANT OF VENICE

Main Roles	Lines	Ensemble	Lines
PORTIA	550	Jessica	83
		Nerissa	80
SHYLOCK	348	Solanio	68
BASSANIO	324	Old Gobbo/Tubal	53
		Stephano (Portia's Servant = Messenger)	23
Gratiano	182	Leonardo (Bassanio's Servant)/Antonio's Servant	3
Antonio	180		
Lorenzo	167		
Launcelot Gobbo	165		
Arragon/Duke	133		
Morocco/Balthazar	108		
Salerio			

HAMLET

Main Roles	Lines	Ensemble	Lines
HAMLET	1358	Marcellus/3rd Player/Fortinbras	93
		Rosencrantz	92
CLAUDIUS	566	Bernardo/Captain/Messenger (= A Lord)/ Priest	77
POLONIUS	345	Guildenstern	48
GHOST/PLAYER/KING/ GRAVEDIGGER	337	Voltimand (= Cornelius)/Reynaldo/Sailor/ Ambassador	43
HORATIO (= Gentleman)	276		
Laertes	187		
Ophelia	163		
Gertrude	140		
Francisco/Player Queen/2nd Gravedigger/ Osric	105		

A MIDSUMMER NIGHT'S DREAM

Main Roles	Lines	Ensemble	Lines
THESEUS/OBERON	452	Egeus/Snout	63
		Flute	57
BOTTOM	259	1st Fairy/Cobweb	41
		Snug	15
Helena	223	Starveling	12
Philostrate/Puck	222	Peaseblossom	6
Hippolyta/Titania	172	(Indian Boy)/Mustardseed	5
Lysander	170	2nd Fairy/Moth	5
Hermia	161		
Demetrius	131		
Peter Quince	123		

MUCH ADO ABOUT NOTHING

Main Roles	Lines	Ensemble	Lines
BENEDICK	460	Friar Francis	80
LEONATO	333	Margaret	70
DON PEDRO	324	Antonio	54
CLAUDIO	273	Ursula	46
BEATRICE	262	Messenger/Sexton	46
Dogberry	182	Balthasar	37
Hero	129	Conrade	36
Borachio	126	Verges	28
Don John	115	1st Watch/A Lord	21
		Boy/2nd Watch	21

THE TAMING OF THE SHREW

Main Roles	Lines	Ensemble	Lines
PETRUCCIO	575	2nd Huntsman/Messenger/Baptista Servant/Curtis/Vincentio	89
LORD/LUCENTIO	319	1st Huntsman/3rd Servant/Philip (= Peter)/Pedant	73
TRANIO	287	Bianca	67
Sly/Grumio	233	Hostess/Page/Nathaniel/Widow	34
Katharina	207	2nd Player/1st Servant/Nicholas/Tailor	34
Hortensio	202	1st Player/2nd Servant/Joseph/Haberdasher	20
Baptista	171		
Gremio	162		
Biondello	104		

ANTONY AND CLEOPATRA

Main Roles	Lines
ANTONY	729
CLEOPATRA	585
OCTAVIUS	368
ENOBARBUS	317
Pompey/Caesar Soldier (= Caesar 1st Watch)/Clown	150

Ensemble	Lines
Charmian	84
1st Messenger (1²)/Ventidius/Ambass. = Schoolmaster/Proculeius	79
Philo/Mess. (2⁵3²) 2nd Sold. (4³) = 2nd Guard (4¹⁴5²)/Decretas	73
Soothsayer/Dolabella	66

Ensemble	Lines
Menas/Servant (3¹³)/Caesar/2nd Watch	63
Lepidus/Captain/Seleucus Mess. (1⁴)/Soldier (= 1st Soldier–Armed Guard = 1st Guard)	56
Demetrius/1st Pompey Serv./Canidius/3rd Soldier (4³) = 3rd Guard	55
Messenger (1⁴)/Eros	45
Agrippa	45
2nd Messenger (1²) = Attendant/2nd Pompey Servant/Scarus	43
Menecrates/Thidias/Caesar's Sentry	41
Alexas/Messenger (4⁴) Egyptian	33
Maecenas	30
Octavia	29
Iras	22
Mardian	16
3rd Mess. (1²) Silius/Taurus/4th Soldier/Gallus	16
Varrius/Messenger (3⁷)	7

OTHELLO

Main Roles	Lines
IAGO	1040
OTHELLO	815
DESDEMONA	348
CASSIO	258
Emilia	221
Brabantio/Gratiano	125
Roderigo	109

Ensemble	Lines
2nd Sen./2nd Gent./Lodovico	89
Duke/Herald	75
Officer/(Gent.) = Montano	58
1st Sen./1st Gent./Clown	53
Bianca	30
Messenger/3rd Gent.	24
Sailor/Musician	10

THE WINTER'S TALE

Main Roles	Lines	Ensemble	Lines
LEONTES	593	Antigonus	97
		Lord = Officer	76
AUTOLYCUS	292	Emilia/Servant (4⁴)	54
PAULINA	290	2nd Serv./Mariner/1st Gent.	40
CAMILLO	264	1st Servant/2nd Gent.	40
		1st Lady/Mopsa	26
Polixenes	238	Dion	23
Hermione	190	Cleomenes	19
Clown	187	Mamillius	17
Florizel	169	2nd Lady/Dorcas	13
Old Shepherd	133		
Archidamus/Gaoler/Time/3rd Gentleman	129		
Perdita	107		

KING LEAR

Main Roles	Lines	Ensemble	Lines
KING LEAR	721	Cornwall	94
		Lear's Gentleman/Herald	81
EDGAR	372	Oswald	68
KENT	341	France/3rd Cornwall Serv./2nd Officer	36
EDMUND	299	Burgundy/2nd Cornwall Serv./Regan's Mess. (= Gentleman)	34
GLOUCESTER	290	Curan/Old Man/Doctor	32
Fool	230	Lear's Knight/1st Cornwall Serv./1st Officer	25
Goneril	195		
Regan	170		
Albany	129		
Cordelia	102		

AS YOU LIKE IT

Main Roles	Lines	Ensemble	Lines
ROSALIND	691	Amiens = Hymen/1st Lord (Duke S)	84
		Phebe	83
ORLANDO	309	Silvius	75
TOUCHSTONE	284	Adam/Martext	68
CELIA	276	Charles/2nd Lord (Duke F.)/J. de Boys	62
Jacques	232	Dennis/1st Lord (Duke F.)/2nd Page	59
Duke Senior/Duke Frederick	172	2nd Lord (Duke S.)/William/Page	39
Oliver	149	Audrey	19
Le Beau/Corin	120		

THE COMEDY OF ERRORS

Main Roles	Lines	Ensemble	Lines
ANTIPHOLUS (Syracuse and Ephesus)	484	Luciana	93
		Angelo	88
DROMIO (Syracuse and Ephesus)	388	Emilia	62
		Luce (= Messenger)/Courtesan	55
ADRIANA	258	Jailer/2nd Merchant	34
Egeon	143	1st Merchant/Officer	27
Duke/Balthazar/Pinch	128		

JULIUS CAESAR

Main Roles	Lines	Ensemble	Lines
BRUTUS	682	Portia	90
		Cobbler/3rd Pleb./Octavius	80
CASSIUS	472	Decius/Titinius	72
		Marullus/2nd Plebeian/5th Soldier (5^4)	59
MARK ANTONY	321	Flavius/1st Plebeian/Cato	56
		Artemidorus/Messala	54
Julius Caesar	144	Metellus/Lucilius	44
Casca	130	Carpenter/4th Plebeian/Varro/4th Soldier (5^4)	32
		Lucius	31
		Cinna/Pindarus	31
		Ligarius/Cinna Poet	28
		Calpurnia	26
		Antony Servant/2nd Soldier (4^3) /Dardanius	22
		Soothsayer/Volumnius	19
		Caesar Servant/Strato/Popilius/1st Soldier(4^3)	16
		Publius/Octavius Servant/3rd Soldier (4^3)/ Clitus	16
		Cicero/Poet	16
		Trebonius/Lepidus	11

THE TEMPEST

Main Roles	Lines	Ensemble	Lines
PROSPERO	593	Sebastian	91
		Alonso	86
Ariel	172	Boatswain/Spirit	46
Caliban	172	Iris	40
Stephano	164	Ceres	22
Gonzalo	152	Master/Adrian	14
Antonio	133	Mariner/Francisco	13
Ferdinand	120	Juno	7
Miranda	112		
Trinculo	103		

KING RICHARD II

Main Roles	Lines	Ensemble	Lines
RICHARD II	748	Aumerle	83
		Lord Marshal/Berkeley/Gardener	83
BOLINGBROKE	410	Greene/Fitzwater	59
DUKE OF YORK	280	2nd Herald/Welsh Captain/Scroop	59
		Bushy/Surrey	49
Mowbray/Bishop of Carlisle	198	Willoughby/Gardener's Man/Exton	43
John of Gaunt	191	Harry Percy	38
Northumberland	144	Salisbury/Abb. of Westminster	30
Duchess of Gloucester/Duchess of York	141	Bagot/Another Lord/Exton Servant	27
Queen Isabel	113	Ross/Keeper	27
		1st Herald/Servant/Groom	23
		Lady	5

KING RICHARD III

Main Roles	Lines	Ensemble	Lines
RICHARD III	1127	1st Murd./Ratcliffe (= York Mess.)	97
		2nd Murd./2nd Cit./Vaughan/Devon Mess.	80
		Edward IV/Bishop of Ely/Urswick/Surrey	80
BUCKINGHAM	345	Gent./Pomfret Mess./Mayor/Tyrrell/Blunt (= Lord)	68
QUEEN ELIZABETH	265	Brakenbury/3rd Cit./Archbishop of York	67
Queen Margaret	216	Dorset/Oxford	57
Clarence	166	Catesby	57
Lady Anne	162	Rivers	52
Hastings	144	Prince of Wales	47
Duchess of York	139	Duke of York	42
Richmond	137	Keeper/Stanley Mess./Priest/Sheriff/Ghost Henry VI	36
Stanley	106	Archbishop of Canterbury/Scrivener/Norfolk	35
		Halberdier/1st Cit./Lovel/Wales Mess./Ghost Prince of Wales	21
		Boy	20
		Grey/Kent Mess.	18
		Girl/Page	12

293

KING HENRY V

Main Roles	Lines	Ensemble	Lines
KING HENRY V	1045	Grey/Williams	88
		Bardolph/Montjoy	82
CHORUS/ELY/ ERPINGHAM/BURGUNDY	330	Boy	80
		Gower	73
ARCHBISHOP OF CANTERBURY/CHARLES V	313	Mistress Quickly/Queen Isabel	68
		Nym/(French Mess. = Bourbon	66
		Katharine	66
FLUELLEN	298	English Amb./MacMorris/Rambures	46
		Orleans	44
Pistol	165	Jamy/Bretagne/French Soldier/Herald	40
Exeter	128	Cambridge/Bates	34
Constable	119	Alice	30
Dauphin	117	Westmoreland (= Warwick = Salisbury)	28
		French Mess./Gov. Harfleur/Grandpré	27
		Scroop/Court	14
		Bedford (= Gloucester = York)	12

THE MERRY WIVES OF WINDSOR

Main Roles	Lines	Ensemble	Lines
FALSTAFF	447	Robin/Anne Page/William	54
		Nym/Rugby/1st Servant	45
MRS PAGE	322	Bardolph	26
FORD	309		
MRS QUICKLY	277		
Hugh Evans	237		
Mrs Ford	184		
Pistol/Caius	154		
Page	152		
Fenton/Simple/2nd Serv.	146		
Slender	139		
Shallow	123		
Host	117		

CYMBELINE

Main Roles	Lines	Ensemble	Lines
IMOGEN	531	1st Gent./British Lord/Jupiter	88
		Lucius	87
POSTHUMUS	416	1st Ld/1st Tribune/Mess. (5⁴)/Soothsayer	86
		Cornelius/Captain	78
IACHIMO	403	Frenchman/Attendant/1st Gaoler	69
		Philario/1st British Captain/2nd Brother	47
BELARIUS	299	2nd Gent./Mess. (2³)/2nd British Captain/1st Brother	23
Cymbeline	236		
Cloten	235	Lady/Mother	20
Pisanio	180		
Queen	148		
Guiderius	134		
Arviragus	107		
2nd Lord/1st Senator/Sicilius Leonatus	100		

KING HENRY IV PART 1

Main Roles	Lines	Ensemble	Lines
FALSTAFF	617	Poins/Lancaster	87
		Gadshill/Douglas	87
PRINCE HAL	563	1st Carrier/Mortimer	81
		2nd Carrier/Vernon	77
HOTSPUR	540	Lady Percy	56
		Hostess	49
HENRY IV	337	Blunt	40
		Westmoreland	40
Worcester	182	Chamberlain/Sheriff/Sir Michael	34
Northumberland/Glendower/Scroop	131	Bardolph	29
		Francis	16
		Peto	15
		2nd Traveller/Hotspur Servant	12
		Lady Mortimer, say,	10
		1st Traveller/Vintner	8

KING HENRY IV PART 2

Main Roles	Lines	Ensemble	Lines
FALSTAFF	650	Hastings/Silence/Messenger	98
		Morton/Bullcalf	93
PRINCE HAL/HENRY V	306	Mowbray/Davy	91
		Rumour/L.C.J. Serv./Gower/2nd Drawer/ Harcourt	75
HENRY IV	291	Page/Shadow/Epilogue	67
Shallow	200	Bardolph	47
Northumb./Warwick	176	Snare/Francis/Feeble/Clarence	47
Mistress Quickly	174	Fang/3rd Drawer/Mouldy/Beadle (= Fang)	34
Poins/Lancaster	165	Travers/Lady Northumberland/Colville	27
Lord Bardolph/Pistol	156	Peto/Wart/Gloucester	23
Lord Chief Justice	154		
Archbishop of York	143		
Lady Percy/Doll	126		
Westmoreland	107		

MEASURE FOR MEASURE

Main Roles	Lines	Ensemble	Lines
DUKE	822	Claudio	96
		Elbow/Barnardine	90
		Juliet/Mariana	67
ISABELLA	399	1st Gent./Froth/Abhorson	54
LUCIO	291	Friar Thomas/Justice	41
ANGELO	290	Mistress Overdone/Francisca	40
Escalus	188	2nd Gent./Servant (= Messenger = Angelo's Man)	22
Pompey	163		
Provost	143		

LOVE'S LABOUR'S LOST

Main Roles	Lines	Ensemble	Lines
BEROWNE	607	Dumain	85
		First Lord/Nathaniel	79
KING OF NAVARRE	303	Longaville	67
		Jacquenetta/Maria	52
PRINCESS OF FRANCE	270	Katharine	46
		Dull/Forester/Marcade	38
Don Armado	237		
Boyet	218		
Costard	190		
Holofernes	185		
Rosaline	170		
Moth	151		

CORIOLANUS

Main Roles	Lines	Ensemble	Lines
CORIOLANUS	797	2nd Sen. C./1st Off./Adrian/Lt. to Aufidius	59
MENENIUS	517	6th Cit./3rd Rom./3rd Serv./Man/3rd Volsc. Lord	58
VOLUMNIA	296	Titus Lartius	52
		1st Sen. C./2nd Off./2nd Mess. (4^6 5^4)	48
Aufidius	244	Valeria	40
Cominius	237	1st Sen. R./Cit. Ant./1st Sent. R./2nd Cit./2nd Volsc. Consp.	35
Sicinius	225	Mess. R./1st Sold. C. (1^{10})/Nicanor	34
Junius Brutus	218	Virgilia	30
Ensemble		8th Cit./Mess. (1^4,1^6)/Herald (= Aedile)/4th Volsc. Consp.	26
4th Cit./1st Sold. C(1^4)/1st Serv. Man/1st Volsc./Watch/1st Volsc. Lord	91	2nd Sen. R. (= Patrician)/1st Mess. R. (4^6, 5^4)/2nd Sent. R.	19
1st Cit./1st Volsc. Consp.	91	7th Cit./Gentlewoman	4
3rd Cit. (= Mess.2^1)/1st Rom./3rd Volsc. Consp.	76	Y. Martius	1
5th Cit./2nd Rom./2nd Serv./Man/2nd Volsc. Watch/2nd Volsc. Lord	61		

TROILUS AND CRESSIDA

Main Roles	Lines		Ensemble	Lines
TROILUS	527		Prologue/Menelaus/Priam/Calchas	96
ULYSSES	459		Diomedes	94
PANDARUS	416		Ajax	79
CRESSIDA	294		Paris	78
THERSITES	278		Patroclus	73
Hector	202		Cassandra	33
Agamemnon	190		Alexander*	30
Achilles	180		Helen	27
Nestor	153		Paris Servant*	18
Aeneas	139		Andromache	15
			Helenus*	4
			Margarelon*	3
			Troilus Servant*	3
			Deiphobus*	2
			Diomedes Servant*	1
			* Myrmidon	

ALL'S WELL THAT ENDS WELL

Main Roles	Lines		Ensemble	Lines
HELENA	440		4th Lord/1st Soldier	83
PAROLLES	368		Widow Capilet	58
KING OF FRANCE	364		Steward	41
COUNTESS	272		(3rd Lord)/Duke of Florence/2nd Soldier/G. Astringer	35
LAFEW	271		Mariana	20
Bertram	248		Page (= Messenger)	5
Clown	195			
1st Lord Dumain	167			
Diana	117			
2nd Lord Dumain	112			

KING HENRY VIII

Main Roles	Lines	Ensemble	Lines
HENRY VIII	403	1st Gentleman/Keeper/One Within	93
WOLSEY	387	Brandon/Suffolk	87
QUEEN KATHARINE	351	L. Abergavenny/Vaux/Surrey/Garter	86
BUCKINGHAM/GARDINER	254	T. Lovell/Crier/Gentleman (Q. Kath)	62
		3rd Gentleman/Gent. Usher/Dr Butts	61
Norfolk	177	Old Lady	60
Prologue/Campeius/Griffith/Lord Chancellor/Epilogue	171	L. Sandys/Bishop of Lincoln/Capuchius	53
Lord Chamberlain	131	Anne Bullen	43
Surveyor/Cromwell/Porter	123	H. Guildford/Sergeant/Denny	17
Cranmer	120	Patience (= Lady)	15
2nd Gentleman/Man	104	Servant/Scribe/Messenger	10

KING HENRY VI PART 1

Main Roles	Lines	Ensemble	Lines
TALBOT	401	Winchester	87
JOAN LA PUCELLE	254	1st Mess./Gargrave/Somerset	83
		Master Gunner/Mess. (C of Auv.)/Gen./Shep.	82
Richard of York	183	Warwick	79
Humphrey of Gloucester	180	Countess of Auv./Margaret	75
Henry VI	179	2nd Mess./Glansdale/Porter/Captain (3²)/Y. Talbot	63
Suffolk	171	Exeter	60
Bedford/Lucy	152	Salisbury/Burgundy	58
Charles, King of France	132	Reignier	57
3rd Messenger/Mortimer/Falstaff	141	Alençon	49
		Mayor of London/Basset	45
		Talbot Mess./Vernon	33
		Bastard of Orleans	29
		1st Warw. Serv./Sergt./Lawyer/Watch/Mess. (4³)/Servant (4⁷)	20
		Off./1st Sent./1st Serv. (3¹)/Scout	20
		1st Serv. (1³)/Sold. (2¹)/3rd Serv. (3¹)	17
		2nd Warw. Serv./Woodville/Capt. (2²)/Keeper/1st Sold./Legate	17
		M. G. Boy/2nd Serv. (3¹)	6

KING HENRY VI PART 2

Main Roles	Lines
RICHARD OF YORK	363
SUFFOLK/RICHARD OF GLOUCESTER	318
QUEEN MARGARET	316
HENRY VI	310
HUMPHREY OF GLOUCESTER	299
CADE	243
Warwick	132
Duchess of Gloucester	119
Beaufort	115

Ensemble	Lines
Salisbury	96
Hume/1st Neighbour/Master/Clifford	91
One/Stanley/Lieutenant/L. Scales	80
Buckingham	74

Ensemble	Lines
Peter/Servant/Dick	65
1st Pet./3rd Neighbour/Messenger (4⁷)/Iden	65
Messenger (1²)/2nd Prent./1st Gent./Y.Clifford	57
Beadle/Post/Lord Say	55
Horner/Herald/Holland/Messenger (4⁹)	48
Simpcox/Smith	46
Bolinbroke/Sherriff/Bevis	44
Somerset/1st Citizen	29
2 Pet./Whitmore	25
Mayor/2nd Neighbour/1st Murderer/H. Stafford	24
Vaux/2nd Murderer/W. Stafford/2nd Messenger (4⁴)	24
Michael/1st Messenger (4⁴)/Soldier	16
Spirit/1st Prent/Mate/Clerk of Chatham/Edward of York	15
M. Jourdain/Simcox/Widow/2nd Gentleman	15

KING HENRY VI PART 3

Main Roles	Lines
WARWICK	434
EDWARD IV	427
RICHARD OF GLOUCESTER	389
HENRY VI	365
QUEEN MARGARET	279
Richard of York/Hastings	192
Clifford/Huntsman	141
Westmoreland/Father kills Son/Lewis XI/Montgomery	117
Clarence	106

Ensemble	Lines
L. Grey, later Q. Elizabeth	73
Northumb./2nd Keeper/3rd Watch/M. of York	59
York Mess. (2¹)/Somerset	54
Sir J. Mortimer/1st Keeper/Oxford	51
Edward, Prince of Wales	45
Rutland/Son kills Father/Henry of Richmond	45
York Mess. (1²)/Post (War)	33
Tutor/Exeter	22
Montague (= Falconbridge)/Rivers	22
Henry VI Mess./2nd Watch/Oxford Mess.	16
Norfolk/Nobleman/Soldier/Somerville	13
D. of N. Mess./1st Watch	11
Lady Bona	9
Lieut./Montgomery Mess.	4

PERICLES

Main Roles	Lines	Ensemble	Lines
PERICLES	567	1st Tyre Lord/1st Pent. F./1st Pent L.*/1st Sailor/1st Eph. L./1st Pirate/1st Myt. L.	96
GOWER	307	Dionyza	84
Helicanus/Cleon	220	Thaisa	71
Ant. daughter/Marina	174	2nd Tyre Lord/2nd Pent. F./2nd Pent. L./2nd Sailor/2nd Eph. L./2nd Pirate/2nd Myt. L.	65
Antiochus/Boult	150	3rd Tyre Lord/3rd Pent. F./3rd Pent L./3rd Sailor/3rd Eph. L./3rd Pirate/3rd Myt. L.	34
Simonides	149	Tarsus Lord/1st Knight	15
Thaliard/Leonine/Lysimachus	140	Escanes/3rd Knight	12
Lychorida/Bawd/Diana	130	Antiochus Mess./2nd Knight (4th Knight)/1st Tyre Gentleman	1
Cerimon/Pandar	128	(5th Knight)/Philemon	1
		* (= Marshal)	

TWO GENTLEMEN OF VERONA

Main Roles	Lines	Ensemble	Lines
PROTEUS	434	Lucetta	68
VALENTINE	373	Panthino/Host	66
JULIA	317	Thurio	54
Launce	207	Antonio/1st Outlaw	54
Speed	198	Servant/2nd Outlaw/Eglamour	41
Duke	198	3rd Outlaw/Singer	40
Silvia	149		

TIMON OF ATHENS

Main Roles	Lines
TIMON	808
Apemantus	230
Steward	188
1st Lord/1st Senator	152
Alcibiades	149
Poet/1st Stranger	129

Ensemble	Lines
(2nd Lord) = Lucius	86
Painter/2nd Varro Serv.	67
Ventidius/2nd Sen.	62
Vent. Mess. = Hortensius/Fool/1st Bandit	50
Lucius Serv. (= 2nd Serv.)/1st Serv./2nd Bandit	50
Lucillius (= Timon 3rd Serv.)/Hostilius/Mess.	45
(3rd Lord) = Sempronius/3rd Sen.	42
(1st Timon Serv.) = Flaminius	41
2nd Alcibiades Mess. = Sold./1st Varro Serv.	40
Lucullus = (4th Ld)/4th Sen.	40
Merchant/Servilius = (Timon 2nd Serv.)	33
Jeweller/Lord's Serv. = Caphis/Philotus	29
Old Athenian/2nd Stranger	28
(Lucullus 3rd Serv.) = Titus/3rd Bandit	28
Cupid/Page	14
2nd Lady/Timandra	5
1st Lady/Phrynia	3

KING JOHN

Main Roles	Lines
BASTARD	508
KING JOHN	425
QUEEN CONSTANCE	260
King Philip	204
Hubert	187
Pandulph	161
Salisbury	155
Prince Arthur/Prince Henry	145
Lewis	138
Chatillon/Pembroke	119

Ensemble	Lines
Queen Eleanor/Lady Faulconbridge	69
Robert Faulconbridge/Melun	61
Austria/Peter of Pomfret/Messenger (5³)	41
Blanche	40
English Herald/Messenger (4²)	24
French Herald/Bigot	20
Essex/1st Executioner/French Messenger (5⁵)	11
Gurney/(2nd Executioner)	1

TITUS ANDRONICUS

Main Roles	Lines	Ensemble	Lines
TITUS	708	Demetrius	90
AARON	352	Bassianus/Clown	85
MARCUS	322	Lavinia	58
TAMORA	257	Martius/2nd Goth	53
		Chiron	49
Saturninus	209	Young Lucius	42
Lucius	180	Quintus/1st Goth	36
		Captain/Aemilius	27
		Tribune/Mess./Publius	26
		Nurse	17
		Mutius/3rd Goth	8

Acknowledgements

First ACT Shakespeare began life as a project under the title *The Shakespeare Pack* shortly after my retirement from business in 1994. My retirement present to myself was a painting by Ronnie Copas called *The Poet and the Painter* which was displayed for a year by the Royal Shakespeare Company at Stratford and subsequently on tour to Newcastle and Plymouth, thanks to David Brierley, a previous General Manager of the RSC. He also allowed me to see years of box office data from Stratford that I collated into a pamphlet – *The Seven Stars* – to suggest a popularity rating for all the plays which I have retained in this book. *The Poet and the Painter* is now on permanent display at Shakespeare's Globe Theatre in London, and my thanks are due to Pete Le May of the Globe for undertaking this.

The Shakespeare Pack was produced by the Ivy Press for which my thanks are due to Peter Bridgewater.

The production of this book has been a splendid team effort. Clive Francis has updated many of his original designs for *The Shakespeare Pack* and his input has been superb. I thank Richard Ritchie who introduced me to Sam and Alice Carter of Tandem Publishing, and my wife Sheila, and ex-secretary Sharon Clay for their efforts in producing the final copy.

Many Tower Theatre colleagues have added to my appreciation of Shakespeare; from my earlier days Terry Marlowe, Tom Tillery, Patanne Fairfoot and Derek (Malcolm) Mudie; and from more recent times Penny Tuerk (to whose memory this book is dedicated), Martin Mulgrew, Haidee Elise, Peter Novis, John Morton, Ian Recordon, Jill Batty, Jonathan Norris, Jill Ruane, Annie Connell and Richard Pedersen. Laurence Tuerk, Dinah Irvine and Stephen Ley have been my long-time colleagues on the technical side, the latter with Sarah Ambrose and David Taylor having carried the company into its new theatre in Stoke Newington. To all those, and many not mentioned, my personal thanks and admiration. Thanks too to my most recent collaborators at the Tower Theatre, Ruth Sullivan and Ian Hoare.

Thanks also to Chris Beetles and staff of the Chris Beetles Gallery for the launch of the book.

My involvement in professional theatre has been enriched by my various associations with the late Paul Marcus, Robert Gillespie, the late Michael Burrell, Sue Plummer, David Cavendish, William Dudley, Lucy Bailey and Waris Hussein. I would like to add Andy Bargilly of the Cyprus National Theatre and Nikos Karanikis of the British Council in Cyprus for their efforts on my behalf to set up a filming of my version of *Pericles* called *Fathers and Daughters.*

Finally to my family my thanks for their enthusiasm and support, to Sheila, Owen, 'the lively' Helena, Declan, Lily and Alana, the latter two in hopes that they and their generation might profit from this book and come to delight in Shakespeare as much as I do. Lily, then aged about six, paid me the ultimate compliment as I launched into another impromptu quotation. "What is Robert being?" she asked her Grannie. Not "What is he saying?" or "What is he doing?" but "What is he *being?*" Can any actor ask for more?

References

The primary edition of Shakespeare used for this book is the 1985 University Press Arden Shakespeare published by Methuen.

Other editions used include:

The Plays and Poems of Shakespeare Edited by A. J. Valpy, Henry G. Bohn 1844

The Chiswick Shakespeare Edited by John Dennis, George Bell 1899

Shakespeare Complete Works Edited by W. J. Craig, Oxford University Press 1905

The Works of Shakespeare for Shakespeare Head Press, Basil Blackwell for Oxford University Press 1934

The key reference books are:

A New and Complete Concordance by John Bartlett, MacMillan 1894

A Shakespeare Glossary by C. T. Onions and Robert D. Eagleson, Oxford University Press 1986

Shakespeare's Words by David and Ben Crystal, Penguin 2002

The Shakespeare Sampler section owes much to:

The *English Sampler* by S. S. Sopwith, G. Bell 1938

Other References:

Shakespeare's Imagery by Caroline Spurgeon, CUP 1935

The Ages of Man: *a Shakespeare Anthology*, George Rylands, Heinemann 1935

Shakespeare's Bawdy by Eric Partridge, Routledge and Keegan Paul 1947

Shakespeare by Ivor Brown, Collins 1949

On Producing Shakespeare by Ronald Watkins, Michael Joseph 1950

A Companion to Shakespeare Studies by H. Granville-Barker and G. B. Harrison, CUP 1955

Playing Shakespeare by John Barton, Methuen 1984

Year of the King by Antony Sher, Chatto and Windus 1985

Shakespeare and Multiplicity, Brian Gibbons, CUP 1993

The Genius of Shakespeare, Jonathan Bate, Picador 1997

Shakespeare's Language by Frank Kermode, Penguin 2000

Shakespeare and Co. by Stanley Wells, Penguin 2006

The Year of Lear by James Shapiro, Simon and Schuster 2015